Foucault and Educational Leadership

School principals are increasingly working in an environment of work intensification, high stakes testing, accountability pressures and increased managerialism. Rather than searching for the latest leadership fad or best practice model, this book suggests that in order to better understand these pressures, the work of educational leadership requires more sophisticated theorisation of these practices. In so doing, the book draws upon the work of Michel Foucault to provoke new thought into how the principalship is lived and 'disciplined' in ways that produce both contradictions and tensions for school principals. Amidst claims of a shortage of applicants for principal positions in a number of Western countries, what is required are more sophisticated and nuanced tools with which to understand the pressures and constraints that face principals in their work on a daily basis. This book provides a powerful example of theory working through practice to move beyond traditional approaches to school leadership.

Key features of the book:

> Provides a well theorised analysis of leadership practices
>
> Acknowledges the messy reality of life for school principals
>
> Provides key insights to the 'real' work that principals undertake every day
>
> Examines the production of principals' subjectivities in education, foregrounding issues of gender and race
>
> Includes the principals' voices through rich interview data.

The book will be of significant interest to principals and those working and researching in educational leadership, including researchers in the field and academics who teach into educational leadership and administration courses. The book will also be of great interest to those working with the ideas of Foucault in education.

Richard Niesche is a Postdoctoral Research Fellow in the School of Education at the University of Queensland, Australia, where he teaches and conducts research in the areas of educational leadership, social justice and Indigenous education.

Foucault and Educational Leadership

Disciplining the principal

Richard Niesche

Routledge
Taylor & Francis Group

LONDON AND NEW YORK

First edition published 2011
by Routledge
2 Park Square, Milton Park, Abingdon, Oxon OX14 4RN

Simultaneously published in the USA and Canada
by Routledge
711 Third Avenue, New York, NY 10017

Routledge is an imprint of the Taylor & Francis Group, an informa business

British Library Cataloguing in Publication Data
A catalogue record for this book is available from the British Library

Library of Congress Cataloging-in-Publication Data
A catalog record has been requested for this book

ISBN: 978-0-415-57170-8 (hbk)
ISBN: 978-0-203-81897-8 (ebk)

Typeset in Garamond
by Wearset Ltd Boldon, Tyne and Wear
Printed and bound by TJI Digital, Padstow, Cornwall

Contents

Acknowledgements   vi

1   Introduction   1

2   A Foucauldian toolbox for educational leadership   17

3   Discourses of educational leadership   41

4   Disciplinary regimes under self-governance   64

5   Leading and managing as ethical work   104

6   'Doing' leadership differently   136

Notes   140
Bibliography   141
Index   159

Acknowledgements

I would like to thank the two principals whose stories are portrayed in this book. They were incredibly generous in their time and responses to my questions. While their portraitures are not intended to be examples of 'best practice', they are nevertheless doing excellent work in very difficult and complex environments. This book has also benefited from the valuable assistance, critique and input from a number of friends and colleagues. Special thanks to Martin Mills, Pam Christie, Bob Lingard, Pat Thomson, Jill Blackmore, Tom O'Donoghue, Robyn Jorgensen, Clare O'Farrell, Amanda Keddie, Carmen Mills, Malcolm Haase, Christina Gowlett and Alison Gable. Thanks to everyone at Routledge for their assistance in making this book better and special thanks to Anna Clarkson for supporting the book from the beginning. And as always, the love of my life, Christine Mason for her unwavering support and refusal to read the manuscript in any form...

Some parts of this book have appeared before. Parts of Chapter 4 first appeared as 'Discipline through documentation: A form of governmentality for school principals', in the *International Journal of Leadership in Education* Vol. 13 No. 3 pp 249–263 (2010). Some sections of Chapter 5 first appeared in the article 'Emotions and ethics: A Foucauldian framework for becoming an ethical educator', published in *Educational Philosophy and Theory* (online first, 2010).

1   Introduction

My point is not that everything is bad, but that everything is dangerous, which is not exactly the same as bad. If everything is dangerous, then we always have something to do.

(Foucault, 2000a, p. 256)

If you ask most people what they think of when they hear the word leadership, they will typically relate stories of exceptional individuals with a variety of characteristics or attributes that have brought about a transformation in a particular field. In both the popular media and academic literature, studies of leadership are similarly dominated by studies of 'great' individuals and the repetitious search for a blueprint of competences, capabilities and models that can be implemented to achieve similar results (Wood & Case, 2006). If we need any reminding that, in fact, we haven't moved away from such crude understandings of leadership, one only need look into recent government policy documents outlining leadership frameworks. In countries such as the US, the UK and Australia, government policy directives typically outline leadership approaches that require transformational, charismatic, heroic models of leadership. For instance, in the UK, documents such as the *National Standards for Headteachers* (DfES, 2004) and bodies such as the National College for School Leadership (NCSL) not only privilege 'top-down' notions of leadership but are also involved in what Peter Gronn calls 'designer leadership' (Gronn, 2003a).

Similarly, in the state of Queensland, Australia, the *Leadership Matters* framework and technical paper, developed by the state education authorities (Education Queensland, 2005, 2006), cite the following capabilities as necessary for quality leadership: 'courage, tough mindedness, intuition, passion, self-confidence, optimism, wisdom' (2005, p. 14). What is particularly alarming here is the similarity of these capabilities with the characteristics of sound battle command in Sun Tzu's *The Art of War* from around 600 BC. For example, Sun Tzu states, 'By command I mean the general's qualities of wisdom, sincerity, humanity, courage, and strictness' (2005, p. 93). Perhaps our understanding of this complex phenomenon called 'leadership' has not come as far as we'd like to think.

The problem with many of these frameworks of leadership is that they not only fail to acknowledge much of the work that is being done by numerous leaders across a range of areas, but also construct leadership as something that exists as 'exceptional practice' and results in a normalising of leadership into models dominated by stories of heroic endeavours. Drawing on Foucault's quotation above, such concepts of leadership are 'dangerous' and need continual problematising and questioning. Just as a new fad of leadership comes around, there is new work to do to unmask the power relations that ascribe particular meanings to the work of leaders and, the focus in this book, school principals.

In the current educational climate of Western countries such as the UK, the US and Australia, school leaders are finding themselves increasingly confronted by governance structures that are heavily based upon principles of high-stakes accountability, competition, work intensification and managerialism (Anderson, 2009; Thomson, 2009). In response to such demands placed upon school leaders, the field of educational leadership has predominantly been preoccupied with research into exploring models of 'best practice'. Without doubt educational leadership is a key aspect of schooling, however, the normative assumptions underlying many of these traditional approaches to leadership at best largely ignore the complex and messy reality of the day-to-day work of school leaders and at worst normalise leaders into highly gendered, racially stereotyped 'hero' paradigms. As a result of this constant search for an idealistic model, some have become disillusioned with studies of leadership (Sinclair, 2007), and others have questioned the futility of studies of exceptional leaders for the 'right' model (Gronn, 2003a). Pat Thomson has also recently provided a thorough and sobering look into the 'risky business' of school headship in the UK (Thomson, 2009). Such examinations that provide necessary illumination into the difficulties faced by school leaders are still too rare in the field.

In order to better understand the complexities of school leadership, there is a need to cast a wider theoretical net in order to analyse the multitude of challenges that face many school principals. In this book I use the work of Michel Foucault to provoke new thought into how the principalship is lived and 'disciplined' in ways that produce both contradictions and tensions for school principals. If, indeed, the principal is an essential ingredient for effective school improvement and the development of sound teaching and learning environments, then more insights are needed into the work that principals are required to do, not from the perspective of job competences, capabilities or job requirements but their daily work practices themselves.[1]

Throughout this book I draw upon the examples of the work practices of two white, female school principals of Indigenous schools in Australia. These choices indicate a complex intersectionality of the issues of leadership, gender and race that provide fertile ground for examining the complexities of daily life for school principals. The two case studies have been chosen to allow for a richness of data through the use of portraiture and the voices of the two principals in telling their stories. However, it is not their life stories that I share. Not that these do not play an important role in their work. They do. Rather, it is an examination of their work practices that I use to illustrate the positioning of these women within a range of power relations and discursive regimes. These portraits will, hopefully, resonate with the experiences of a range of school leaders, not just women leaders or principals of Indigenous schools. Instead, more important is the exploration of principals' work practices through a range of discursive regimes evident across numerous contexts that construct school principals as particular subjects.

To do this I draw upon Foucault's notion of genealogy, as well as his concepts of disciplinary power, governmentality and ethics. It is through these concepts that I interpret these principals' work practices and demonstrate the multiple subjectivities of these principals. School principals are constructed as subjects through school leadership and management discourses (Lingard et al., 2003) and I aim to show that these 'theories' of leadership and management fail to adequately recognise and explain the positioning of these principals in the complex arrangements existing in the two case studies.

Foucault's work is important for providing an alternative way of understanding principals' work through examining educational leadership from the level of the principals' practices themselves in specific, local contexts. I argue against using over-arching theories in an attempt to explain and understand what goes on in schools. It is through their work practices and the power relations invested in these actions that the principal is made a subject. Progressively through the book I provide a rich tapestry of these principals' experiences of working in their respective schools and explore both the constraints and possibilities for action that occur for these principals.

While the use of Foucault has been extensive in educational research generally,[2] there has been very little use of his work specifically in the field of educational leadership. However, Foucault's work can be valuable for providing fresh insights into our understandings of principals' work and principals' subjectivities. By examining the principal as a site of power relations and exploring principal subjectivities, it becomes possible to find the cracks and spaces in which principals are able to operate within normalising discursive regimes such as leadership frameworks and self-management. It is then a further aim in this book to explore how principals may be able to use these spaces and avenues to act within a variety of disciplinary regimes to influence their daily work practices and, in turn, the outcomes of their students.

Research context

It is my aim that this book is read as much a text drawing on empirical research as a theoretical text. There is a huge corpus of literature discussing Foucault and his work across numerous disciplines, and education is no exception. However, there is still a need for research that 'uses' Foucault rather than discusses Foucault. Sawicki (1991) argues for the need to do more genealogies and while I do not regard this book as a genealogy of leadership per se (and this still needs to be done, in my opinion), it is a book that uses a number of Foucault's concepts through which to analyse and make sense of empirical research. This is why I use the term 'toolkit' from which I take out particular Foucauldian concepts to use at my disposal. As Foucault states:

> I would like my books to be a kind of tool-box which others can rummage through to find a tool which they can use however they wish in their own area ... I would like the little volume that I want to write on disciplinary systems to be useful to an educator, a warden, a magistrate, a conscientious objector. I don't write for an audience, I write for users, not readers.
>
> (Foucault, 1994, pp. 523–524)

This book is not designed to be a blueprint for how research using Foucault should be conducted. This book is an example of one of numerous possibilities for employing Foucault's work to understand, analyse and interpret how school principals undertake their work. Methodologically this book draws upon the notions of Foucauldian genealogy and Sara Lawrence-Lightfoot's concept of portraiture (1983; and with Jessica Hoffman Davis, 1997), the first of which I explain in the next section.

Genealogy

This book is in part a study of the principal; more specifically, a 'genealogical reading' of the principal's work. It is my aim here to take up Foucault's challenge of writing genealogies: to use his analytical tools and to use genealogy as a method of analysis. For Foucault, 'Genealogy is a form of research that is aimed at activating "subjugated" historical knowledge, that is, knowledge which has been rejected by mainstream knowledge, or which is too local and specific to be deemed of any importance' (O'Farrell, 2005, p. 68).

It is this subjugated level of knowledge that I highlight using elements of Foucault's genealogy. That is, knowledges that exist at the local and specific level which cannot be explained or understood by mainstream discourses of leadership and management. It is at this level where power/knowledge operates, where the division between true and false exists (O'Farrell, 2005). Genealogy questions the truth that is claimed by 'scientific' discourses of leadership and management. Genealogy entails a questioning of our existence, that is, an historical investigation into the events that have led us to constitute ourselves as subjects (Bernauer & Mahon, 2005). Foucault states that 'beneath what science knows about itself is something that it doesn't know', and through genealogy we can identify 'its history, its becoming, its periods and accidents' (Foucault, 1996, p. 54). Thus, Foucault's notion of genealogy is primarily concerned with tracing the descent of particular discourses, the emergence of different interpretations that serve to dissolve the unity of the subject (Foucault, 1977a). The playful analogy by Kendall and Wickham perhaps provides a simpler way of understanding what it is that Foucault's notion of genealogy aims to do. They claim that genealogy is:

> A methodological device with the same effect as a precocious child at a dinner party: genealogy makes the older guests at the table of intellectual analysis feel decidedly uncomfortable by pointing out things about their origins and functions that they would rather remain hidden.
>
> (Kendall & Wickham, 1999, p. 29)

Central to the notion of genealogy are the different modalities of power (Davidson, 2005) and the way that the relationship between power and knowledge produces particular subjectivities for these school principals. The specificities of power relations in local settings are central themes of this approach. Others have used the notion of a policy genealogy (Gale, 2001) to seek out discontinuities in the emergence of certain policy frameworks to problematise the valorisation of certain policies and discourses rather than viewing them in a continuous sequential fashion. Therefore, I undertake in this book a reading of the principal's role and practices in these two schools that targets the emergence of the principal as a discursive construct within systems and policy that through its own limitations cannot acknowledge other conditions of possibility. This use of 'genealogy as critique' (Visker, 1995) provides a useful method of analysis of the modern power–knowledge mechanisms of subjectivity of the principal that have emerged under systems of self-governance.

Foucault's analysis of a 'regime of practices' is central to this process. I examine how the relations of power invested in policies of self-governance are rationalised, how the discursive practices and techniques are affected upon, through and by principals. This is not to focus on the institution of schooling itself but those regimes of practices, 'practices being understood as places where what is said and what is done, rules imposed and reasons given, the planned and the taken for granted meet and interconnect' (Foucault, 1991a, p. 75). It is these practices that discipline principals and construct them as subjects in these discursive regimes. Practices such as management teams, shared governance councils, parent involvement models (Anderson and Grinberg, 1998), alongside principal competence tables, school effectiveness and performance examinations all serve as disciplinary practices that attempt to control actions carried out in schools. These governmentalities all attempt to 'know' the principals, to prescribe a certain truth to their work and their being, and, as such, are both disciplining and self-forming. Anderson and Grinberg further argue that empowerment also needs to be seen as a disciplinary practice that 'embodies forms of unobtrusive control or

non-overt control in contemporary organisations in which control no longer
appears to come from outside the organisational members' sphere of activity'
(1998, p. 337). It is this notion of 'steering at a distance' (Ball, 1994) inherent in models of self-governance that subjectifies principals through methods
of accountability, while governments are seen to have less of a direct role.
Therefore, I analyse the self-forming practices that principals must employ
through self-governance by studying the 'interplay between a code that
governs ways of doing things and a production of true discourses that served
to found, justify and provide reasons and principles for these ways of doing
things' (Foucault, 1991a, p. 79). A genealogical approach to leadership and
management is about retracing specific ways of doing and knowing, to
identify how particular assumptions work together and change over time.
Typically, mainstream historical approaches tend to look at the development
of policies and changes over whole periods of time with little examination of
the multitude of specific and often minute events through which these discourses and policies are formed.

The difficulty in employing the work of Foucault is that there is no such
thing as a Foucauldian theory or methodology (Tamboukou & Ball, 2003).
It is not my aim to search for a singular, best perspective as this would be
against the intent of Foucault's work, but to examine the discursive regime
of practices of self-governance of the principal through a multifarious range
of methodologies. I do not aim to improve current best practice in educational administration and leadership, but rather to analyse the practices and
discourses that create principals as subjects particularly under recent educational reforms to self-governance. It is through these examinations that it
may be possible to understand the subject formations of principals within
regimes of self-governance opening up lines of inquiry into the possibilities
and constraints for action.

These representations of principals' practices are all saturated in discourses, histories, biographies, local narratives and situated perspectives
(Thomson, 2001). It is important to note that these representations are not
simply reflections of reality. They are constructions with the intention of
'developing contestatory political and public spaces which open up in relation to existing systems of governance' (Yeatman, 1994, p. ix). For example,
views such as that of self-governance as a disciplinary practice that I present
in Chapter 4 are but one of many representations of the practices of self-
governance.

I have used multiple methods of gathering data for the purposes of creating this in-depth portraiture of the schools and their principals, not so much
as a means of triangulation but as providing a 'venue' for dialogue between
the differing approaches, or that of 'building bridges' (Miller, 1997, p. 25).
Specifically I use a comparative case study method incorporating qualitative
measures such as interviews with the principals, teachers, school staff and
community members; observations of the principals at work; and school and
government document analyses. For this book I use Yin's definition of a case

study: 'A case study is an empirical inquiry that investigates a contemporary phenomenon within its real life context, especially when the boundaries between phenomenon and context are not clearly evident' (Yin, 2003, p. 13).

The research project consisted of case studies of two Indigenous schools and their principals over a period of 18 months. The research findings have been reflexively interpreted in relation to the broad literature on educational leadership and self-governance using the work of Michel Foucault. More specifically, I have analysed the data through the lens of the Foucauldian concepts of disciplinary power, governmentality and ethics. These concepts are used to undertake three different levels of analysis: the broader systemic level (governmentality), the school level (disciplinary power) and the individual (ethics). It is important to note, however, that the issues represented in these analysis chapters occur concurrently and are intertwined; they should not be read as sequential and separate as the chapter order might imply.

Portraiture and initial sketches

In addition to Foucault's genealogical concepts I use Lawrence-Lightfoot's notion of portraiture (1983) of the case study schools to provide a picture of the particular contexts within which each principal operates. These initial sketches are largely based on narratives as well as observations and interview material. As Thomson states:

> Narratives of the real life of schools attempting to change, narratives based on empirical study that do not seek to create 'best practice' and models, but rather tell particular stories that exemplify potentially useful principles for ways of working, have some hope of connecting with the reform efforts of other real life schools.
>
> (Thomson, 2002, p. 189)

The notion of portraiture is concerned with a blending of both empirical research and an aesthetic approach to examining the complexities of human experience and organisational life (Lawrence-Lightfoot & Davis, 1997). The portraitist plays a central role in the construction of the portrait, bringing to light the researcher's own voice alongside the stories of the participants. An important distinction of the portraitist against, say, an ethnographer is that the portraitist is 'looking *for* a story rather than listening *to* a story' (Hackmann, 2002, p. 54). The use of portraiture has received criticism as a methodology (for example, see English, 2000; Merriam, 1988); however, it can be a particularly useful approach to studying educational leaders (Hackmann, 2002; Wolcott, 1999). In the remainder of this introductory chapter I begin the portraits of the schools and their principals with some initial sketches.

Riverside Community School

Walking through the gate of the Riverside Community School, to the casual observer it could be any school in any suburb of a major Australian city. It is not outwardly apparent that this school is an Indigenous school, apart from the new sign that went up in late 2004. There are all the usual signs of a regular school, children playing, teachers on playground duty, yet this is not a regular school. This is a school with a particular set of histories and circumstances that help to define its being. It is a school that is not just assisting in the participation of Indigenous children in the education system but it is striving towards the ownership of learning outcomes for Indigenous communities. Not only does the school signify a struggle for Indigenous peoples to obtain community control and ownership of schools and other educational facilities, but also for understanding the importance of cultural beliefs and practices in the children's development (Downey & Hart, 2000).

Riverside is an independent community-based school in an urban area of Queensland, Australia. It has been operating since 1986 and has progressed from a focus on primary school to now incorporating both high school and community-based education services. For its first 10 years the school was located in a disused Catholic primary school. At this site there were only three classrooms and almost no playing areas for the students. The school then moved to its current location, where it is now more able to suitably meet the needs of the children.

The school is currently a mixture of the old dilapidated buildings that still stand from the previous primary school and the modern classrooms and canteen block that signal the recent changes for this school. The architecture of the school beautifully understates the current transformation from the old primary school site to one that is more modern and in keeping with the vision of the school for the future. In a sense the school is working within the spaces of old school architecture as both compliance with and resistance to traditional schooling spaces. The architecture and design of the school is important as it is significant in the formulation of both disciplining regimes and patterns of resistance (this is discussed in more detail in Chapter 4).

This school has a number of key contextual factors that provide not only an excellent example of a success story for Indigenous education in Australia but also a fascinating case study. Some of the factors that contribute to the 'thisness' (Thomson, 2000, 2002) of the school include things such as the school being the only community-based independent Indigenous school in the region. Judy, the principal, is white and female and has been its only principal for a period of 12 years. Before this, the role was in a very different capacity, as Judy states:

> When I first joined, the role of principal didn't exist. It was education co-ordinator. They had two people, an education co-ordinator and an administrator. They had been without an education co-ordinator for

about six months as they hadn't been successful in finding somebody. So I was asked if I'd like to come and join. So I went to my first Board meeting which was my interview apparently and after that they asked if I would come, so it was more of a different kind of situation. So I joined the school in term four, 1994. It was a very different kind of school then. We were in a disused Catholic School, we had two class rooms, no playing space for the children, and there were 28 students.

As a result the job for the newly appointed principal was challenging, to say the least. Starting a school from such humble beginnings proved to be no easy task for the new principal and the community as there were a number of challenges, particularly in the area of finance:

When I started in term four, 1994, no one had received their group certificate for that year and there were no wages books to be found. The school hadn't received any of its funding for that year either and it was all because in the previous year no acquittals had been done. So it was quite an administrative slog at first to get things back in order. Now, as you are aware, the school has a strong reputation for being financially clever. Things are always in on time. So we've been able to do that. At the same time we have gone from 28 to 280 students. And not having any premises of our own. This is all owned by the community. In 10 years we have gone from 0 assets to an asset of 7.5 million now.

Over the years the school has responded to the needs of the students by implementing a number of programmes and strategies to enable a successful schooling experience for the students. For example, the school runs a private bus system to transport the students to and from school each day, often travelling long distances. The school also runs a nutrition programme whereby the students are provided breakfast, morning tea and lunch so that they are guaranteed regular meals during the school day. The school also runs a health out-clinic to monitor general health and wellbeing as well as a learning skills centre that caters for the wider Indigenous community, including adult education. In terms of staff, it is school policy to ensure a large percentage of teaching staff are of Indigenous background. There is also a full-time child and family support worker as well as a speech therapist/pathologist.

These are just some of the important services offered at the school to meet the wide-ranging needs of the students and Indigenous community in general. The school maintains a fee-free structure for parents, as a significant percentage of parents receive welfare benefits and/or are in low-income employment. This is an example of the commitment the school has in achieving the participation of Indigenous children in primary and secondary schooling, although as discussed later in Chapter 5, this fee-free structure does create more work and further complexities, particularly for the principal. The role of the community has also been of particular importance for the school and has provided significant emotional and financial support for the school and the tutoring programme.

The Aboriginality of the students, staff and school is something that is celebrated and is part of the school's philosophy. In addition, the school's vision states: 'In respect of our peoples, our cultures, our land, we foster an inclusive learning environment which promotes empowerment, identity and success through education' (*School Handbook*, 2005, p. 1). Upon meeting my students for the first time I was asked questions such as 'Are you married?', 'Do you have kids?' Upon learning that yes I was married but had no kids, the children were incredulous that I could be married for five years and not have any children. This demonstrated to me the profound importance for Indigenous culture on one's family. Most often, the students in the school would know each other and the staff by who they were related to. It was very important for the students and community at this school to situate them-selves in relation to each other by their families as a child's family is a valu-able source of assistance and understanding if issues arise at school or at home.

One of my most enduring moments while both visiting and working at Riverside was witnessing the late arrival of a little boy, probably aged six or seven, to his classroom. He was at least half an hour late to school but instead of chastising the child for being late, the teacher immediately made sure the child had something to eat for breakfast and sent him off to the canteen in search of cereal, as the school has an extensive nutrition pro-gramme for the students. In some cases such as this, the teacher later told me, it is important for some of these kids that they are coming to school regularly and that when they do come to maximise the learning environment for them. Riverside's holistic approach is displayed through such initiatives as ensuring that each child is able to fully participate in the learning experi-ence even if it means feeding them breakfast so that they can learn effectively during the day. The nutrition programme ensures that each child has three meals during the school day so that they can fully participate in class. The importance of this programme in the school needs to be acknowledged and has been one of the central features of the school's approach.

Pine Hills State School

Driving into the town of Pine Hills in rural Queensland for the first time, the observer is instantly confronted with this country's poor treatment of its Indigenous inhabitants. Run-down, dilapidated dwellings and buildings, often housing large extended families are the norm in this town and are reminiscent of those found in the 'third world'. As I took the large bend in the road into town, I got the sense that I had left mainstream rural Australia and entered a place that by today's standards and expectations should not exist in such conditions. Pine Hills is only located a few kilometres outside a larger rural town and yet when you arrive, you feel miles away from white mainstream Australia.

Like many Indigenous settlements, this town has had a troubled history. It was established in 1903 by the Queensland government as an Aboriginal settlement. Many Indigenous people were forcibly removed from their families and settled here, and it was only in the mid-1980s that the community was given title to the land. High levels of unemployment and welfare dependence are common, with alcoholism, petrol and paint sniffing, sexual and domestic violence and abuse being issues of great concern to the community. Years of racism and discrimination are issues that the community has had to cope with. It was not so long ago that racial segregation was an issue in this community, as Ruth, the school principal, explains:

> The community came through being a mission; they had a superintendent as it was very hierarchical and it was very controlled and I read a thing the other day, when I was having one of my kids in 1984, the hospital down here, the dining room and that were still segregated. That's pretty recent in my history that this dining room and the kitchen and that were segregated and I think that well a lot of my staff are women older than me who having their kids who have been through that system, in such recent memory.

While this description paints a bleak picture, the situation is not all bad. The town recently celebrated its centenary and increasingly has much to be proud of, particularly the fact that the community and school have survived generations of discrimination, racism and low expectations for Indigenous people.

The much publicised achievements and turnaround of Pine Hills State School from 1998 to 2004 have played a significant role in improving the situation for the students, the community and the school's profile. This turnaround has been instrumental in restoring a sense of pride in the town's community and their Aboriginality. After a long period of poor performance and outcomes, coupled with low expectations of the students on behalf of much of the school staff and community, the school was appointed its first Indigenous principal in 1998. The challenges the school presented at that time were vast, as he explains:

> When I came here, lots of kids were fighting with each other. Paint was all over the ground. There was no pride in the place. It shouldn't have been like that. There's enough people out there ready to put us down and kick us in the guts without us doing it to ourselves. I saw children walking around like empty skeletons. The community was complex, the issues that the children brought to the school were complex, but somehow we managed to get them to believe in themselves, to believe they can be young and black and deadly. And now, when you look

around, you can see they're young and black and deadly. The first couple of weeks here, there were children literally running up and down on top of the two-story buildings and nobody was really gonna say anything about it. There was no pride in the school, there was no sense of, 'This is our school. We love our school. This is where we come to learn.' There was none of that. And that had to change.

(Interview from Message Stick, 2003)

The principal then set about changing the culture of this school by adopting the motto 'Strong and Smart', which the school still uses today, 'Strong' meaning proud of their Indigenous heritage and 'Smart' meaning working hard to be just as good as kids in any other school. The principal was able to dramatically reduce truancy rates and implemented a range of policies to improve the performance and outcomes of the students, particularly in the area of information technology.

The school was initially started in 1903 with 32 students in a bush shelter with just one teacher. Now, Pine Hills is a community school that caters for around 250 local children. It is a state-run school that delivers educational programmes ranging from Kindergarten and Pre-school through to Year 7. Like Riverside there is a transient nature to some of the school population which adds a complexity to the school's operations. Interestingly there is a high percentage of transience between Riverside and Pine Hills. However, as yet, there have been no formal discussions around this issue.

Today, the school has approximately 12 classroom teachers, with four specialist teachers and a Remote Area Teacher Education Program (RATEP) teacher to deliver a range of programmes. In addition to this there are a large number of Indigenous teacher aides and support staff, cleaners and maintenance staff to contribute to the day-to-day operations of the school. This large number of staff contributes to the complexity of running the school and leading and managing such a large workforce. The school also hires a number of part-time staff under the Community Development Employment Project (CDEP) programme which adds to this dimension. While leading and managing such a large workforce is a challenge in a school of this size, there are a number of perceived benefits to having local community members working at the school. One of these is the direct link to the community through the school staff. As a result, the school is better equipped to be able to understand issues that may arise at the school due to concerns within the community. For example, when a student is truanting or misbehaving, the school is able to call upon a number of its local Indigenous staff to be able to communicate with the student's family or relatives and find out if there may be any reasons why this behaviour is occurring.

Pine Hills is a very insular community where a lot of family and social issues have a direct impact on the school. These issues are brought to the school on a daily basis by both teachers and students. For example, as a local community member explained to me, the day after welfare payments are sent out, many of the children can be distracted and inattentive at school as the parents may have been drinking the night before. This can sometimes result in those children witnessing alcoholism and violence which can affect their concentration at school. As a result the school is very much trying to deliver more than just an educational role; there is the social wellbeing role as well. The complexities of this aspect of the school are discussed in greater detail in Chapters 4 and 5.

As a result of this close community engagement with the school, some staff do make home visits to discuss students' progress and any concerns that may be arising, so there are also some services that the school is able to offer that most schools wouldn't be able to. However, the school still continues to struggle with the state government on some key issues that affect the school and students' performance. For instance, Emma, a teacher at Pine Hills, commented that

> Even to get acknowledged that the Aboriginal English spoken at Pine Hills qualifies for English as a second language. That hasn't been readily accepted. We've actually had to do a whole heap of research and data gathering to prove something that has been accepted by the teachers in this school for years. Aboriginal English at Pine Hills is a language with different grammatical structures and syntax, so kids have to code switch between home language and school language and they find it very difficult.

In addition, the school does have a reputation for being a challenging place to work. This has been recognised by some of the staff at the school who travel from outside the town. For instance, Lois, a school staff member, remarked that

> It's like well you might be at Pine Hills so well bite the bullet and get on with it. Do your job here or go somewhere else if they don't like it. Lots of community issues from what I can gather which causes a lot of upheaval.

The high turnover of staff also supports this perception. However, the current principal is working hard to restore positive attitudes towards the school. The principal, Ruth, started at the school at the end of 2004 and quickly found that there was still much hard work to be done after the previous principal had left. Even though the success of Pine Hills was widespread in education and other circles, the reality for the incoming principal was perhaps not as optimistic as she was led to believe. She was actually headhunted for the job, but since her appointment there has been a lot of criticism directed at the school and herself from within and outside the community. This has brought a complex dimension to the new principal's job that for most principals may not exist. A white, female principal coming into Pine Hills after the success of the previous male, Indigenous principal certainly raised some eyebrows, as this interview with Emma, a teacher at the school, demonstrates:

> I'd say it'd be difficult for anybody to come in. I was really shocked when I heard a female principal was coming in. There has been a history that there have been female principals before but because of the paternalistic culture within Indigenous communities, the men are the ones that hold power and I thought it was going to be interesting but as far as that goes she has won respect where she has needed to win respect. Yes, I think that anybody coming in after the previous principal had a big show to follow.

The Executive Director of Schools for that region also expressed some of the difficulties for the new, incoming principal:

> The difficulties Ruth has had has been following someone of such high profile. If the previous principal had none of his profile the degree of difficulty wouldn't be as great. It's going to happen to anyone, the old principal is such a substantially influential, fantastic person. It's not just him, it's the presence. He put that place on the map so it wouldn't have mattered who followed him.

The job for Ruth has certainly been difficult, but the school, despite some criticisms, seems to be moving forward and she has conducted extensive reviews of systems and processes and is now putting in place a range of mechanisms and strategies for long-term growth such as the Indigenous Knowledge Centre (IKC), a whole-school intervention model, a new Indigenous Studies programme and a new Special Education position to support students with disabilities.

An additional complexity for Ruth at Pine Hills is the extraordinary number of staff working at the school, particularly for a school of its size. For example, when I asked Rob, a staff member at the school, about what constraints exist for Ruth, this is what he had to say:

> In this particular school the biggest one would be staff. Because of the way they band schools, they're banded on student numbers but they don't realise that for the student numbers we have twice as many staff. Because we can use CDEP workers which in a regular school you might only hire two people but they would be full time to do all of the cleaning. We have five cleaners but they're only working x numbers of hours to cover the CDEP work, to keep people in the community active in the workforce and the same with the tutoring and the teacher aides. So it's managing a massive workforce of almost 60 people with the resources delegated to a school that would probably have 16 or 17 workforce, so she's tripling the amount of paperwork, the funding.

The Executive Director of Schools also believed the large staff that Ruth has to manage to be particularly challenging:

> Pine Hills is most unusual in that it has a very large number of staff, 50+ staff which is actually the equivalent in staff numbers to our larger schools, what we call a Band 8 and some of our smaller Band 9, so it's what we call very complex. You're dealing with a lot of HR issues, a lot of people management, more than the number of kids. The banding of the school is based on the number of kids, not the number of staff. So that's why it's most unusual, it's a small school that has very large HR demands and the management of people.

These added complexities of managing a large staff are a constant source of distraction and added workload for not only Ruth but also the administrative officer. These issues are returned to in Chapters 5 and 6 where the portraits are progressively filled out in greater detail.

Outline of the book

In the next chapter, Chapter 2, I provide the theoretical basis for the book by introducing the particular concepts of Michel Foucault through which I analyse these principals' work. The purpose of this chapter is twofold: first, to argue for the usefulness of Foucault's concepts to the study of educational leadership and management; and second, to introduce the Foucauldian tools that frame the rest of the book. In particular I draw upon Foucault's notions of disciplinary power, governmentality and ethics to explore the webs of power that shape principal subjectivities.

In Chapter 3 I provide a genealogical reading of a range of leadership and self-management literature to demonstrate how certain leadership policies and discourses have been privileged over others. In so doing, I show how the principal is uneasily positioned within these discourses and I analyse how such constructions of the principal are problematic when attempting to understand their roles and work. I argue that such leadership and management discourses not only fail to adequately grasp the complexities of the job but can also create problematic constructions of principals' leadership that can lead to a normalised and disciplined subject position.

Chapter 4 begins with a daily snapshot of the principals' day to provide a rich account of the messy work that principals are involved in. Drawing on these experiences, this chapter then uses Foucault's notions of governmentality and disciplinary power to illustrate how each of the two principals is positioned within discourses of school management. I argue that the two principals are inserted differently within these regimes and that the government of individualisation is an important figure of power. I demonstrate how elements of this power can be both totalising and also productive in each principal's capacity for resistance. I use Foucault's notions of docile bodies and panopticism in particular to show how the principals are placed within disciplinary regimes that use them as both objects and instruments of the exercising of disciplinary power. At the same time I juxtapose the notion of governmentality (that is, the conduct of conduct) through specific practices of the principals in both schools, using the writing of submissions and grants as examples. Following this, I then demonstrate how the principal is constituted by particular accountabilities and relationships by their respective communities, staff and controlling bodies. Such relationships with the local communities play a significant role in the way that each principal frames their work and, indeed, how their work is perceived.

In Chapter 5, I use Foucault's work on ethics as the basis for examining the principals' understandings of their own actions, work practices and technologies of the self. Thus, while the previous chapter examined power relations on a broader, school-based level, this chapter explores the principals' work on the self, a more individual level of analysis. The first section revisits Foucault's notion of ethics and the four dimensions to this self-forming process, which are: the ethical substance, modes of subjection, forms of elaboration and telos. The second part of this chapter explores the telos of each principal in terms of the work they do on themselves and on the school as principal. The third section examines in much more detail the work that each principal does to become a moral subject. The final section of this chapter compares and contrasts the fourfold work that both principals do and demonstrates that even though they may have a similar telos, through the different contexts of each school, they must do different work. As a result of this exploration of Foucault's notion of ethics and principals' work, I demonstrate how contextual factors play such a significant part of these principals' leadership in their schools and cannot be ignored.

The significance of this book is that principals and educational leadership do matter and can make a difference to the lives and educational outcomes of students (Lingard, Hayes, Mills & Christie, 2003). At a time when there is a number of principals leaving their positions and there is a shortage of applicants for principal positions (Gronn, 2003a, 2003b), albeit for a range of reasons (Barty, Thomson, Blackmore & Sachs, 2005; Thomson, 2009), it is important to have more diverse perspectives and understandings of leadership (Sinclair, 1998; Sinclair & Wilson, 2002) and to recognise multiple dimensions of educational leadership (Blackmore, 1999). In this book, I show an examination of principals' everyday practices that enable a textured reading of educational leadership, rather than conceptualising leadership as a range of competences and models that are common in many of the popular leadership discourses.

2   A Foucauldian toolbox for educational leadership

> My role is to raise questions in an effective, genuine way, and to raise them with the greatest possible rigor, with the maximum complexity and difficulty so that a solution doesn't spring from the head of some reformist intellectual or suddenly appear in the head of a party's political bureau.
>
> (Foucault, 2002a, p. 288)

There has been an enormous volume of literature published discussing Foucault and his work generally and in the field of education. So rather than attempt to provide a review of Foucault's œuvre, I focus on a few key Foucauldian concepts. This is because one cannot regard Foucault's body of work as 'an immediate unity nor as a certain unity nor as a homogeneous unity' (Foucault, 1972, p. 27). Therefore I draw upon specific concepts to make up my toolkit and consciously draw more heavily on Foucault's original works than interpretations of his work by others.

The fact that there is a limited use of Foucault in educational leadership is surprising, given the wide use of his methodologies in other fields and education more broadly. Perhaps this is in part due to education being very much accepting of modernist ideals, particularly assumptions deriving from Enlightenment thought (Usher & Edwards, 1994). As Lingard, Hayes, Mills and Christie (2003, p. 2) argue: 'Western schools have a strangely old fashioned, perhaps modernist feel. Their solid buildings, local embeddedness, rigid timetables, clearly defined curricula and formalized relationships and rituals seem out of step with times of liquid global change.' While targeted at schools generally, it could be argued this point is valid for educational leadership also. Jill Blackmore (1999), for example, questions the recent conceptualisations of educational leadership in theory, policy and dominant top-down visionary leadership and strategic management to highlight the need to examine and unravel the genealogies of the technologies of gender implicit in educational leadership.

Only a handful of writers have challenged the traditional bastions of educational leadership and administration through Foucault's work. For example, Anderson and Grinberg (1998) have introduced the importance of Foucault's view of power, discourse and method to educational administration.

Meadmore, Limerick, Thomas and Lucas (1995) have argued for Foucault's notion of 'governmentality' as crucial in an examination of the discourses of devolution in a particular school. Stephen Ball has written extensively on the British educational system and has extensively utilised Foucault's ideas (Ball, 1990a, 1990b, 1994). Others in the field of leadership in education who have used Foucault include Angus (1996), Blackmore (1999), Lingard *et al.* (2003), Maxcy (1991, 1994), Popkewitz (1991), Popkewitz and Brennan (1997, 1998) and Quicke (2000). A survey of this literature highlights the need for further research and analysis of Foucault's work for application in the field of educational leadership and management. The importance of Foucault's work is that it can be used to provide different ways of understanding discourses of educational leadership. The dominant paradigms of leadership through heroic performances, leader designer frameworks and best-practice models that are so pervasive have little or no rigorous theoretical underpinnings, and as such the feasibility of these 'more traditional' approaches in terms of providing a means for critical self-reflection needs to be seriously questioned. Issues such as power relations are essential to the study of leadership and administration. Therefore in this book I attempt to fill two gaps in the existing literature: first, that of Foucault and references to educational leadership; and, second, the use of Foucauldian concepts in studies of educational leadership and management.

In this chapter I specifically aim to demonstrate the usefulness of Foucault's work in the examination of educational administration and leadership through the concepts of disciplinary power, governmentality and ethics. Such themes are still relevant today, and in fact May (2005) argues that if we need to question the relevance of Foucault's work for today, then we must become *more* Foucauldian rather than less.

Why Foucault?

Foucault provides an original critical framework through his notions of archaeology and genealogy, with particular reference to his detailed focus on the emergence and operation of power in modern society. Foucault describes archaeology as 'the appropriate methodology of the analysis of local discursivities' and genealogy as 'the tactics whereby, on the basis of the descriptions of these local discursivities, the subjected knowledges which were released would be brought into play' (1980a, p. 85). It is these local tactics that I am particularly interested in throughout this book. Foucault also works within an historical framework in his archaeological and genealogical approaches that account for the constitution of the subject.

In later works, Foucault's genealogies investigate the links between rationalisation and power in specific fields rather than society as a whole. He has investigated the regimes of practices invested in insanity and mental illness (1967), medicine (1975), penal institutions (1977b) and sexuality (1981a). It is through these examinations of practices and how power operates that it is possible to understand how the subject is placed and constructed in complex power relations. Thus, Foucault is attempting to provide methods of analysis for power relations for which there were previously no tools for study (Foucault, 1983). Best and Kellner agree as they argue, 'the overriding emphasis of Foucault's work is on the ways in which individuals are classified, excluded, objectified, individualised, disciplined and normalised' (1991, p. 55). Foucault's work on disciplinary power is particularly important for an examination of the subjectification of leaders through the multifarious disciplinary regimes of school-based management. Foucault emphasises power as a central notion in the understanding of how subjects are constructed. It is therefore the examination of practices undertaken by and upon the principal that is important in this analysis of power relations.

On a more macro level, Foucault's notion of governmentality is also important for emphasising and analysing the formation of a whole series of government apparatuses and the development of a whole complex of *savoirs* (Foucault, 1991b) that work to control the population for purposes of social administration (Meadmore et al., 1995). Usher and Edwards similarly argue that 'education is not simply that which goes on in schools but is an essential part of governmentality, a crucial aspect of the regulatory practices of a range of modern institutions' (1994, p. 84). It is not only the managing and ordering of students' 'docile bodies' that is imperative in this framework, but also the managing and ordering of principals' bodies through a range of practices associated with regimes of self-management. It is the discourses that subjectify and normalise principals that require unpacking. Another point that needs to be considered is the discourses that principals use to normalise others, for example, teachers, staff and students. Principals have at their disposal a range of discursive practices and techniques with which they can normalise others within their school in order to achieve certain outcomes. The principal is uniquely positioned through a range of discourses that create particular subjects for particular purposes. These are specifically examined throughout Chapters 4 and 5.

Foucault and discourse

Foucault's concept of discourse is central in any attempt to analyse and apply Foucault's work, and it is here that I start. Of particular importance is Foucault's notion of analysing power as it is exercised through discourse. Foucault argues that

> In a society such as ours, but basically in any society, there are manifold relations of power which permeate, characterise and constitute the social body, and these relations of power cannot themselves be established, consolidated nor implemented without the production, accumulation, circulation and functioning of a discourse.
>
> (1980a, p. 93)

Furthermore, Foucault states that 'it is in discourse that power and knowledge are joined together' (1981a, p. 100). An understanding of Foucault's concept of discourse is essential to the study of power/knowledge and disciplinary power. For Foucault, discourses are mechanisms and practices that frame what can be said and thought, as he argues: 'discourses are practices that systematically form the objects of which they speak' (1972, p. 54). Blackmore also describes discourses as 'the institutionalised use of language, which can occur at a disciplinary, political, cultural and small group level' (1999, p. 16). Although language is important, as it constructs the individual's subjectivity in ways that are socially specific (Weedon, 1987), Foucault is more concerned with analysis of institutional practices and power relations that produce meaning. He states that

> Discourses are composed of signs; but what they do is more than use these signs to designate things. It is this more that renders them irreducible to the language (langue) and to speech. It is this 'more' that we must reveal and describe.
>
> (1972, p. 54)

Foucault goes on to further explain the complexities associated with the notion of discourse as he points out that he has used discourse 'sometimes as the general domain of all statements, sometimes as an individualisable group of statements, and sometimes as a regulated practice that accounts for a certain number of statements' (1972, p. 90). It is this pluralist approach to discourse that provides an originality and complexity to Foucault's approach. Such a conceptualisation of discourse provides a wide array of tools with which to approach his study. Discourse is more than just language; it is also the emphasis of a complex set of practices that engage some statements while at the same time excluding others. Furthermore, it is the regulation of discourse that interests Foucault:

> In every society the production of discourse is at once controlled, selected, organised and redistributed by a certain number of procedures whose role is to ward off its powers and dangers, to gain mastery over its chance events, to evade its ponderous, formidable materiality.
>
> (1981b, p. 52)

The notion of analysing power through discourse is a central task throughout his book. Concepts such as leadership and management, for example, are constituted and sustained through certain discourses, and, as such, 'leadership is not what it claims to be, but rather it is an effect of a discourse, a superficial surface, a mask that deflects attention from its genealogy and effects' (Lingard et al., 2003, p. 128). Roland Bleiker similarly argues that 'discourses render social practices intelligible and rational – and by doing so mask the ways in which they have been constituted and framed'

(2003, p. 28). The way terms such as 'leadership' and 'management' are used and the way they are joined together within discourses constitute leadership in certain ways. For example, the impact of the proliferation of management texts as discourses of principals' work disciplines and normalises leaders towards a more management-oriented paradigm (this issue is expanded upon in Chapter 3). To reiterate Foucault, discourses should be viewed as practices that systematically form the objects of which they speak, and as such can become mechanisms of disciplinary power. As Pat Thomson argues:

> The habits of categorization are alive and well in much of the educational administration literature, in which there abound multiple varieties of leadership and various foci for management. These scholarly abstractions, because of their imbrication with the work of educational administrators and bureaucracies, indeed become active in the construction of principals as technicians; they become disciplinary.
>
> (2001, pp. 15–16)

Thomson further argues that publications such as *The Practising Administrator*, published by the Australian Council of Educational Administration, emphasise the technical and operational matters of the everyday processes yet neglect issues of pedagogy and the growing body of research into educational reform. As Thomson suggests, 'it is what is left out that is significant' (2001, p. 7). It is in this way that discourses can create systems of exclusion in which one group of discourses is prioritised while others are neglected and excluded. It is these practices and techniques that prioritise management issues while ignoring issues of pedagogy, social justice and ethics in leadership discourses. It is a complex web of 'discontinuous segments whose tactical function is neither uniform nor stable' (Foucault, 1981a, p. 100). Foucault here is referring to a multiplicity of discursive elements at play at any given time rather than a situation of one dominating the other.

Foucault is very much a pluralist in that he refutes the claim to identify cause-and-effect linkages to render apparent the polymorphous interweaving of correlations (1991c, p. 58). There are a number of complex interweaving discourses and strategies at play at any given time. It is for this reason that Foucault's approach to discourse is important as he rejects simple causality as an answer to problems. Foucault is also careful to emphasise the productive capacity of discourse. For Foucault, 'discourse transmits and produces power; it reinforces it, but also undermines and exposes it, renders it fragile and makes it possible to thwart it' (1981a, p. 101). Of course here Foucault is referring to the idea of power being synonymous with resistance.

It is necessary to work both inside and outside the discourses to examine the exercise of power and to identify normalisations. It is for this reason that I incorporate Foucault's work on governmentality while simultaneously using the earlier work on disciplinary power. This is a complex task as Foucault moved through phases in his writing, and the notion of governmentality was developed later. That is not to say that the two concepts cannot be used together, but rather to acknowledge the complexities associated with using both concepts simultaneously. In the examination of principals it is necessary to look at power/knowledge formations outside the institution of the school, that is, in the social body as well as inside the school itself. Foucault writes about the importance of defining the play of dependencies between the transformations of intradiscursive, interdiscursive and extradiscursive dependencies (1991c). Foucault uses the term 'discursive field' to describe the difference between what one could say correctly at one period and what is actually said at a specific moment. This discursive field 'consists of a whole group of regulated practices which do not merely involve giving a visible outward embodiment to the agile inwardness of thought, or providing the solidarity of things with a surface of manifestation capable of duplicating them' (Foucault, 1991c, p. 63).

It is for this reason that Foucault argues, and this is his notion of conducting a history of the present, that 'discourse must not be referred to the distant presence of the origin, but treated as and when it occurs' (1972, p. 28). It is important to grasp statements in their specific occurrences: that is, the conditions of their occurrence, correlations with other statements and what statements are excluded. It is this discursive field that I explore, that is, the inter-correlation of discourses in notions of leadership as they occur, for example, leadership and management discourses as disciplinary practices that create principals as particular subjects.

Foucault also argues that 'discourse is not a place into which the subjectivity irrupts; it is a space of differentiated subject-positions and subject-functions' (1991c, p. 58). This notion of the subject is important as Foucault is referring to the idea that subjects are not only shaped by social structures, but actively take up their own discourses through which they are shaped and by which they shape themselves (Blackmore, 1997). The notion of the subject is one that Foucault argues has been at the centre of his research (Foucault, 1983) and is also central to this book. Foucault argues that the subject is placed in power relations that are very complex, and it is important to analyse these power relations that make individuals subjects. Foucault uses the word 'subject' to mean 'subject to someone else by control and dependence and tied to his [*sic*] own identity by a conscience or self knowledge' (1983, p. 212). The notions of agency and structure are always present when looking at educational leaders, as they are expected to formulate visions and enable change, but at the same time are constrained and normalised by bureaucratic processes and mechanisms (see, for example, Thomson, 2001).

It is not my aim to re-explore the age-old agency/structure debate but more so to understand this notion of agency through the concept of discourse (Bleiker, 2003). Bleiker argues that discourses not only frame and subjugate our thoughts and behaviour but also offer possibilities for human agency. It is here that there is possibility for resistance to systemic and discursive practices, through these fissures and cracks, for Foucault sees power as productive and can be seen as an instrument of resistance. I would argue against the notion of transformative pathways, however, as these would lead to further normalisations and power/knowledge formations consistent with another set of discourses. Furthermore, one must analyse institutions from the standpoint of power relations, that is, to analyse power relations from outside the institution, deep in the social nexus (Foucault, 1983, p. 222). This is why the notion of governmentality also forms a significant concept in my toolkit.

Power/knowledge

The early foundation for the notion of power/knowledge first surfaced in *Madness and Civilisation* (Foucault, 1967), where Foucault attempted to pursue the production of knowledge in complex institutional systems, that is, 'in what network of institutions and practices the madman was both enmeshed and defined' (2000b, p. 5). It was through this study that he developed the pursuit of identifying the formation of knowledge on the basis of social practices (2002a). These social practices and strategies form discourses that construct subjects. It is here that Foucault (2002a) draws upon Nietzsche's work to illustrate, historically, the birth of a certain type of knowledge (*savoir*) without granting the pre-existence of a subject of knowledge (*connaissance*). Foucault draws the distinction between *connaissance* (knowledge) and *savoir* (knowledge). Foucault (2002b) sees *savoir* as the process that enables one to both modify the subject and to construct the object. *Connaissance*, on the other hand, is more a relation between a fixed subject and a domain of objects. *Savoir* is more a process, whereas *connaissance* is the things that one knows. In forming his notion of knowledge, Foucault uses Nietzsche to argue that knowledge was invented, it is not something that is inscribed in human nature. Foucault states that

> Knowledge is simply the outcome of the interplay, the encounter, the junction, the struggle, and the compromise between the instincts. Something is produced because the instincts meet, fight one another, and at the end of their battles finally reach a compromise. That something is knowledge.
>
> (2002a, p. 8)

The importance of what Foucault is saying is that at the centre of this conception of knowledge are power relations and it is through these struggles that power relations form knowledge. To therefore understand knowledge it is imperative to examine power relations. Knowledge does not exist in itself, it exists through power relations. In effect, knowledge is always a strategic relation in which one is placed (Foucault 2002a). One of Foucault's tasks was to examine how domains of knowledge have been formed through social practices (for example, *Discipline and Punish* and *The History of Sexuality, Volume 1*).

In *Discipline and Punish* (1977b), Foucault's task was to examine historically how it is that the disappearance of the public spectacle of punishment, a hold on the body, became an infusion of punishment, surveillance and constraint of the soul. It was Foucault's intention to outline:

> A correlative history of the modern soul and of a power to judge; a genealogy of the present scientifico-legal complex from which the power to punish derives its bases, justifications and rules, from which it extends its effects and by which it masks its exorbitant singularity.
>
> (Foucault, 1977b, p. 23)

In this statement Foucault is outlining a number of methodological approaches that he uses in this text. He works historically and he plans to use genealogical analysis to examine juridical practices and disciplinary power and normalisation. It is this genealogical approach, although not so much historically, that I use throughout this book, to expose the normalisation and subjectification of principals through discourses and practices at work through regimes of school-based management. To provide an alternate reading of school-based management, it is necessary to examine the practices and discursive regimes that are not readily apparent; that is the practices that normalise educational leaders on a daily basis.

Foucault's concern is with 'power at its extremities, in its ultimate destinations, with those points where it becomes capillary, that is, in its more regional forms and institutions' (1980a, p. 96). In order to analyse power, it must be seen in a radically different way than had previously been done. This was one of the processes that became evident in, and in fact central to, Foucault's analysis of the emergence of the modern penal institution. Foucault emphasises the analysis of power from its bases, its lowest levels. It is at this level that the formation of knowledges is circulated, through the micro-mechanisms of power. These power relations that produce knowledges can be seen through such procedures as principal and school accountabilities, competence characteristics, school effectiveness tables and managerialism. Meadmore et al. (1995) argue that devolution by documentation is one example of the power/knowledge nexus. The principal is held accountable through these webs of documents and is ultimately 'knowable' through these forms of management (see Chapter 4). Foucault emphasises that

> Power produces knowledge; that power and knowledge directly imply one another; that there is no power relation without the correlative constitution of a field of knowledge, nor any knowledge that does not presuppose and constitute at the same time power relations.
>
> (1977b, p. 27)

Whether it is employed in penal institutions or schools, the exercise of power and the manifestation of power relations are implicit with the production of truth. This question of truth is important for Foucault as he argues that every society has its regimes of truth; that is, what discourses are accepted and function as bearing true statements and the mechanisms and practices that allow these discourses to distinguish true and false statements. Foucault states that

> Each society has its regime of truth, its 'general politics' of truth: that is, the types of discourse which it accepts and makes function as true; the mechanisms and instances which enable one to distinguish true and false statements, the means by which each is sanctioned; the techniques and procedures accorded value in the acquisition of truth; the status of those who are charged with saying what counts as true.
>
> (1980b, p. 131)

Essentially Foucault is arguing that truth is not lacking in power, it is a thing of this world. Truth is 'the ensemble of rules according to which the true and false are separated and specific effects of power are attached to the true' (1980b, p. 132). It is therefore the role of the intellectual to ascertain the possibility of a new politics of truth by detaching the power of truth from the discourses within which it operates. For this book that means unpacking discourses and practices that normalise principals and position them as subjects within the complex web of school-based management and educational leadership. In so doing it is possible to not only deconstruct leadership discourses but also introduce a constant instability into assumptions of how leadership is constituted and understood (Lingard et al., 2003).

Foucault's view of power emphasises the point that it is not possessed but rather it is exercised through networks of relations that are constantly in tension. Foucault states that

> Power must be analysed as something which circulates, or rather as something which only functions in the form of a chain. It is never localised here or there, never in anybody's hands, never appropriated as a commodity or a piece of wealth. Power is employed and exercised through a net-like organisation. And not only do individuals circulate between its threads; they are always in the position of simultaneously undergoing and exercising this power ... individuals are the vehicles of power, not its points of application.
>
> (1980a, p. 98)

Thus, these relations of power go through all aspects of society, and it is this investment through the individual that is important. The individual is not only an effect of these micro relations of power but power is also constituted through the individual. It is this analysis of power from its infinitesimal points that Foucault is concerned with, an ascending analysis of power (1980a, p. 99). This leads Foucault to emphasise the subjection of the individual and the body as being crucial in this power/knowledge system (1977b, pp. 25–26).

Disciplinary power

In a series of lectures entitled 'Truth and Juridical Forms' (2002a), Michel Foucault outlines the formation of disciplinary society that he argues is a central feature of contemporary society. It is his aim to show how the formation of domains of knowledge through social practices (particularly through control and supervision) serves to give rise not only to new techniques and concepts but also to new subjects and subjects of knowledge. Foucault attempts to show 'the historical construction of a subject through a discourse understood as consisting as a set of strategies which are part of social practices' (2002a, p. 4). It is here that Foucault focuses on juridical practices and, in particular, the inquiry. It was in the search for truth within the juridical order in the middle of the medieval era that the inquiry was founded. Furthermore, Foucault argues, during this period the inquiry developed as a particular way of knowing, 'a condition of possibility of knowledge whose destiny was to be crucial in the Western world' (2002a, p. 40). Foucault claims that the inquiry's emergence was a complicated political phenomenon that had both administrative and religious origins. Of particular importance is the emergence of the inquiry in medieval Europe as a governmental process, an administrative technique, a management method; in other words, a particular way of exercising power (Foucault, 2002a). Thus the inquiry emerges as a form of knowledge, a political form that became a way of authenticating truth, a form of power/knowledge.

Infractions against this form of knowledge resulted in penalties performed by a whole network of institutions of surveillance and correction, not by the judiciary itself (Foucault, 2002a). It is here that we see the beginnings of a disciplinary society. The ultimate mechanism for this composition of disciplinary power is Bentham's 'panopticon'. Foucault outlines the main concerns of the panopticon as 'individualising observation, with characterisation and classification, with the analytical arrangement of space' (1977b, p. 203). Bentham's panopticon is an architectural mechanism that, though applied to prisons, could readily be used by any closed institution. The idea behind the panopticon was the division of inmates into separate cells whereby they are constantly under surveillance, with the central observer unseen. Thus the inmates are separated and always on view. This state of conscious and permanent visibility ensured the automatic functioning of power (Foucault, 1977b, p. 201). Bentham's view that power should be visible and unverifiable is crucial to this arrangement and underscores the importance of the panopticon, for:

> It automatises and disindividualises power. Power has its principal not so much in a person as in a certain concerted distribution of bodies,

surfaces, lights, gazes; in an arrangement whose internal mechanisms produce the relation in which individuals are caught up.

(Foucault, 1977b, p. 202)

The panopticon is therefore the ultimate disciplinary mechanism that not only provides an apparatus for supervising inmates but also can supervise its own mechanisms. This notion is particularly important for the architectural design of the school, as it is not only for the supervision of the students but also for the supervision of those in charge. It is therefore my aim to demonstrate how the panopticon operates for principals, through his/her daily operations, in their daily existence. Foucault states that

The individuals over whom power is exercised are either those from whom the knowledge they themselves form will be extracted, retranscribed, and accumulated according to new norms, or else objects of a knowledge that will also make possible new forms of control.

(2002a, p. 84)

A point that Foucault constantly reiterated was that power is productive through the body and its subjection to these power relations. It is one of the purposes of education to produce knowledge, but one needs to recognise that it is not just the ordering and subjection of children's bodies but also those of teachers and principals of schools who are constructed by these power/knowledge relations. These methods of control over the body are what Foucault refers to as 'disciplines' (1977b, p. 137). These disciplines have their own discourses and produce and subjectify 'docile bodies'. It is not only the emergence of these micro powers that is able to control the body and make it more docile, but also through self-management and regulation. It is in the small things, the details that bodies are made more pliable. Foucault outlines the notion of enclosure, the specification of a place heterogeneous to all others and closed in upon itself (1977b, p. 143). This results in the individualisation of bodies through the organisation of space. This disciplinary method of division 'individualises bodies by location that does not give them a fixed position, but distributes them in a network of relations' (1977b, p. 146).

These 'dividing practices' (Foucault, 1980a) are no more evident than in the school. This form of disciplinary power is readily apparent in the organisation of students' bodies. Similarly, principals and administration staff are organised into segmented and functional spaces to maximise the efficiency and obedience of bodies and tasks. School administration is usually accorded its own building or organised space in which its tasks can be carried out efficiently, as are departments and faculties in high schools. This arrangement of bodies into specific departments allows sufficient differentiation so that specific activities can be undertaken without distraction. Equally as important as the arrangement of space is the regulation of time–space. The control of activity through timetables is also significant as it makes efficient use of time in the regulation of activity, as Foucault states, 'time penetrates the body and with it all the meticulous controls of power' (1977b, p. 152). The school bell signals any deviance from regulated activity. Thus, what emerges is a disciplinary penalty based upon time, for example, lateness, absenteeism and interruption of tasks.

The success of disciplinary power, according to Foucault, derives from the use of simple instruments: hierarchical observation, normalising judgement and the examination. Hierarchical surveillance is presupposed in the idea that the networks of observation work from top to bottom, bottom to top and also laterally (Foucault, 1977b, p. 176). It is a mechanism that 'coerces by means of observation; an apparatus in which the techniques that make it possible to see induce effects of power and in which, conversely, the means of coercion make those on whom they are applied clearly visible' (Foucault, 1977b, pp. 170–171).

This notion of visibility is crucial to the functioning of disciplinary power since, for this power to be effective, those subjects involved in its perpetuation must be aware of their observation. At the same time it is also organised as 'a multiple, automatic, and anonymous power' (1977b, p. 176). These disciplinary institutions secrete a machinery of control that functions like 'a microscope of conduct; the fine, analytical divisions that they created formed around men an apparatus of observation, recording and training' (1977b, p. 173). Thus it was initially in the construct of the school building in which these mechanisms of observation and surveillance could be produced. With the current move to a more market-oriented schooling system, it is the gaze of the parents that is increasingly becoming a factor for school principals. Schools are now more accountable to the parents, or clients. Principals must now, in panoptic fashion, act as though the parents are observing and judging them even though their physical presence is not felt (Usher & Edwards, 1994, p. 114). Thus, this disciplinary power can be exercised over schools and principals as well as through them.

Disciplinary power also relies upon a number of penal mechanisms that enjoy a kind of 'juridical privilege with its own laws, its specific offences, its particular forms of judgement' (Foucault, 1977b, p. 178). Schools, in particular, were privy to penalties related to even slight departures from strict regimes according to time, behaviour, speech, sexuality and the body. The differentiation of individuals through these rituals, rules and regimes of truth is a normalising function of disciplinary power, 'the perpetual penalty that traverses all points and supervises every instant in the disciplinary institutions compares, differentiates, hierarchises, homogenises, excludes. In short, it normalises' (Foucault, 1977b, p. 183).

The third of these disciplinary instruments is the examination. With the advent of the panopticon, a new type of knowledge is founded, not upon the inquiry but the examination. The examination is a particularly important aspect of normalisation, for it not only combines the techniques of an observing hierarchy and those of normalising judgement, but its formal and informal roles in education have been and still continue to be a bedrock of disciplinary power. Foucault describes the examination as:

> A normalising gaze, a surveillance that makes it possible to qualify, to classify, and to punish. It establishes over individuals a visibility through which one differentiates them and judges them ... the examination is highly ritualised. In it are combined the ceremony of power and the form of the experiment, the deployment of force and the establishment of truth. At the heart of the procedures of discipline, it manifests the subjection of those who are perceived as objects and the objectification of those who are subjected.
>
> (1977b, pp. 184–185)

The ceremony and ritualised nature of the examination is still a strong presence in schools today. The examination's power lies in the establishment of truths through the objectification of individuals as well as their comparison with each other. Through the examination, each 'case' is individualised so as to uncover specific abilities and features while at the same time allows a comparative mechanism to be established through documentation. Foucault emphasises that this 'power of writing' (1977b, p. 189) is an essential part of the mechanisms of discipline. Education has very much revolved around this documentary accumulation through the examination for it allows an environment in which 'the individual may be described, judged, measured, compared with others, in his very individuality; and it is also the individual who has to be trained or corrected, classified, normalised, excluded, etc.' (Foucault, 1977b, p. 191).

It is not only the formal examination undertaken by students that is the issue. It is also the disciplining of teachers and school administration in the construction of examinations and the formulation of their documentation. Teachers and schools are judged by the performance of students in public examinations. Teachers must also submit to evaluations and competence tests. Similarly, principals are constantly subjected to leader-competence reports, school performance tests and the like in a constant stream of performance examinations and accountability procedures (Anderson, 2009; Thomson, 2009).

Foucault argues that, historically, the development of the bureaucracies and administrative structures of the Imperial Period increased the amount and role of writing in the political sphere (2000a). This in turn evolved into the notion of constant writing being closely linked to the idea of taking care of oneself (Foucault, 2000c, 2000d). The intensification of principals' work in today's schools is an indication of this link between constant documentation and taking care of oneself and one's school (see Chapter 5). The use of performativity and target-related funding is also central to the operation of school-based management, not only the market form, but also that of corporate managerialism. The introduction of market forces, particularly, has shifted the emphasis of schooling to one of competition and choice (Whitty, Power & Halpin, 1998). Thus, marketing and income-generation combine with an insistence of output measures (for example, examination perform-ance) to shift the focus to one of consumption. This emphasis on perform-ance is one of the lynchpins of a market perspective of school-based management, as prospective clients are forced to rely on such mechanisms when 'choosing' a school for their children. The use of such terms as 'con-sumers' and 'clients' signals this shift towards a market perspective.

It is through normalisations such as hierarchical observation, normalising judgement and the examination that disciplinary power is wielded. These practices are central to policies of devolution where principals are subjected to increased visibility, accountability and responsibility for the constraints of power so that they become self-governing (Meadmore et al., 1995). It is also important to note that disciplinary practices cannot be escaped, but it is my aim to question those practices such as school-based management that claim to be more democratic and participatory, while in fact they result in more effective technologies of control (Anderson & Grinberg, 1998). For example, the changed form of the distribution of finances to schools now requires the principal to be responsible for writing the submissions and managing the funds. As a result, the subject position of the principal has shifted to one that is now bound into rules, regulations and constant examination.

Foucault and feminism

As I stated at the start, while issues of gender are not the object of this book, they do play a notable role in the construction of any principal's subjectivi-ties. For the two principals in this study, there are particularities to being female principals that need to be acknowledged. The position of principal in Australia is still largely dominated by men, so any examination of the prin-cipal must take this into account. As I discuss in Chapter 3, leadership is still often conceptualised from a top-down, 'heroic' style of leading that is masculinist in scope and results in a normalised view of leaders according to this paradigm. Such a normalisation is problematic for both women and men who are principals, but has particular implications for women principals. As Jill Blackmore states:

> Populist versions promoted in the media of feminist discourses about women's styles of leadership being more caring and sharing have con-flated 'being female' to 'being feminist' in highly essentialist ways. It is a conflation that ignores both the differences amongst women and the difficult political context in which leading women work.

> (1999, p. 3).

In education we are still faced with a situation where the vast majority of teachers, particularly in primary schools, are female, yet there is an overwhelming majority of men in positions of authority. Traditional 'masculinist' leadership theories have served to 'sanitise the unequal power relations within an organisation' (Watkins, 1989, p. 11). As a result: 'White, middle-class, heterosexual males continue to wield cultural and financial power derived from contemporary educational discourses that associate masculinity with economic rationality, being strong, making 'hard' decisions, the 'hard' knowledge areas of science and technology and entrepreneurship' (Blackmore, 1999, p. 4).

Foucault's work has much to offer some feminists in terms of a critique of essentialist accounts of women's oppression. Foucault's analysis of historically specific power relations has provided a useful framework in which women can be viewed as subjects that are constructed through language and discourse (McNay, 1994) rather than biologically determined. The body is produced through power and is as such a cultural entity rather than a natural one. Foucault has also been criticised for ignoring the gender configurations of power relations and the gendered character of many disciplinary techniques, therefore conflicting with the feminist project of rediscovering and revaluing the experiences of women (McNay, 1994). This silence may be seen in some feminist circles as contributing to the oppression of women. Some writers (see Diamond & Quinby, 1988; Hartsock, 1990; Said, 1986) have also argued that Foucault's work leaves subjects with few avenues for resistance. Critics of Foucault's work have claimed that while revealing injustice and cruelty, his theorisations let them go more or less unchecked (Said, 1986, p. 152).

A number of feminist authors have also found shortcomings in Foucault's work. For example, Diamond and Quinby (1988, p. xiv) state that Foucault's discussions gloss over the gender configurations of power, and Hartsock (1990, p. 159) argues that Foucault's work, among other poststructuralists, serves to hinder rather than help the plight of the marginalised. While I would acknowledge and agree in part with these arguments, it must be stated that it was not Foucault's purpose to 'arrive at moral or intellectual judgements on the features of our society produced by such forms of power, but to render possible an analysis of the process of production itself' (Gordon, 1980, p. 237). Thus, the importance of Foucault's perspectives on power is not as a blueprint for breaking boundaries on behalf of disadvantaged groups, but rather it 'encourages us to take a closer look at how power works in relation to the lived experience of groups and individuals in local contexts' (Quicke, 2000, p. 312).

The criticism that Foucault's work is not useful for women or oppressed groups is largely misleading, as Foucault makes it clear that it was not his intention to outline any of these things. It is only the attempt to apply Foucault's work to these issues that proves problematic. Certainly there is an underlying theme of a concern for social justice throughout Foucault's writing (O'Farrell, 2005) but to apply his concepts with the purpose of sustaining a subjective viewpoint where there was none intended is fraught with difficulties.

In relation to educational leadership and administration, Foucault's work would suggest that educational administration is incapable of asking critical questions because it is trapped within discourses of efficiency, productivity and performativity (Anderson & Grinberg, 1998). Due to the normalisation and constitution of such power relations being so widespread, it is difficult to escape these discourses in order to provide competing discourses. Thus, the importance of Foucault, for this book, is not to try to outline best practice within educational administration, but more so to call into question the taken-for-granted ways of thinking and processes that occur through normalisations. To try to promise solutions would be to create a new regime of truth that would then need to be unmasked (Anderson & Grinberg, 1998). Foucault's work suggests that to undertake more appropriate school reforms would be to take up struggles at the local, community level, to give a voice back to those who have previously not been allowed to speak. This is one of the contentious issues associated with school-based management as proponents of the move towards self-management advocate that it gives a voice back to the schools themselves.

Foucault's intention was to underscore problems, to raise questions in their complexity so that solutions come from the grassroots, from restoring people's right to speak. What needs to be done is:

> To criticize the working of institutions which appear to be both neutral and independent; to criticize them in such a manner that the political violence which has always exercised itself obscurely through them will be unmasked, so that one can fight them.
>
> (Foucault, 1974, p. 171)

It was not Foucault's intention to offer solutions, as he argues that

> I have absolutely no desire to play the role of a prescriber of solutions. I think that the role of the intellectual today is not to ordain, to recommend solutions, to prophesy, because in that function he [*sic*] can only contribute to the functioning of a particular power situation that, in my opinion, must be criticised.
>
> (2002b, p. 288)

What Foucault argues here is that such solutions would also then need to be unmasked as they would be themselves constituting new regimes of truth; in other words, school reform needs to take place as a local struggle to create the schools their communities need, not through large-scale re-engineering or re-culturing policies (Anderson & Grinberg, 1998). Foucault would argue in favour of more local resistances, as Walzer writes, 'Foucault's political theory is a tool kit not for revolution but for local resistance' (1986, p. 55). Walzer also goes on to argue that Foucault's refusal to propose solutions is the 'catastrophic weakness of his political theory' (1986, p. 67), yet I would counter this by saying that it is for this reason that Foucault's genealogies are so powerful and thought-provoking. Veyne writes that 'the originality of Foucault amongst the great thinkers of this century has been that he does not convert our finitude into the foundation for new certainties' (Veyne, cited in O'Farrell, 1989, p. 129). Ultimately, Walzer contradicts his earlier statements about Foucault's ideas being described as toolkits when he criticises Foucault for not prescribing solutions. Perhaps the importance of Foucault's discussion of resistance lies in the notion of resistance being a struggle to find a place of less domination within mainstream institutions such as schools rather than against such institutions.

Governmentality

Foucault's notion of governmentality can be a useful way of understanding the practices of government with respect to school-based management and the principal. In other words, how the practices of government make some form of that activity thinkable and practicable both to its practitioners and to those upon whom it is practised (Gordon, 1991). This notion of governmentality provides an overall framework within which to examine more specific issues of power relations and the mechanisms that bring power/ knowledge frameworks into place. I believe that this concept has specific implications for the work of principals in the management of their schools. The principal needs to be viewed as somebody who is not only subject to the practices of government but also a vehicle through which government can regulate the population. In other words, it is the surface practices of school-based management and the effects on individuals, in this case the principal, through the deployment of a range of tactics and procedures. It is at the surface that I explore the concept of school-based management, not for any underlying rationale or purpose. It is therefore through the practices and techniques of government that the subject becomes manageable. It is through this 'analytics of government' that question the taken-for-granted assumptions of how things are done that the principal's work and principal as subject can open up spaces where alternative viewpoints can operate.

Using governmentality to inform an analysis of school-based management or devolution is not a new concept (see Meadmore et al., 1995), but it is one that is particularly useful and needs further exploration.[1] Foucault's concept of governmentality is an attempt to analyse the problematic of government and to trace its emergence. The term itself refers to a combination of the words government and mentality. In *The History of Sexuality, Volume 1*, Foucault describes the emergence of 'bio-power', a notion of power that has two forms: one centred on the body and the other on the population (Foucault, 1981a). It was specifically in this issue of the regulation of population that the emphasis on government has emerged. Foucault's work on this emergence of government has some key ideas that have a profound influence on the questions of government that emerge under issues of school-based management. The importance of Foucault's work in this area needs to be emphasised as he is attempting to sketch an alternate analytic of political power (Miller & Rose, 1992).

Foucault's notion of 'government' can be defined as the 'conduct of conduct' (Dean, 1999; Gordon, 1991; Foucault, 1983). This particular notion of government is to do with the efficient management of 'men [*sic*] and things' (McNay, 1994, p. 115). The word 'conduct', however, has specific reference to behaviours and actions and also has particular importance for the notion of self-conduct. Dean argues that 'government entails any attempt to shape with some degree of deliberation aspects of our behaviour according to particular sets of norms and for a variety of ends' (1999, p. 10). It is this idea of self-conduct or self-government for which one can view the governor and the governed as two aspects of the same actor (Dean, 1999). By getting schools and principals to be self-governing means that the government increasingly relies on the individual principal (particularly in smaller schools) to assess their own conduct and the conduct of staff and students in order to improve efficiency and effectiveness. It is also where the government can expect parents to assess the conduct of principals and their schools, even though, often, parents' expectations may not align with the government's view. This is Foucault's concept of not only governing states and populations but also how one governs oneself. Dean also follows this line of reasoning, for example:

> Government concerns not only practices of government but also practices of the self. To analyse government is to analyse those practices that try to shape, sculpt, mobilise and work through the choices, desires, aspirations, needs, wants and lifestyles of individuals and groups.
>
> (1999, p. 12)

It is these practices of government that are important, particularly the rationalities of government, that is, the discourses that address the questions concerning how to conduct the conduct of the state and of the population (Hindess, 1996, p. 98). It is not for the purpose of overturning or emancipating from these disciplinary rationalities of government that I use Foucault, for this would constitute the same universalistic discourses that Foucault avoided. Nor do I aim to suggest reforms that would result in little more than the substitution of one set of powers for another (Hindess, 1996, p. 152). It is more for an appraisal of the techniques, practices and rationalities of government that, while not readily apparent, do discipline and normalise principals, thus exposing them to subjectification within discourses of school-based management as this can further undermine the confidence of both practitioners and subjects of a power relation (Ransom, 1997, p. 60). It is important to remember that 'The production of individuals through disciplinary mechanisms and the management of populations through the "art" of government produces an image of power that is formidable, to be sure, but hardly monolithic or impervious to critical reflection' (Ransom, 1997, p. 60).

Foucault uses the metaphor of governing a ship to help illustrate the notion of government. Using this metaphor, Foucault shows how government means taking charge of not only the sailors but also safely bringing the boat and its cargo to port through the dangers associated with winds, rocks and storms (Foucault, 1991b, p. 93). This is to be done by establishing a relationship between the sailors and the boat and its cargo. It is this forming of a relationship that is important as Foucault describes government as the 'complex composed of men and things' (1991b, p. 93). This metaphor can easily be transferred to the school, whereby the governing of a school involves taking charge of the teachers and also establishing a relationship between the teachers and the processes of teaching and learning, to weather the storm and bring students safely to the conclusion of their schooling to become active participants in society, that is, to a convenient end for the things that are to be governed (Foucault, 1991b, p. 95). It is in this way that Foucault moves away from posing the problem of the state in terms of sovereignty and in terms of employing tactics:

> With government it is a question not of imposing law on men [*sic*], but of disposing things: that is to say, of employing tactics rather than laws, and even of using laws themselves as tactics – to arrange things in such a way that, through a certain number of means, such and such ends may be achieved.
>
> (1991b, p. 95)

It is not in the proliferation of laws that government becomes possible but in the use of a range of tactics. It was during the sixteenth century, Foucault argues, that the problem of government explodes. At this time there occurred the intersection of two movements, one of state centralisation and the other of religious dissidence. It is at this intersection that the problematic of government emerges. Although Foucault is specifically referring to the sixteenth century, his analysis proceeds through to the eighteenth century. Furthermore, this analysis of the emergence of the political form of government still has relevance today, as Foucault states, 'we live in the era of a governmentality first discovered in the eighteenth century' (1991b, p. 103). Foucault uses Machiavelli's *The Prince* as a basis for comparison with other government literature to outline the establishment of the art of government as being concerned with the introduction of economy into political practice (1991b, p. 92). This has particular relevance for self-management as it is becoming imperative that principals of schools maximise efficiency from shrinking educational budgets and resources; the problematic for principals is fast becoming one of introducing economy into their management of schools. It is at the intersection of devolved responsibility to the schools and the recentralisation of education through approaches to effectiveness and efficiency that one of the problematics of government occurs for the principal. The principal is situated within a range of discourses. For example, they are governed by state-level policies, surveillance and accountability procedures as well as being in charge of their own 'households' (Foucault, 1991b, p. 92). It is not in the imposition of its will on principals that the government exercises its will but in the employment of tactics, practices and mechanisms through which the required ends may be met. Examples include state-wide testing of students' literacy and numeracy; principal and teacher competence and accountability frameworks under school-based management; and the ever-increasing government, parent and student gaze.

This new art of government that Foucault describes has as its target the population both as a subject which is the end of government and as the mechanism through which its aims are met. Foucault also points out that the issue of sovereignty, while playing a lesser role under this art of government, is far from being eliminated. In fact, Foucault argues that the problem of sovereignty is made even more acute than ever (1991b, p. 101). Nor is discipline eliminated either, as he states:

> Discipline was never more important or more valorised than at the moment when it became important to manage a population; the managing of a population not only concerns the collective mass of phenomena, the level of its aggregate effects, it also implies the management of population in its depths and its details.
>
> (1991b, p. 102)

It is therefore in this triangle of sovereignty–disciplinary–government (Foucault, 1991b, p. 102) that we need to view this issue of government and its target, the population. Foucault therefore conceptualises governmentality to mean three things:

1   The ensemble formed by the institutions, procedures, analyses and reflections, the calculations and tactics that allow the exercise of this very specific, albeit complex, form of power, which has as its target population, as its principal form of knowledge political economy, and as its essential technical means of apparatuses of security.
2   The tendency which, over a long period and throughout the West, has steadily led towards the pre-eminence over all other forms (sovereignty, discipline, etc.) of this type of power which may be termed government, resulting, on one hand, in the formation of a whole series of specific governmental apparatuses, and, on the other, in the development of a whole complex of *savoirs*.
3   The process, or rather the result of the process, through which the state of justice of the Middle Ages transformed into the administrative state during the fifteenth and sixteenth centuries, gradually becomes 'governmentalised'
(Foucault, 1991b, pp. 102–103)

What is significant about Foucault's notion of governmentality is that it challenges the taken-for-granted practices of government, or what Dean calls the 'mentalities of government' (1999, p. 36). It is concerned with how thought operates in our regimes of practices and is linked and embedded in the technical means for the conduct of conduct in practices and institutions (Dean, 1999, p. 16). This view of governmentality stands in contrast to the prevalence of state-oriented conceptions that cannot adequately describe the multitude of power relations that exist throughout the social body. Hunter (1994) argues that the treatment of schooling has been dominated by statist views of sovereign power, whereby power is transmitted in a repressive fashion to fulfil principled beliefs of education. Hunter goes on to propose that the emergence of the modern schooling system was founded upon a hybrid of administrative technologies and a system of pastoral discipline.

The importance of Hunter's genealogical approach is that he emphasises not only the unplanned nature of this development of the bureaucratic-pastoral school system but also the idea that the schooling system was not founded upon principled ideals of democracy or popular struggle (Hunter, 1996). Linking back to Foucault, the aim of the schooling system was thus not the development of children according to any particular ideology but rather the reinforcement of the state itself through the political technology of individuals. As Foucault states, 'reason of state refers neither to the wisdom of God or to the reason or the strategies of the prince: it refers to the state, to its nature, and to its own rationality' (2002c, p. 407). Thus we can infer from *Discipline and Punish* that it is not educational principles that are central to educational systems but school premises (Hunter, 1996).

One of the crucial ways in which governments could govern the population in a continuous and permanent way was through the development of power techniques oriented towards individuals (Foucault, 2002b, p. 300). Foucault describes this phenomenon as pastoral power. In doing so, he attempts to illustrate the paradoxical nature of modern techniques of government (McNay, 1994) or, more specifically, how pastoral power is both totalising and individualising.

Ethics

The final concept in my Foucauldian toolkit is his notion of ethics and how it can be used to illuminate the moral subjectification of principals through their own actions. Foucault gives the term 'moral' to the set of values and rules of action that are prescribed by agencies such as the family, educational institutions and churches; and 'ethics' as the real behaviour of individuals in relation to these prescribed codes, whether these values are respected or disregarded (Foucault, 1992). It is this relationship that Foucault emphasises as important, for it refers to the way one conducts oneself according to these moral codes, a relationship with the self. Foucault proposes that ethics is generally the relationship one has with oneself. This is closely linked with the notion of practices of freedom, as Foucault states that 'ethics is the considered form that freedom takes when it is informed by reflection' (2000e, p. 284).

The role of the principal is both moral and ethical in that principals have a range of codes of behaviour, competences and roles in their job description and they are constantly making ethical decisions based on the matter at hand in relation to these expectations. Using the four main aspects of Foucault's genealogy of ethics (1992), I consider the self's relationship to itself as a key notion of the way I look at principals' work. The four aspects of ethical work Foucault puts forward include:

1   Ethical substance: this refers to the part of oneself or of one's behaviour that is relevant for ethical judgement in order to achieve moral conduct, for example feelings; or more specifically the act linked with pleasure and desire.
2   Mode of subjection: this is what Foucault refers to as the way in which people are invited or incited to recognise their moral obligations. For example, this may refer to divine law in a holy text such as the Bible or the Koran, social customs, natural laws or rationality.
3   Forms of elaboration: these are the self-forming activities by which we can transform ourselves into ethical subjects. Such activities can include a range of physical and mental techniques such as self-discipline, meditation, writing and training one's body.
4   Telos: this refers to the achievement of a certain mode of being, a mode of being characteristic of the ethical subject. More specifically, the accomplishment of a mastery over oneself, the sort of person one wishes to be (Foucault, 1992, 2000a; O'Farrell, 2005).

These four aspects will form the basis for a more in-depth look at the ethical work of principals in Chapter 5, but it is also important to recognise that Foucault considers the self's relationship to itself as being at the intersection of forms of governmentality and the history of subjectivity (Davidson, 2005). In his studies of madness, delinquency and sexuality, Foucault emphasises the establishment of 'a certain objectivity, the development of a politics and a government of the self, and the elaboration of an ethics and a practice in regard to oneself' (2000f, p. 116). Thus, while his work on ethics may be seen as a slight departure from previous works, there is still a clear link with his other projects and particularly with the notion of governmentality. Foucault makes it very clear how important the role of governmentality is as a form of analysis in his work on ethics:

Governmentality implies the relationship of the self to the self, and I intend this concept of governmentality to cover the whole range of practices that constitute, define, organize and instrumentalise the strategies that individuals in their freedom can use in dealing with each other.

Those who try to control, determine and limit the freedom of others are themselves free individuals who have at their disposal certain instruments they can use to govern others.

(2000e, p. 300)

Thus, Foucault is making clear the link between the relationship of the self to itself and the governing of others, and I think this is a useful concept to explain the ethical work of principals. The concept of governmentality and its underlying concepts of disciplinary power and pastoral power can in turn also help us to understand the relationship of the principal to him/herself and to others. Essentially the point is that in order to not abuse your power over others, you must consider what it means to be a good principal of a school (telos). That is, ultimately exercising power over your self: 'The good ruler is the one who exercises his power as it ought to be exercised, that is, simultaneously exercising his power over himself. And it is the power over oneself that thus regulates one's power over others' (Foucault, 2000e, p. 288).

In his development of technologies of the self, Foucault draws upon two different historical contexts, those of Greco-Roman philosophy in the first two centuries AD and Christian spirituality and the monastic principles in the fourth and fifth centuries (Foucault, 2000d). Foucault chooses these contexts to highlight a transformation in the moral principles of Western society through a shift from the principle of 'take care of yourself' to that of 'know yourself'. The significance of this is that principles had prohibitive codes in relation to sex and sexual conduct, but it was the way those prohibitions were integrated in relation to oneself that is different. Foucault argues that in Stoic ethics, the emphasis was an aesthetic existence, that is, a belief in a beautiful existence rather than one that attempted to normalise the population (Foucault, 2000a). It is this genealogy of the subject, the study of the constitution of the subject across history that, Foucault argues, has led to the modern concept of the self (1993, p. 201). It is the understandings the subject creates about oneself that are important, and Foucault uses the example of sexuality to draw out such analyses. For example, he argues that the transformation at the beginning of the Christian era of the principle of 'know yourself' became one based upon confession (1993, p. 204).

It is important to note that Foucault is not advocating Ancient Greek ethics as a model to be put forward in today's society but rather to provide ideas and tools that may provoke analysis and change of current practices. As he states:

We don't have to choose between our world and the Greek world. But since we can see very well that some of the main principles of our ethics have been related at a certain moment to an aesthetics of existence, I think that this kind of historical analysis can be useful.

(2000b, p. 261)

This chapter was by no means meant to be an exhaustive look at Foucault's work but rather to introduce the central theoretical concepts that are utilised throughout this book. I have argued that Foucault's work is useful for analysing the positioning of principals in a range of discourses that construct them as subjects. It is important to reiterate that power is not only repressive but also productive and transforms individuals into subjects through the formation of various knowledges, organisational practices and techniques of the self. In the next chapter, I examine a range of discourses and literature that address more specifically educational leadership and school-based management. In particular, I critique a range of leadership models and theories that, I argue, do not provide an adequate reading of principals' work.

3 Discourses of educational leadership

> Educational leadership is an effect of discourses of schooling, rather than a set of practices or dispositions adopted by individuals who occupy certain positions within schools.
>
> (Lingard, Hayes, Mills & Christie, 2003, p. 143)

The body of literature around leadership and even educational leadership is staggering in both its size and scope. As a result, mapping the field is no easy task. However, substantial and useful mapping has come from Leithwood, Jantzi and Steinbach (1999), Christie and Lingard (2001), Gunter and Ribbins (2002), Harris (2005a) and Heck and Hallinger (2005). Rather than provide another survey of the field, in this chapter I examine some key discursive formations in the field. This is for the purpose of illustrating the variety of ways these discourses create the particular objects of which they speak.

I begin by clarifying some of the ways in which the term 'leadership' is used and taken up by certain discourses. It then becomes possible to understand how principals are created as subjects through particular discourses of educational leadership. Using the work of Christie and Lingard (2001), I unpack the terms 'leadership', 'management' and 'headship'. Within this frame I briefly examine a range of the most prevalent models of leadership. Following this, I then undertake a brief genealogical reading of the notion of transformational leadership, as this is a model that has had a significant impact in the field of educational leadership. Specifically, this includes a textured analysis of the work of Burns (1978) and follows the way such discourses of transformational leadership have been taken up by writers such as Bass (1985), Bass and Avolio (1993, 1994), Leithwood (1992) and Leithwood and Jantzi (2000a, 2000b) in the field of educational leadership. It is also important to note the influence of feminist leadership literature to show how these discourses construct principals in different ways and show how the gendered aspect of leadership needs to be considered.

In the second part of this chapter, I examine how the notion of school-based management has positioned school principals differently, using the work of Caldwell and Spinks (1988). The moves towards self-management in countries such as the US, the UK and Australia have had a profound effect on the work of school principals and through this section of the chapter, I identify a key link between models of leadership promoted by Caldwell and Spinks as a part of the self-managing school and recent leadership policies and documents to argue how these discourses result in school principals being positioned as disciplined subjects. Discourses of exceptionality (Gronn, 2003a) have also become normalised into the everyday lexicon of principals' work through their incorporation into state-wide policy in Queensland, Australia and do not provide adequate ways of understanding the complex, messy, unpredictable nature of the experiences of the two principals in this study.

What is leadership?

The term 'leadership' is a heavily contested one and discourses of leadership are now largely ubiquitous given the breadth of both conceptual and research literature (Gronn, 2003a). There has been a huge growth in the business of leadership studies in recent years, as it seems that the term 'leadership' has become privileged over other terms such as 'management' or 'administration'. Leadership has often been associated with notions of influence, power, authority, control and supervision (Yukl, 2002), although certainly recently the term 'leadership' has gained significant favour. To understand leadership, Gunter and Ribbins (2002) argue that leadership needs to be understood not just as tasks and behaviours, but through the gathering of professional experiences within different contexts coupled with a theorising of agency and structure. Christie and Lingard (2001) conceptualise leadership as a form of influence that can exist at any point within (or outside) an organisation, and not just considered synonymous with the head of an organisation or a particular individual. More specifically, leadership should be seen as being 'practised by many teachers, principals and parents in a range of educational sites and in a number of informal as well as formal administrative positions' (Blackmore, 1999, p. 6). This view of leadership as being exercised at all levels of the school is synonymous with distributed, dispersed or parallel leadership (Crowther, Hann, McMaster & Ferguson, 2000; Crowther, Kaagan, Ferguson & Hann, 2002; Gronn, 2002, 2003b, 2006; Spillane, 2006). Thus, leadership is not exclusive to any one position, and certainly does not only revolve around the position at the head of an organisation. Leaders can emerge from anywhere within the organisation. This is where the notion of headship differs from leadership, as the term 'headship' designates that a person's responsibilities come from a formal position in the organisation, for example, as a Principal, Headteacher or Head of Department (Christie & Lingard, 2001). However, it is the principal that is constructed as the centre of control in the school by numerous leadership and schooling discourses. This can be seen as a form of normalisation in itself, as the principal is placed in the position of 'head' of the school. It is through such discourses and structures that the principal is positioned in relation to a range of formal powers constituted through that position. The structures of schools make it very difficult for others to participate in decision-making processes if they are not within this hierarchical structure. As stated by Lingard et al.:

> Discourses of schools constitute principals as their 'heads'. Indeed it is difficult to imagine schools without principals because it is common for the administrative heart of the school to be clustered around the principal's office and for this to be the point of interface between the school and the community. The principal's office is also commonly constituted as the locus of control and discipline and there is also a line of command designed to ensure the seamless transfer of power in the event of the principal's absence.
>
> (Lingard et al., 2003, p. 141)

It is therefore crucial that leadership be understood in terms of an ongoing relationship between participants, not just in terms of a great visionary individual and not just as a top-down one-way flow of authority. In order to avoid this type of dominant and pervasive discourse, it is necessary to examine the contextual factors upon which leadership discourses are constituted. This links to the arguments of both Gronn (2003a, 2003b) and Blackmore (1999) about avoiding a view of leadership that sees it as something exceptional but rather to see it as everyday practice. Further to this, Christie and Lingard argue that 'leadership needs to be understood in terms of the complex interplay of individual, organisational and the broader social, political and economic contexts' (2001, p. 19). This type of approach is both difficult and complex, yet necessarily so in order to adequately convey the multitude of factors at work.

In a search for new perspectives on leadership, Sinclair (2004, 2005) and Sinclair and Wilson (2002) argue that leadership must be understood through its political, cultural and historical contexts. Dimmock (2003) and Dimmock and Walker (2005) have also emphasised the importance of culture in educational leadership. Initiating a study of leaders through their 'complex cultural roots', Sinclair and Wilson (2002, p. 2) provide an illuminating analysis that may diffuse the need to conform to traditional leadership stereotypes. Exploring leadership through a discourse of complex cultural roots is an avenue of study that takes the notion of leadership away from the dominant discourse that constructs leaders as white, male and with exceptional visionary purpose. Similarly, Sinclair's work (2004), through personal narrative, emphasises a view of leadership that moves away from objectified, disembodied, de-gendered and positivist approaches. These types of contributions to the field promote leaders as coming from a variety of backgrounds, whether it is on a basis of gender, ethnicity, race or socio-economic factors. As can be seen in later chapters, these factors are important to the work and leadership of the two principals of the case study schools. It is in this way that context needs to be more strongly recognised in approaches to leadership.

Another point worth noting is that leadership can be understood as an ongoing life process. Gronn (1999) writes about understanding leadership as a longitudinal and developmental career. Taking this idea further, Limerick (1995) stresses the importance of reconceptualising careers as 'lifestreams' and recognising the notion of 'accommodated careers' for both men and women. This alternative to more traditional, mainstream notions of leadership has value when attempting to view leaders outside of dominant discourses.

Leading and/or managing?

The use of the terms 'leadership' and 'management' in studies of educational leadership is an issue that is both complex and problematic. These two terms are often used interchangeably yet are qualitatively different (Gronn, 1999). While some (Krantz & Gilmore, 1990) argue against a splitting of leadership and management, it also may be necessary to separate the two concepts in order to problematise their use. This by no means indicates that leadership should be viewed as something that is separate from management, nor as something that is possessed by individuals of extraordinary abilities, as one can split the two terms without resorting to visions of heroic leadership. Nor do I argue that one person cannot lead and manage, as principals regularly do this in their daily work. The separation of terms is relevant for the highlighting of particular discursive constructions of principals' work. It is not so much my intent to suggest that such roles cannot be carried out by a single person, but rather that management tasks are more easily 'distributed' through teams.

It is clearly important for principals to engage in both leadership and management activities. However, in the face of constantly changing political environments and educational restructuring, principals are finding that they are spending increasing portions of their time on administrative and managerial tasks. It is the reduction in time and resources spent on 'leading' through recent disciplinary mechanisms such as performance indicators, school-effectiveness measuring, marketisation of schools and the competition for dwindling resources that discipline principals in a more neo-liberal managerial paradigm. Within this framework, issues such as budgeting, marketisation, effectiveness and performance tables can all function as forms of disciplinary power on principals. As Ball writes, 'management provides a paradigm case of disciplinary technology, a form of bio-power, which employs scientific categories and explicit calculations to objectify the body – the worker – and to render individuals docile and pliable' (1990a, p. 7). Thus, the management discourses constitute leaders according to this paradigm as management discourses are easier discourses of control for states to use than leadership discourses. Perhaps this is due to management being a more controlling discourse than the potentially untameable aspect of leaders, particularly in discourses of charismatic leadership where it is easier for people to be 'led astray'. Clegg (1990) also argues that management is essentially a modernist activity rooted in the application of formal logic to the solution of problems. It is important to remember that, as Haber (1994, p. 86) puts it, 'if power is instantiated in mundane social practices and relations, then efforts to dismantle or transform the regime cannot ignore those practices and relations'. I certainly do not argue for a transformation or dismantling of the regime, but more so to focus on the practices and relations themselves to identify such discursive regimes. In doing so, it becomes possible to challenge these dominant leadership and management discourses and disrupt and destabilise the ways leaders are constructed by examining the operation of power within and outside these discourses. This can be done through a process of 'disembedding' (Lingard et al., 2003) the concepts of leadership, management and headship, as there is a certain amount of overlap between these terms. Foucault's work can help examine how leadership discourses operate to produce particular principal subjectivities, illustrating different and more complex ways in which terms such as 'leadership' and 'management' operate in the two case study schools. In doing so I provide a diverse reading of leadership that does not necessarily conform to the prescribed models and theories that are so prevalent in much of the leadership literature.

Dominant theories of leadership

In recent years the discursive constructions of leadership have become more numerous, so much so that they constitute an industry by itself, with the introduction of leadership centres and university courses, as well as the enormous field of academic (and in some cases not so academic) literature. What this demonstrates is that the production of the discourse itself generates power nodes such as leadership centres and courses that are used to institutionalise power. This then becomes a matter of justifying the exercise of power through the production of discourses and theories about the discourses in institutionally sanctioned ways. If, indeed, as Gronn claims, 'leadership is in the eye of the beholder' (2003a, p. 274), then one considers that the search for a theory of leadership is a futile one (Leithwood, 1996). Dimmock and Walker also question this quest when the consequence of this search is that 'for a definition to gain even a modicum of agreement, it needs to be generalised and somewhat bland' (2005, p. 11). Calder (1977) argues that leadership is little more than an everyday term that has been commandeered for the purpose of constructing leadership as a field with scientific status. Kerr and Jermier (1977), in their work on substitutes for leadership, canvassed the idea that it may be factors other than the leader that can act as a substitute for leader behaviour (Tosi & Kiker, 1997).

There have been a number of shifting attempts to pin down the discursive and polysemic notion of leadership over the years. Such discursive constructs as trait, situational, contingency, transactional, transformational, authentic, servant, instructional, invitational, moral, sustainable and distributive have not been able to fully resolve the quest for a definition of leadership. Nor do I aim to do this. What I aim to highlight in the following section is to outline how a number of different discourses tackle this concept of leadership in different ways to frame how these discourses speak about the subject. It is not possible, here, to examine all of these notions in sufficient depth, so I consider those theories that have had the most purchase across the field of educational leadership. It would also be valid to argue that by selecting some concepts and not others I am also actively constructing a particular discourse of leadership that speaks about and forms the subject in particular ways.

Trait theories

Discourses of leadership that emphasise the notion that leadership resides in the attributes or characteristics of an individual are commonly referred to as trait or heroic models. Such models construct a particular type of individual that has certain qualities or attributes that result in 'good leadership'. More often than not these models have formed subject positionings that are heavily white and masculine in origin (Blackmore, 1999). For example, Wolcott's (1973) ethnography of a school principal, while an important contribution to research into principals and their work, constructs a subject positioning of a white male principal in a normalised fashion. Earlier research into the notion of traits (Stogdill, 1948, 1974) attempted to ascertain whether certain traits could be identified as being essential for effective leadership. This empirical research found little evidence of any universal leadership traits (Yukl, 2002). While the flaws in this kind of theory are apparent, there is still a tendency to resort to such interpretations when explaining how leaders do what they do. The appeal of such theories is partly reliant on the fact that there do exist people who fit this stereotype and continue to provide examples of qualities that are considered desirable. Other research into trait theories included competences in managerial effectiveness (Boyatzis, 1982); physical stamina and stress tolerance of leaders (Bass, 1990a; Howard & Bray, 1988); self-confidence (Bass, 1990a); and emotional intelligence (Goleman, 1995). These attempts to identify the individual traits of leaders necessary for organisational success continue to construct a view of leadership that is inherently individualistic and often fail to acknowledge broader contexts in which these leadership forms take place nor do they take into consideration leader behaviour and the relationship with the 'followers'.

Situational and contingency theories

Using Christie and Lingard's (2001) template, a second line of inquiry into understanding leadership consists of a shift away from individual leader qualities and characteristics and towards the inclusion of context and styles of leadership behaviour. These are referred to as contingency and situational theories. These theories move beyond the role of the individual and stress the behaviour of leaders and situations in which they occur. Research into contingency and situational theories has consisted of McGregor's Theory X and Theory Y (1960); Fiedler's Contingency Models (1964, 1967, 1978); Path–Goal Theories (Evans, 1970, 1974; House, 1971, 1996; House & Dressler, 1974; House & Mitchell, 1974); and the situational theories of Hersey and Blanchard (1974, 1993). One of the main problems with these approaches, in particular those of Hersey and Blanchard (1974), is that they fail to take into account the issues of ethics and morals of leaders' behaviour, and when applied can result in the manipulation of followers (Christie & Lingard, 2001). The research into these theories has also indicated that there is little evidence that these approaches actually improve the effectiveness of leaders and managers (Yukl, 2002). These theories have generally been hampered by a complexity that is difficult to test and they also lack sufficient attention to leadership processes.

Transformational leadership

The notion of transformational leadership emerged in the 1980s and has spawned an enormous amount of research on a concept that has proven to be very resilient. Due to the significant attention this model has been given and also due to the long-lasting impression these ideas have had in the field, I undertake a brief genealogical reading of the importance of the taking-up of James MacGregor Burns' work (1978) as a pivotal moment in studies of educational leadership. This discourse and those from Burns' followers such as Bass (1985), Leithwood (1992) and Leithwood et al. (1999) have privileged a particular understanding of leadership and reading of Burns' work that positions leaders within a 'power over' paradigm. Such a paradigm closely aligns with the leader-as-hero perspective that continues to ignore other factors such as context, race and gender.

The theory of transformational leadership owes much to the work of James MacGregor Burns (1978). Burns makes the distinction between transactional and transformational leadership. Transactional leadership occurs when 'one person takes the initiative in making contact with others for the purpose of an exchange of valued things' (1978, p. 19). Transformational leadership, on the other hand, occurs when 'one or more persons engage with others in such a way that leaders and followers raise one another to higher levels of motivation and morality' (1978, p. 19). Burns emphasises values and morals in his description. This may explain why such an approach has been favoured by some writers on educational leadership due to the emphasis on morals and values which are compatible with normative views of education. It should also be pointed out that Burns was, in fact, writing for the political arena, so his focus was not intentionally directed towards educational priorities.

There are a number of concerns with Burns' notions of leadership that need to be unpacked. The assumptions in Burns' analysis of leadership need to problematised as these assumptions have tended to be wholeheartedly adopted by a number of educational leadership discourses. The first of these is the assumption that it is possible to generalise about the leadership process across cultures and across time, which Burns argues is a central purpose of his book (1978, p. 3). The notion of generalising across place, time and space is one that does not take into account the specific contexts or 'thisness' of the school setting as well as the complex interplay of power relations at work within schools and across educational systems. As Christie and Lingard state:

> Educational leadership involves storied individuals, within the organisational contexts of schools as institutions for systematic teaching and learning, at particular times and places, while also recognising that there are multiple and contingent factors which come together in the creation of educational systems and schools.
>
> (2001, p. 8)

All of the leadership models presented so far do not allow for the production of context-specific principal subjectivities which are formed through multiple and competing discourses (Mills, 1992, 1997; Sawicki, 1994; Weedon, 1987). A result of this decontextualising of leadership is the drawing-up of leadership frameworks based upon standards and competences which leaders much exhibit. Such leadership-by-design frameworks (Gronn, 2003b) emphasise the search for distinctive leadership roles and qualities, which is the second notion Burns puts forward that is problematic (Burns, 1978, p. 4). The way that such discourses operate is to normalise leaders through their disciplined subjectivity. Disciplinary regimes of control such as standards for school leaders take hold when school principals willingly subjugate their own identities and dispositions to these normative regimes through the acquisition of desirable and required aptitudes and behaviour (Gronn, 2003a). The subjugation of these principals' bodies through such disciplinary regimes as competence frameworks succeeds through the gaze consisting of supervisory and other surveillance practices, examined in more depth in Chapter 4. However, it is primarily the disciplinary functioning of discourses through the notion of individual leader design frameworks that I am concerned with here. It is when principals position themselves within this normalised field that they subject themselves to the gaze and normalising judgement. This self-normalisation occurs through the principals positioning themselves within this designer leadership framework. This is not to say that this form of self-discipline is all-pervasive, as there are spaces in which these principals can resist disciplined subjectivity, as is evidenced in Chapter 5.

The third problematic assumption Burns makes concerns his notion of power. That is, he views power as something which is possessed. As he states:

> I view the power process as one in which power holders, possessing certain motives and goals, have the capacity to secure changes in the behaviour of a respondent, human or animal, and in the environment, by utilizing resources in their power base, including factors of skill, relative to the targets of their power-wielding and necessary to secure such changes.
>
> (1978, p. 13)

Here Burns is articulating the assumptions that are largely made by all of the theories of leadership referred to thus far. This understanding of power stands in contrast to Foucault's view of power. Such a 'power over' modality, as used by Burns, aligns closely with the 'leader as hero' paradigm (Allan, Gordon & Iverson, 2006). This point links with the fourth problematic notion in Burns' work, and that is that the study of leadership in general will be advanced by looking at particular leaders (1978, p. 27). I acknowledge that Burns' work was to examine leaders within the political sphere, a path I have no issue with. What I do have concern with is the uptake of Burns' work into the field of education where such representations and understanding of leaders and leadership from politics are qualitatively different, with different concerns, intentions and contexts from the work of school principals, for example. As I outline in Chapters 4 and 5, there are a whole range of tactics, surveillance mechanisms and regimes of practice particular to schools and school principals that form their subject positioning in different ways from those of political leaders. A fifth concern with Burns' work is his search for a true nature of leadership (1978, p. 11). The way that his search for truth operates is to privilege a political setting at a particular moment in history. The use of political leaders in developing his models of leadership frames the rules and limits of a 'true nature' of leadership, that is, transformative capacities and characteristics of charismatic leaders are constructed as the true form of leadership.

A final concern with Burns' concept of transformational leadership is that the notion of a transformation implies that there is a beginning and an end, with a focus on a particular outcome. There are two important questions that need to be considered here. The first of these is, according to whose view has a transformation taken place and how has this information been gathered? The second concerns the point at which leadership is deemed transformational (Gronn, 1995). The literature on transformational leadership is very focused on positive outcomes and the profound effects on followers. Rarely mentioned, if ever, are the potential negative aspects of leadership; as Clements and Washbush argue, 'It is clear that effective leadership can be instrumental in promoting social good, but what should be equally clear is that effective leadership can also be instrumental in promoting social disaster' (1999, p. 2). Not only can the actions of a leader sometimes be disastrous but also those of followers. Clements and Washbush further state: 'Failure to acknowledge and examine the dark side of leadership and influence can distort efforts to learn about the leadership process and may encourage a blind eye approach to examining the results of influence attempts' (1999, p. 2). This tends to be a possibility overlooked by not only much of the transformational leadership literature, but also leadership studies in general.

The taking-up of Burns' work into transformational leadership provides a pivotal moment in the development of educational leadership discourses. The notion of transformational leadership has received significant attention in the education literature over the last 20 years.[1] Transformational leadership discourses have been taken up in the field of education through the quantitative work of Bass (1985) and then Leithwood (1992). One of the most active proponents of transformational leadership has been Bernard Bass, who drew heavily upon Burns' work in his book *Leadership and Performance beyond Expectations* (1985). Bass initially differentiated strongly between transactional and transformational leadership. Transformational leadership, in Bass's view, goes beyond a follower's material and psychological needs as:

> Transformational leaders attempt and succeed in raising colleagues, subordinates, followers, clients or constituencies to a greater awareness about the issues of consequence. This heightening of awareness requires a leader with vision, self-confidence and inner strength to argue successfully for what he [*sic*] sees is right or good, not for what is popular or is acceptable according to the established wisdom of the time.
>
> (1985, pp. 17–18)

Gronn (1995) argues that the critical ingredient in Bass's work on transformational leadership is charisma, which builds on Weber's concept of charismatic authority (Weber, 1978). Bass also drew heavily upon the work of House (1977) discussing the effects of charisma, and also Zaleznik (1977, 1983), who argues that leaders and managers were qualitatively different types of individuals and it was inspiration that was significant (Gronn, 1995).

The work of Bass and his followers relied heavily on questionnaires and surveys.[2] This has led to some researchers being confined either to orthodox tick-a-box or circle-a-number respondent surveys of superiors or to structured interviews with diverse informant samples (Gronn, 1996). As Gronn (1996) argues, one of the most significant deficiencies in these approaches has been that the claims made in favour of transformational leaders far outrun the data's capacity to sustain them, thus resulting in the failure to prove the uniqueness, superiority and effectiveness of the transformational leader. Much of the above research has highlighted the correlation between leadership qualities and well performing schools, and yet has continually failed to outline direct causation. There has been too much focus on the personal qualities and styles of the individual leader without adequately taking into account broader contextual factors. A significant number of these leadership studies have followed the pattern of the research programmes of the Ohio State University and University of Michigan that were conducted during the 1950s and 1960s (Yukl, 2002). These research studies (for example, Fleishman & Harris, 1962; Katz, Maccoby & Morse, 1950; Katz, Maccoby, Gurin & Floor, 1951) were heavily dominated by survey questionnaires based upon leaders' behaviour. One of the downsides to this type of research is that co-relational studies do not establish cause–effect relations between variables (Gay & Airasian, 2003). Determining causality is very difficult, as many of these researchers would usually assume that causality is from the leaders' behaviour to the criterion variable. This may not necessarily be the case as, when a correlation is found, it is difficult to identify the direct cause.

Like Burns, Bass did draw upon biographies of famous leaders, but these were for the purposes of justifying his notion of transformational leadership rather than using them to analyse long-term behaviours and practices that may have provided some useful data. Instead Bass and his followers relied heavily on a process of continual modification of surveys and questionnaires. The significance of the work of Bass and others into transformational leadership is that these discourses privilege the hero model of leadership. Such models continue to captivate researchers into leadership as it is seductive to be able to pinpoint the actions of particular leaders that will make the difference in the end. From this perspective stems the need to then 'design' leaders according to such paradigms and the evidence of this can be seen in policy documents and leader-competence and standards frameworks which I examine in the next section.

Distributed leadership

The notion of distributed leadership is not a new one, however, there has been an increasing amount of attention given to this concept in recent years (see, for example, Gronn, 2002, 2003b, 2006; Harris, 2005; Hartley, 2007; Hatcher, 2005; Spillane, 2006; Spillane, Halverson & Diamond, 2004; Spillane & Orlina, 2005; Spillane, Camburn & Pareja, 2007; Woods, 2004). The use of the notion of distributed leadership is now so widespread that there is also some confusion about what the term means (Mayrowetz, 2008; Woods, Bennett, Harvey & Wise, 2004). The emergence of distributed leadership as a concept appears to have come about due to the 'failure' of charismatic hero models of leadership such as transformational leadership, as well as recognition of the greater complexity of tasks that now confront many school principals (Hartley, 2007; Spillane, 2006). Gronn (2002) argues that distributed leadership begins with the division of labour within organisations that sets out to capture the complexity of leadership through either aggregated or holistic forms. An aggregated pattern of distributed leadership is one that Gronn describes as when 'a number of individuals, on different occasions, as part of different activities, for varying periods of time and for a variety of reasons, are believed by their colleagues to exercise leadership' (2006, p. 4). A holistic pattern of distributed leadership is 'when the parts are combined to form a whole resulting in a functioning unit with structural integrity that can act back on parts themselves' (2006, p. 5).

Some critics of distributed leadership, and for that matter a number of the leadership models and frameworks, argue that they are not supported by strong theoretical foundations (Hartley, 2007). Hartley argues that much of the distributed leadership literature adopts a functionalist and normative stance within the field that Grace (2000) has termed Education Management Studies (EMS). Similarly, Thrupp (2003) argues that much of the educational administration and leadership literature serves to 'prop up' recent managerialist reforms in education. Thrupp's polemical approach serves to further categorise and divide authors and their work into categories of 'problem solvers', 'overt apologists', 'subtle apologists' and 'textual dissenters'.

Other critics of distributed notions of leadership argue that they appear to incorporate democratic procedures, but arguably do no such thing (Woods, 2004) or they underestimate the micro-political aspects of leadership practice (Hatcher, 2005; Storey, 2004). Crowther et al. (2000) prefer the term 'parallel leadership', while Lambert (1998) uses terms such as 'density of leadership' to describe similar phenomena. Lingard et al. (2003) prefer the term 'dispersed leadership' to represent the spreading of leadership across the school to avoid the notion of power being understood as a possession that is given away in a zero-sum manner. It still needs to be ascertained what is to be distributed through these leadership models, as often what is to be distributed remains within governmental rationalities where hierarchical forms of accountability are still dominant.

Instructional and authentic leadership theories

The constructing of leadership through models such as authentic, instructional or educative leadership has received some attention in recent years. These 'post-transformational' leadership models (Day, Harris, Hadfield, Tolley & Beresford, 2000; Thrupp, 2003) have emerged from the realisation that there has been little or no evidence that transformational leadership on its own actually has improved consequences for student outcomes (Earley & Weindling, 2004). While instructional leadership is more concerned with a focus on those factors that directly impact upon student learning, there are more similarities than differences between the two approaches (Hallinger,

2003), so much so that Marks and Printy (2003) use the term 'integrated leadership' to signify the leader of instructional leaders. Another notion that has developed from transformational and instructional models of leadership is that of 'learning centred leadership' (Southworth, 2003), which also emphasises a distributed style of operating with a focus on learning and pedagogy.

So far in this section, I have provided a brief examination of a number of the significant models and notions of leadership that still largely inform our understandings of leadership. As stated earlier, the leadership literature is so vast that it is beyond the scope of this book to do more than provide an introductory look at these dominant leadership theories. In the following section, I examine a range of feminist perspectives of leadership that have been very critical of the way the leadership field has been constructed.

Feminist perspectives on leadership

The vast body of literature in the field of educational leadership has proven to be remarkably impermeable to feminist critiques and gender discourses. Although, in recent years, there has been an increase in the number of more nuanced approaches to gender and leadership (see, for example, Alvesson & Billing, 1997; Billing & Alvesson, 1994, 2000; Blackmore, 1999, 2005; Blackmore & Kenway, 1993; Collard & Reynolds, 2005; Halford & Leonard, 2001; Lambert, 2007; Limerick & Lingard, 1995; Ozga, 1992; Sinclair, 1995, 1998, 2004), the work of school leaders, and in particular school principals, continues to be largely viewed as individualised and decontextualised practice (Blackmore, 2005). Leadership is most often constructed through various discourses as a range of attributes, competences and capabilities that are to be implemented in schools to make them more effective. 'Good leadership' continues to be constructed within a masculinised framework (Blackmore, 1999). In fact, Lambert (2007) asserts that in recent years there has even been a re-masculinisation of leadership through leadership ideals such a transformational leadership. Such positions need to be viewed within a general shift seen by some towards a masculinisation of education in recent years (Blackmore, 1999, 2005; Mac an Ghaill, 1994; Mills, Martino & Lingard, 2004; Skelton, 2002). This seems to suggest that there is much more to be done in terms of a critique of the gendered effects of leadership discourses on educational leaders.

Much of the earlier work on feminist critiques of educational leadership/management/administration has focused on the lack of women moving into more senior positions within educational organisations. There has been significant research into the lack of women in senior leadership and management positions (Hall, 1996, 1997; Halford & Leonard, 2001; Limerick, 1991; Limerick & Lingard, 1995; Sinclair, 1998), although there have been shifts towards more women moving into these positions in recent years (Collard & Reynolds, 2005). The phrases 'glass ceiling' for women and 'glass escalator' for men have been used to describe the different trajectories of males and females into senior positions. Even though there is evidence to suggest that more women are, in recent years, breaking through the 'glass ceiling', Ryan and Haslam (2005) use the term the 'glass cliff' to intimate that once women attain these leadership positions, their positions are risky or precarious. The significance here is that even though more women are making it to these senior positions, when they do, they still face great challenges that perhaps men in similar positions do not (Blackmore, 1999). Others, such as Still (1995) and Carmody (1992), have used terms such as 'greasy' and 'slippery' pole to describe similar phenomenon.

The agenda(er) of educational management and administration did not really receive any significant attention until 1987, when Shakeshaft's book *Women in Educational Administration* raised a number of important questions that needed further examination and research. Shakeshaft's work (see, for example, 1987, 1989, 1995) has been important for raising a number of concerns into the lack of research into gender and educational leadership. However, her emphasis on gender differences of male and female leaders can provide only a limited account of the complex and contestatory environments in which these leaders work. Although emphasising different socialising patterns as being the most influential factor in these gender differences (1995), Shakeshaft's work in this text is highly assumptive and generalised. More account needs to be given to different groups of men and women as well as historical and cultural settings as important factors influencing leadership behaviours (Billing & Alvesson, 2000). The assumption that there is a feminine style of leadership needs to be problematised as this notion tends to assume fixed singular identities of women. Kanter's work (1977) is important here for showing how women may reject such 'feminine' managerial traits in favour of more 'masculine' models. Using Foucault, it is the exercise of power, that is, the production of knowledge and institutional practices that combine to produce overlapping and contradictory discourses that create different gendered subjectivities (Ford, 2006; Hall, 1996; Weedon, 1987). Blackmore's work (1999) is particularly useful here as she adopts a feminist poststructuralist approach to 'trouble' the way that feminist discourses about women and leadership produce regimes of truth that can be both disempowering and empowering for women. Discursive practices can therefore both shape and constrain possibilities for action.

Halford and Leonard (2001) draw upon a wider theoretical terrain in their approach as they argue for a multiple constitution of power as being the key to understanding the issue of gender and organisations. They argue that no single perspective on power is sufficient to understand the interplay of gender in organisations, and that liberal, structural and poststructural interpretations of power offer different perspectives that are necessary to explain gender inequalities.

While research into gender, leadership and organisational management has greatly increased in recent years, there are still areas of significant silence in the broader literature. For example, Sinclair (1995, 2004) argues that leadership discourses are all too often disembodied, de-gendered and de-sexualised. The silence on sexuality, in particular, she argues, leads many women to camouflage their sexual identity as women. Marshall (1984, 1995) also argues that such evidence of female sexuality is taboo in organisational environments. Acker (1998) argues that questions into both emotions and sexuality can assist to understand male and managerial behaviours in organisations.

Similarly, there is also a significant silence on the issue of emotions and leadership (Blackmore & Sachs, 1998). George (2000) acknowledges the importance of emotions in the leadership process, yet emotions, as an aspect of leadership, are often played down due to the highly gendered perception that emotionality is in opposition to rationality as a desirable leadership characteristic (Blackmore & Sachs, 1998). The work of Beatty (2000a, 2000b, 2000c, 2002a, 2002b) and Hargreaves (2000, 2001, 2004) into the social and organisational dimensions of emotions has been significant for providing the theoretical basis for much of the (limited) research into emotions and educational leadership. This is largely due to a focus on the cultural dimensions of emotions that has attempted to move away from seeing emotions in individualistic terms. Hargreaves uses the term 'emotional geographies' to describe how emotions in education result from shared communities or spaces. Beatty has drawn upon Hargreaves' work to investigate emotions and leadership. However, as Zorn and Boler (2007) argue, these approaches unwittingly fall into seeing emotions in theory and practice in dualistic terms that unintentionally reinforce the problems they are attempting to solve. As a result, emotions are still largely seen as not only individualistic, internal and private (Harding & Pribham, 2002, 2004) but continue to depict emotion as feminised weakness and exclude emotion from 'rational' depictions of leadership that continue to be so prevalent (Boler, 1997). The silence on emotions, and in fact the notion of emotions as a sign of feminised weakness, need to be disrupted, for as can be seen in Chapter 6, the self-regulation of one's emotions were a key part in the way that both principals in this study went about their daily business.

Self-management as a powerful discourse of leadership

School-based management and its various interpretations have played a significant part in educational reforms in a number of Western countries. School-based management, while having different meanings in different countries, signifies a shift away from centralised distribution of human, material and financial resources to the individual school, allowing them more autonomy in decision-making (Caldwell, 2005; Pang, 2008). These shifts to local autonomy have tended still to be framed within a centrally determined framework to ensure some sense of the system is maintained (Caldwell, 2005). This has usually involved the creation of school councils and the decentralisation of power and/or school budget to the school from the central/state government (e.g. New Zealand, Australia) or the school district/local education authority (e.g. US, UK) (Pang, 2008). More recently, similar moves have been occurring to differing extents in China and Malaysia (Cheng, 2006) and parts of Europe.

One of the main aims of this book is, through the use of Foucault, to understand how regimes of self-management operate in the two case study schools. School-based management should not be perceived as a singular notion or entity or as a repressive force of power relations exercised by the state. Rather, it should be viewed as a multitude of strategies, techniques, instruments, statements, discourses and rationalities of government. The idea of school-based management is one that presents many faces depending upon the changing political contexts (Lingard, Hayes & Mills, 2002) and broader social, economic and political agendas (Rizvi, 1993), not to mention the complexities of policy implementation (Bishop & Mulford, 1999; Fullan 1993, 1999, 2001, 2003; McLaughlin, 1987; Niesche & Jorgensen, 2010) that are heavily dependent upon the personal agendas of principals, administrative staff, teachers, parents and students. Each state in Australia also has a differing interpretation of school-based management and is in constant flux moving towards or away from self-prescribed ideals. The 'facelessness' of school-based management as a concept is a result of these competing factors and priorities, so that any meanings can only be gained from analysing the uneasy co-existence of statements within the fields of discourse in which they reside. Foucault states that 'so many diverse meanings are established beneath the surface of the image that it presents only an enigmatic face' (1967, p. 20). It is no longer easy to ascribe meanings to the notion of school-based management based upon perspectives of social democracy, corporate managerialism and the market (Rizvi, 1993). These rationalities of school-based management can no longer safely speak for themselves. Hunter (1994) argues that in fact this type of approach is based upon principled positions of educational discourses and as such can only lead to the failure of mass schooling from these perspectives. Such 'grand narratives' as social democracy, corporate managerialism and the market can longer ascribe truth to what exists as a series of struggles between the politics of discourses and language games of educational leadership, management and administration for the purposes of government.

Critics of school-based management have argued that this process of educational restructuring, particularly in the education systems of the UK, the US and Australia has shifted the emphasis of schooling as a social and political process to one of managerialism, performativity, efficiency, effectiveness and accountability (Angus, 1994; Smyth, 1993). Government schools are thus urged to come into line with devolution policies that remove the inefficiencies of bureaucracies; making schools more accountable to parents and students; to enable decision-making that is closer to the point of learning; and giving parents greater choice in the education of their children through the adoption of competitive business practices that construct children as customers (Smyth, 2002). The discourses surrounding these moves to devolved education systems are centred on the idea that schools and principals are more empowered to act in their own interests. Along with this view is the notion that control rests with parents, teachers and administrators rather than the centralised bureaucracy.

There has been research (Angus, 1993, 1994; Blackmore, 1997, 1999; Smyth, 1993) to suggest that while the rhetoric speaks of participation and democracy, in fact there is evidence of a further centralisation of power through 'national curricula, statewide testing, national standards and competencies, teacher appraisal and curriculum audits' (Smyth, 1993, p. 4). It is this hidden nature of power that can be so pervasive in its operations that, as Foucault states, 'power is tolerable only on condition that it mask a substantial part of itself. Its success is proportional to its ability to hide its own mechanisms' (1981a, p. 86).

Smyth (1993) goes on to argue that the rhetoric of the self-managing school demonstrates a deliberate process of subterfuge, distortion, concealment and wilful neglect on the part of the state. He states that 'the self-managing school is not fundamentally about choice, grassroots democracy or parent participation. It is absolutely the reverse' (Smyth, 1993, p. 4). He further describes it all as a cruel hoax, 'what we have instead of genuine school-based reforms of participation are increasing forms of managerialism, hierarchy, individual competitiveness and task orientation' (Smyth, 1993, p. 4). This again links to Foucault's notion of the hidden operations of power that are important for its success. Drawing on Hunter (1994), I would argue that Smyth is also arguing from a principled position of educational restructuring. He believes that school-based management needs to be concerned with grassroots democratic principles. However, if school-based management is to be seen as a rationality of government, then it is no surprise that there is evidence of managerialism, hierarchy and individual competition. It is not for the purpose of empowering democratic ideals that school-based management operates, although much of the rhetoric states otherwise. It is for the purpose of government that such tactics and mechanisms are employed. Angus (1993) similarly argues that the only thing that is devolved to many schools is responsibility for a range of management tasks and control of their budgets. The serious consequence is that,

> Principals, who must 'prove' themselves as efficient and entrepreneurial managers, may well feel themselves pressed to become more task-oriented and to push a personal agenda in order to make their mark on the school. There is a strong danger that this press may have the effect of eroding team building and collegiality among principal and staff and of limiting rather than enhancing democratic, school level decision making.
>
> (Angus, 1993, p. 18)

As a result, there is a tendency for these 'democratic practices' and for decision-making in schools to actually become more managerial devices and heighten control mechanisms. Gerwitz, Ball and Bowe (1995) and Thomson (2001) raise questions relating to this move towards a new managerialism. For example, Thomson states:

> The moves by various state and national governments to neoliberalism, with the concomitant adoption of institutional strategies of local school management, intensified accountabilities, and risk management, result in increased workloads, frustration and emotional stress for school principals as their work swings towards rational-technical planning and system quality measurement and data collection, and away from teaching and learning.
>
> (2001, p. 14)

It is not just issues of teaching and learning that principals are being steered away from. There is also the battle for some to attempt to initiate pedagogically progressive and socially just discourses and practices, while minimising the damage of economic rationalist discourses that create enormous struggles for principals (Smyth, 2002). For example, in a case study of educational leadership under school-based management in Victoria, Australia, during the 1990s, Feeney (1998) concluded that the Schools of the Future programme positioned education as a commodity rather than an investment. This, coupled with the relentless reduction in government spending on schooling and the absence of actual educational improvements, resulted in the loss of a significant opportunity for significant education reform.

What all this research and debate point to is a realisation that what is espoused by governments and policy documents is far from reality for those working in schools, as principals are faced with contradictory messages concerning power relations within the schooling system. For example, self-management and the new roles accorded principals means that principals are told to be more collaborative with teachers and school communities, but the uncertainties and ambiguities associated with this due to increased accountability and focus means that some principals may be reluctant to accept these changes. Just because policy states that schools will be more collaborative in their power structures does not necessarily lead to shared decision-making. With the advent of self-managing systems, principals expected that they would have more freedom and authority to act, but find themselves instituting reforms from above that are just replacing those previous top-down style of reforms. In a sense, one set of rules and guidelines has simply been exchanged for another (Wildy, 1999). Principals are still doing the will of the system and this requires principals to therefore bend the will of staff to perform necessary tasks while also working in collaborative ways to reach decisions about school issues (Wildy, 1999). Schools and principals are subjected to a system of punishment and rewards under the guise of being empowered, more democratic, having more choice and better management, but also being held more accountable. While schools are given more responsibility with regard to funding and resources, they are still not able to exercise this power without centralised constraints.

One of the main consequences of these changes is the changing role of the principal. There is significant research that indicates that the principal is quickly moving away from a focus on educational leadership fostering teaching and learning to a focus on corporate governance (Ball, 1994; Blackmore, 1999; Grace, 1995; McInerney, 2001; Smyth, 1993). It is these individualising discourses and dividing practices that are normalising principals into a more management style of paradigm. School-based management as a technique of government operates through as well as 'on' principals to achieve its selected aims. Such a view helps to illustrate the complexities now facing principals under regimes of school-based management and also raises serious questions as to whether principals are now able to continue to effectively foster an environment focused upon sound teaching and learning practices under such competitive systems.

Certainly school-based management is a contested notion (Lingard et al., 2002), yet it is not my purpose to enter into a debate concerning the merits of different perspectives. I prefer to analyse the operations and practices which give birth to certain discourses, those which are said and given preference to and those which are passed over, to conceive of school-based management as discourses that it takes as its own (Foucault, 1972). In particular, it is important to take note of normalising discourses and practices and individualising power relations that can be brought about by these regimes of self-management. It is not my aim to outline an Australian history of school-based management as this has been covered elsewhere (see Chapman, 1990; Lingard et al., 2001; Lingard et al., 2002; Martin et al., 1994; McInerney, 2001; Meadmore, Limerick, Thomas & Lucas, 1995; Rizvi, 1993; Smyth, 1993, 2002; Whitty, Power & Halpin, 1998), nor would this type of research be true to Foucault's genealogy. It is, partly, making visible what is invisible not through an attempt to identify some underlying rationality but through the surfaces of discourse.

The self-managing school and competence frameworks as discourses of leadership

In this section, I provide a brief reading of the work of Caldwell and Spinks, particularly their book, *The Self Managing School* (1988), to argue that this text, and work further developed on this model, privilege a particular type of leadership discourse, that is, a very top-down principal-centred leadership owing much to the notion of transformational leadership. This type of leadership discourse has been taken up through designer leadership frameworks through competences and capabilities in Education Queensland policy documents.

Although Caldwell and Spinks have gone on to further elaborate and expand upon their initial framework of the self-managing school (see Caldwell & Spinks, 1992, 1998; Caldwell, 2006), it is this earlier text itself that paved the way for discourses of self-management both in Australia and overseas. The importance of this work lies in the particular representations and understandings ascribed to principals and principals' work under regimes of self-managing schools. These ideas have continued to retain significant purchase in policy documents in Queensland and other Australian states.

Caldwell and Spinks state that the decentralisation of authority to schools is a move that is administrative rather than political (1988, p. vii). This simple statement speaks great volumes about the assumptions of this management model. The implications are that this model of school management can be implemented and adapted to any political and educational context. The approach that Caldwell and Spinks term the 'Collaborative School Management Cycle' (1988, p. 21) has six phases beginning with goal-setting, policy-making, planning, preparation, implementing and evaluating. This linear cycle of management seems to sit at odds with the portrait of the often messy, complex and multi-faceted work of the two principals that I outline in Chapters 4 and 5. Nor does this management model question the social, cultural and political conditions of their work. Contrary to Caldwell and Spinks' claim, I argue that this move to self-managing schools is very much political, for it is through mechanisms such as self-management that the subject becomes manageable. By their direct involvement in every facet of the school-management model proposed by Caldwell and Spinks, school principals are required now to be wholly concerned with assessing the conduct and performance not only of their staff and students but also themselves. Governmentality is concerned with not only governing others but also governing the self. School-based management is a form of governmentality. By requiring principals to be the key instigator in the management cycle, principals are being constructed as the centre of control in these matters and as such are repositioned at the top of the school's hierarchy. Leadership is therefore being ascribed to a hierarchical position that is the key to achieving organisational goals (Angus, 1994). Caldwell and Spinks claim that

> As a leader and the executive officer of the policy group, the head teacher invariably has responsibility for ensuring that the process works smoothly. In the planning phase of Collaborative School Management the head teacher has responsibility for one or more programmes but must act also as co-ordinator, motivator, and source of information for others with programme responsibility. Collaborative School Management also provides a framework wherein the higher order functions of leadership can be exercised, namely working with and through others to build the enduring school culture which is critically important if excellence in schooling is to be attained.
>
> (1988, p. 54)

The purpose of highlighting this excerpt is that it clearly positions the principal as the source of leadership in the school and also openly claims that 'higher order' types of leadership are necessary for excellence in schooling. There is a more than a striking resemblance here to transformative types of models of leadership that are being valorised. Caldwell and Spinks even explicitly refer to the model of transformational leadership in later work (1992, 1993). A flow-on effect from the search for 'excellence' in schools through exceptional forms of leadership is then the search for skills, competences and capabilities that are considered necessary for principals to have in order to achieve these outcomes. Therefore, we see the emphasis of competence frameworks for leadership evolving throughout many states of Australia and overseas.

Until 2006, with the introduction of *Leadership Matters* in Queensland, the significant leadership policy document had been the *Standards Framework for Leaders* (Education Queensland, 1997). This document was released at a time when the state was undertaking significant moves towards self-managing schools with such policies as *Focus on Schools* (Education Queensland, 1990), *Leading Schools* (Education Queensland, 1997) and, subsequently, *Future Directions for School Based Management in Queensland State Schools* (Education Queensland, 1998), *School Based Management in Queensland State Schools* (Education Queensland, 1999a) and *Implementation of School Based Management* (Education Queensland, 1999b). The significance of this policy terrain for principals is the way power/knowledge works through these discourses to place the principal as the key player in this new decentralisation/centralisation mix of governmentality. The development of a range of competences for principals (Education Queensland, 1997) is aimed at targeting the individual principal as the centre of control in these moves, thus reinforcing styles and models of leadership that emphasise leadership as something that is largely exercised at the top of the school hierarchy. It is from the principal as an 'effective' leader that 'effective' schools come about. Such competence and standards frameworks construct a discourse of leadership that is instrumentalist (Land, 1998). That is, they operate through a range of managerial competences to construct the notion of the ideal principal. The *Standards Framework for Leaders* document outlines a range of best practice and personal performance competences in the areas of Leadership in Education, Management, People and Partnerships, Change, Outcomes and Accountability. Principals are therefore being discursively constituted according to these particular competence frameworks.

These standards-based regimes for school leaders can be viewed as a form of designer leadership (Gronn, 2003a, 2003b) that is not only problematic but also a form of disciplined subjectivity. These standards result in the normalising of leadership into lists of expected qualities, behaviours and anticipated behaviours in the case of capabilities outlined in the *Leadership Matters* document. These standards frameworks are used for assessment and recruitment of aspiring and prospective leaders. For example, the following is an excerpt from the *Standards Framework for Leaders* document:

The standards are the basis for the recognition of an individual's profile. From this profile each leader will select the appropriate professional development and training for his or her respective needs. This professional development plan will become an integral part of the planning and accountability framework at each site within Education Queensland.

(Education Queensland, 1997, p. 2)

And this:

The standards form the basis of Education Queensland's approach to recruitment and selection of leaders. Selection criteria will be based on the six key roles for leaders. Work reports will capture information on a person's site based performance in relation to best practice competencies. Each leader, with the assistance of his or her supervisor, will create a portfolio that will document the required evidence to demonstrate a leader's competence. Education Queensland will credential competent leaders.

(Education Queensland, 1997, p. 2)

Not only aspiring leaders but also current ones are subjected to the gaze of the state through this initial and ongoing accreditation of school leaders. It is possible to identify leaders and potential leaders through this gaze. Actions can then be performed on the bodies of these subjects for the purposes of 'professional development'. As a result, principals (and we are in no doubt as to who these 'leaders' are) become self-disciplined in conforming to these standards and designs. According to Foucault, power is productive, so it is through the self-forming work of these leaders or aspiring leaders that they become disciplined subjects.

Interestingly, the recent *Leadership Matters* document no longer speaks of standards or competences. Instead, the discourse operates around 'capabilities' in the areas of educational leadership, personal leadership, relational leadership, intellectual leadership and organisational leadership. It seems clear that these 'capabilities' operate in a very similar fashion to those of standards or competences in the disciplining of principals. The authors of *Leadership Matters* cite the work of Duignan (2003, 2004), Goleman (1995) and Stephenson (2000) as being influential in their technical paper (Education Queensland, 2005), and while the notion of capabilities is intended to be future-oriented, one could easily substitute 'characteristics' or 'competences' for the word 'capabilities'. The paper even cites a list of qualities and capabilities that include things such as courage, tough-mindedness, intuition, passion, self-confidence, optimism and wisdom (2005, p. 14). These capabilities are far from the central human functional capabilities that Nussbaum (2000) has drawn up for the purposes of moving beyond instrumentalist notions of neo-liberalism. In fact, the capabilities used by Education

Queensland in *Leadership Matters* could be seen as an example of a rearticulation of capabilities discourses to actually further instrumentalist notions of leadership.

In addition, any discussions of the gendered aspect of educational leadership have been ignored in the *Leadership Matters Technical Paper* (Education Queensland, 2005) as well as the *Leadership Matters* document itself. For example, of particular note in the *Leadership Matters* document are two of the capabilities under the area of personal leadership. These are that principals need to be 'emotionally mature' and that they 'remain composed in challenging and complex situations'. My earlier comments concerning the gendered aspect of leadership discourses, and the fact that both principals in Chapter 5 mention that controlling one's emotions are an important aspect of their work, indicates that these are powerful discourses that permeate what principals do and think about in their daily work practices. Such discourses also serve to reinforce particular ideologies about what good leadership looks like. Advancing these heroic, masculinised assumptions about what it means to be a good leader serve to maintain a particular set of power and social relations (Sinclair, 2004).

Additionally, the use of the word 'inspire' is also significant in the *Leadership Matters* document, as it appears in a few of the capabilities. For example, principals 'inspire a climate of mutual respect, trust and support' and they 'inspire and develop a sense of collective responsibility and shared leadership'. Ironically, on one hand the document is promoting a very top-down, principal-directed leadership framework, but the rhetoric also speaks of collective responsibility and shared leadership. Principals are also expected to 'welcome challenge and be open to diverse opinion' while also being able to 'manage and resolve conflicts effectively'. A tall order indeed! The significance of the capabilities is that many of them could have come straight out of the work of Burns or Bass on transformational leadership, and this indicates how strongly the moral, aspirational, transforming and visionary dimensions of leadership are still very influential today.

4 Disciplinary regimes under self-governance

Maybe the target nowadays is not to discover what we are, but to refuse what we are.

(Foucault, 1983, p. 216)

In this chapter I explore the positioning of the school principals within regimes of school-based management. I demonstrate how each of the school principals is differently inserted in discourses of school management. Within these regimes, it is the government of individualisation as the actual figure of power (Masschelein, 2004) that it is important to acknowledge for its normalising and disciplining capacities. While elements of this power also consist of totalising practices, there does exist the productive side of power that can operate through critique, reflection and resistance. Therefore, this chapter reflects these power regimes.

This chapter is structured into four main sections. In the first section, I return to the portraits of the schools using observation notes as illustrative examples of the work practices of each principal in their respective self-managing schools. Second, I examine how each principal is placed within disciplinary regimes that use them as both objects and instruments of the exercising of disciplinary power, using Foucault's notions of docile bodies and panopticism, as well as use of space, time and architecture. In the third section, I use the constant writing and managing of submissions and grants as an example of a disciplinary technique that functions within regimes of governmentality. In the final section, I analyse how the principal is constituted by particular accountabilities and relationships by their respective communities, staff and controlling bodies. I use Rose's (1999) notion of community as a new power game operating in a field of ethico-politics that is implemented as a part of governmentality through school-based management. Within this section I also examine issues of race, and the principals' 'whiteness' operating as a disciplinary regime within their respective communities that creates new and different subjectivities for each principal. This is not to say that this is the only way of approaching this complex issue, but one of a number of approaches that could be taken. The approach I have chosen, however, I feel is more sympathetic to the work of Foucault. In so doing, I recontextualise the work of these two school principals that can be often overlooked and ignored by much of the literature promoting leadership models, such as transformational leadership, for school principals that I raised in the previous chapter. It is through this analysis that it becomes possible to see how each of the school principals is differently inserted within discourses of self-management, as well as illustrating the creation of multiple subjectivities through disciplinary processes existing in forms of governmentality.

A day in a self-managing school

Riverside Community School

As I arrive at the main office of Riverside, the busy preparations for the school day are already in full swing. Teachers and other staff are arriving and signing their names in the record book, children are coming in and out of the office before classes start, an administration officer is attending to a Grade 1 or 2 student that has scraped his arm and is putting on a band aid; all the while the sounds of children playing basketball in the centre playground are easily discerned. I let the receptionist know that I am back today for another day of observations and hopefully another round of interviews. Judy has already given me an illuminating first interview and I have a whole host of follow-up questions to which I know she will provide direct and open responses. In addition to the principal, there are only two other full-time staff members in the administration office: the receptionist and administrative officer.

During the time I was employed at Riverside, I did not have many interactions with Judy, as the literacy programme was almost a separate unit within the school. As principal, Judy organises the funding for the programme to go ahead and then leaves the daily running to the programme co-ordinator. As I spend more time with her, I begin to see why she is so popular with the students and the majority of staff I have talked to. There is an immediate affection for all of the children, displayed often when they come into her office, even for misbehaviour. Judy has a lot of time for the students and devotes a lot of hours in the day to students' concerns, as I witnessed on a daily basis. One staff member remarked to me that sometimes the extra time with the students can be at the expense of time for staff, but even this was said with a tone of respect and admiration rather than genuine complaint.

As Judy comes out of her office her eyebrows immediately rise and she expresses a little surprise at seeing me, saying, 'Oh, I forgot you were coming in again today!' She says this with a smile, as she has commented in the past that she finds it difficult to believe that I will find anything interesting enough about her work day. As I move into her office to set myself up, she says that she is just going to briefly chat with a staff member and will be back in a few minutes. Once she is back in her office, I settle in on the comfortable couch with my notepad, hoping to be reasonably inconspicuous, although Judy does introduce me to a number of people, telling them what I am doing and why I am sitting in the corner of her office.

The following transcript from my field notes for one day's events were chosen because they seem reasonably representative of a day's work for Judy at Riverside Community School. Some days I observed were more hectic and others were quieter, but this day seemed to encompass a broad range of everyday practices that Judy undertakes. The following is from my field notes for that day.

8:30 a.m.	phone call from teacher calling in sick
8:35	phone call to arrange for some students to be picked up by the school bus that weren't ready on time to be picked up by the bus
8:40	discussion with teacher about a problematic student
8:40–9:00	organising for someone to fill in for the teacher away today
9:00	discussion with another teacher about covering some of the sick teacher's classes
9:00	phone call to fill in a playground duty
9:04	discussion with admin staff about a payroll issue
9:10	discussion with relief teacher for the day, which class etc.
9:15	discussion about some incidents (vandalism) which occurred over the weekend
9:20	brief discussion with painters as the school is currently being painted, which buildings, when they will be finished etc.
9:25	makes a phone call about repairs for the vandalism

During these times Judy is also making preparations for speech night at the end of the year.

9:30–9:40	phone call with admin officer and discussion about finances in preparation for the audit
9:40	a student comes in who is out of class (a young boy, probably Grade 3/4). Judy asks why, then, personally takes him back to class
9:50	booking computer room for a seminar
9:55	a staff member comes to discuss an issue about some students
10:00	receives a phone call about the computer room booking
10:00	rings to organise classes this afternoon for the teacher away
10:00–10:15	visits classroom for a discussion with a student

10:15	phone call about getting a student back into school who is not coming at all. Organises a meeting with the students and carer
10:00–10:25	brief admin for speech night
10:25	discussion about pests in the prep room, arranging repairs
10:25–10:30	work on computer
10:30	morning tea – kids come into office, ask for money, just hanging around
10:50–11:10	School Assembly, lets other staff member run parade – they take it in turns. Judy usually takes a back seat and just wanders around quietly talking to people. Disciplines high school kids for graffiti appearing on the new paint
11:10	back in office – student is going home sick, arranges for a taxi and taxi voucher then asks student to ring to say she arrived home safely
11:15–11:25	discussion with teacher about water bottles for Grade 1 students
11:25	orders more boardroom chairs
11:25–11:55	administrative work on computer
11:55	discussion with painter about what needs painting
12:00	eating lunch early to avoid being hassled by kids at lunch time
12:10	talks to student attending school who is at risk – student who is currently only coming for the middle session but Judy wants student to try hard and be able to come back to school for the whole day. Student has a carer outside of school hours
12:15	phone call from one of the bus drivers about students' behaviour on the bus this morning
12:20	visits family worker to discuss the above student
12:30	lunch time, students come into office again, informal chats with staff and students, brief check over and along the top veranda on way to computer room to check kids' behaviour as they have been playing up lately
1:30	after lunch checks voice messages, makes routine phone calls, spends more time organising speech night, rings chairman of the board, phone call to the IT person as the server is down, discussion with admin staff concerning administrative issues, another chat with a student who is upset – takes her back to class; into the playground after school for bus runs and duty.

I have briefly summarised the afternoon session as there was a similar cross-section of work and work practices on a 'typical' day. Overall, a significant portion of this day was spent in the office. Some days required a more visible presence in the school and attendance at formal meetings, etc., while other days allowed Judy more time to do administrative tasks, albeit less often. It seems like much of the administrative work is done outside of school hours, often at home, as Judy states:

> Well I get up at 4 a.m. and I work till 6:30 at home, then I'm here by 8 a.m. and then I'm here until at least 4 p.m. often later and then I would work again for a couple of hours at night and then usually one day of the weekend. A lot of the things I do, most principals wouldn't have to do. I don't know many principals that are entirely responsible for running the financial side of the school. Now, most schools would have a bursar and most principals wouldn't have to search for the funds that I do and I'm not saying that I work harder than other principals, I think my role is a bit different from other principals. Often I get called out here for security issues.

Noticeably, it seems that any tasks or jobs that require a span of uninterrupted time are pushed to the edges and not only outside of the school day but also the school premises. By doing so, the principal is therefore withdrawing her visibility from the school's gaze. As is discussed in more detail in the following section, the panoptic effect on the principal within the school grounds can constrain the principal into certain types of activities involved in the day-to-day running of the school. This does not necessarily operate in a repressive fashion on the body of the principal but, in fact, makes the principal more productive and docile to those types of tasks. Similarly, by withdrawing from the school's gaze to undertake other tasks at home or outside school hours, the principal is able to be more efficient at completing tasks that require their undivided attention such as writing and preparing submissions and grant applications, as well as other time-consuming endeavours such as answering emails.

What this brief snapshot of this principal's day reveals is the high level of personal, direct interactions with other staff members, students and parents, whether it is face-to-face communication or by phone. Each of the encounters with staff, students and parents ranged from a brief discussion about a specific topic or a wide variety of issues discussed with one person. There were few 'formal' appointments as most encounters consisted of people coming into the principal's office or were discussions while the principal was outside the administration block. Other days certainly consisted of more formal appointments but it was usually these more informal and casual encounters that seemed to take up a large part of the day. Judy was often on the phone and would even answer outside calls if the receptionist was busy. On a number of occasions I have spoken to Judy directly when calling the school's reception.

From my observations and interviews with Judy, this type of approach appears to be largely indicative of her personal style of operating, a high level of approachability and an emphasis on building relationships with staff, students and parents. At the same time, according to my interviews with teachers and staff members of the two schools, it is perceived by them that being a principal of a school of this size requires a higher level of visibility and reachability as there are no layers of administration and leadership to 'filter' out some of the competing demands. One cannot forget also the cultural demands of leading an Indigenous school where notions of hierarchy play a much lesser role. For example, in staff meetings at Riverside there is very much an atmosphere and structure of equality where everyone 'sits at the table' and plays an important role in decision-making. One staff member remarked to me how it is a 'Murri'[1] way of doing things to have everyone sitting around a circle with the layers of hierarchy removed and everyone is given the opportunity to have their say. Another example of this 'flatter hierarchy' is the rotating system of staff members running the weekly school assemblies which means it is not always the principal who is seen to be in charge. Interestingly, this is different from the situation at Pine Hills where the principal found a similar method of undertaking staff meetings to be problematic and felt the need to resort to standing while everyone else sat and she took charge of the meeting, as is discussed in more depth later.

Pine Hills State School

The average day for Ruth is often quite different from Judy's, certainly in her early time as principal at Pine Hills. Ruth has expressed to me the importance of being visible (and invisible, at times) for certain tasks and being involved in all aspects of the school in those initial days. The principal's visibility is important in terms of accessibility for staff, students and parents. This idea of being visible and also withdrawing the principal's visibility appears to be an important one and is analysed using Foucault's concepts of panopticism and hierarchical observation in the next section. On this issue, Ruth responds:

> First year here, though, I like to probably do a bit more hands on myself, for example, the mail. You can learn a lot from opening the mail and get a feel for the bills and those sorts of things, what comes in, what other people have contacted the school about and that sort of stuff. In some schools, the principal wouldn't touch the mail, they would only just see the important bits. Again we had our only admin staff member leave when the previous principal left so we had a brand new administration officer as well.

The changeover between Ruth and the previous principal is an issue that Ruth and I discussed at length and in the following transcript she highlights some concerns she has had in regard to this process as well as taking up a principalship in a new school:

INTERVIEWER: So do you think some of the workload for you this year has been from the changeover?

RUTH: Some of it has, I think the first year you go into any school as a new principal and you're trying to get your head around how it all happens, it also depends on how the school has been left too. For example, I've had extra work to do this year because in some of the areas like finance and facilities and other things where we've needed to put some systems in place that haven't been in place and the previous principal would probably agree that there were some systems that could have been operating in a better way but you have to make a judgement, if he's going to do the strategic vision then you just have so many hours in the day and some stuff is not probably where he would want it. So if you've gone into a school where all those systems are working really well and the people are skilled, it's probably less of a workload for the transition.

By making judgements about which tasks to give priority to amid the many competing demands, the principal can shape the job or leave their mark as much in what they do not attend to as what they do attend to given the abundance of demands. The previous principal at Pine Hills focused his efforts on issues of truancy, raising expectations for student achievement, improving student pride in self and their Aboriginality, while being constrained in his capacity to devote time and resources into areas of special education, for example.

The day I use as an example of Ruth's work day consists of a day towards the end of the first year of her tenure as principal in the school. This day was specifically chosen to illustrate how much of the principal's time can be spent outside of the administration office and in classrooms and playgrounds maintaining a high level of visibility. The following excerpts are from my field notes for the day. These notes were revised and edited at the end of the day.

8:30–9:30 a.m. Wednesday: When I arrived at the school the principal was already doing rounds of the school, talking to kids, making sure they were in class at the start of the day. There were a few teachers away today so there was extra organisation necessary for their classes and getting supply teachers in for those classes. I followed Ruth to every classroom as she checked to see everything was running smoothly and there were a number of kids just wandering around and she asked why they weren't in class yet and accompanied them to their classes.

9:30 Ruth had a meeting with a representative from the Pathways to Peace Program. The representative outlined what the programme is and how it is used and implemented in schools. Ruth expressed some interest in some of the ideas put forward and the representative left her card and details.

9:45 Another quick round of the playground and classrooms to check that there weren't any kids hanging around out of class.

10:00 Meeting with the person in charge of the film making projects that the school is running for groups of students in the school and the making of DVDs and documentaries. Also discussed was the setting up of IT courses during the summer over December and January. They are also making a short 5 min. film over 23–25 November in preparation for the Pine Hills's Celebration Day on 29 November. This was quite a long meeting with a number of topics discussed. During morning tea Ruth constantly kept an eye and ear out for any trouble or issues in the playground, from the office windows it is possible to see and hear what is going on in the playground [for more on this and the issue of panopticism, see later in this chapter].

11:30 Back to the school rounds at the end of morning tea

1:00–2:00 Conducted a formal interview with Ruth

2:00–3:00 School rounds, behaviour management etc.

3:00–4:00 Staff meeting in staff room.

Although the day seems fairly structured, there were a number of interruptions and issues that needed to be addressed as they happened, such as arranging home visits throughout the day and in the afternoon for problematic students. Usually these are carried out by a senior staff member from Pine Hills, as he is familiar with most of the families and their situations. Sometimes the teachers also make home visits, and Ruth herself has made some home visits with parents to discuss particular students.

Generally Ruth gets to school early (usually between 6:30 and 7:00 a.m.) as often there are a number of children who arrive at school well before classes start. Ruth also says she needs to be there in case any vandalism needs to be reported, and in case there are any teachers away so that casual staff can be contacted (the administration officer arrives at 8:00 a.m.). Much of the day that I observed was focused on behaviour issues as, similar to Riverside, there is no middle management to carry out discipline and behaviour duties. Therefore administrative duties are usually done outside of school hours. This was an early visit to the school and some practices and behaviours did change as I returned for follow-up visits.

Ruth also works very long hours and remarks that the workload is difficult to get on top of:

I'm usually here by 6:30 a.m. and I probably don't leave till 5:30 p.m., so 11 hour days plus at home a bit and I don't feel that I'm getting it all done.

The workload is a challenge, just the sheer scope and depth of it. The complexity has been a challenge, trying to get yourself up to speed on the complexity of the issues when you're trying to deal with them at the same time. There isn't a time out while you get up to speed, it's like get up to speed while you're dealing with stuff that's coming thick and fast ... You can't just knock off at 2:30 and you're finished, it is just getting started here at 2:30. You have almost got another day's work after 2:30 just about.

This sense of frustration at not only the workload but also the varied nature and complexity of the role appeared to be greater for Ruth than for Judy, for a number of reasons. First among these reasons is that she has only been in the position at Pine Hills a short time. Second, this school is a step up in terms of size from her last school. A third reason may be the difficulty of following in the footsteps of the previous principal, who was the stereotypical 'charismatic leader' who was very popular with the students, staff and community. Fourth, by the same token, there were a number of processes that she claims were not implemented under the last principal that Ruth now has to get established. Lastly, in those early times at the school Ruth spent a lot of time visible in the school and managing by walking around, which could have interrupted time available to spend on the more administrative tasks. The unpredictable nature of working at Pine Hills does affect Ruth's work patterns, as she comments:

Emails I find hard to manage. Some school principals may have a system where they do emails and then they do something else where everything is set, structured and predictable but it's not here. So that impacts on your effectiveness and my state of mind if I've got all this stuff hanging over me. I find that very challenging, you don't ever feel like it's getting much less, that you're knocking some of it on the head and then there's more coming in, especially when you've been away like I was last week. It just piles up again.

One noticeable difference between the two principals was Ruth's lack of use of the telephone and Internet/email during school hours. She reported on a number of occasions that she deals with email and phone messages after school hours and often at home. Again, the personal nature of the job is one aspect that stands out. The majority of the principal's time was in face-to-face interactions with staff, students and parents. It is also clear that both principals value this personal nature of the job as highly important and one of the most rewarding aspects of the job. While being principal entails a range of administrative tasks, it seems that both principals engage with these outside of school hours as during school hours their total focus is on the daily needs of students and staff.

In summary, the presence of each of the principals in their schools is an important factor in their work activities. Their need to be present and in view as part of the operation of both schools, though for different reasons, is part of the disciplinary processes functioning under the notion of govern-mentality. This is examined in more detail in the next section. As a result both principals have pushed substantive work to the edges of the day in favour of the fragmentation of 'being available'. These brief sketches of both principals at work have provided a brief glimpse of what a typical day might look like in these two schools. In addition, these glimpses of typical work practices provide an important context and basis for the examination of disciplinary processes and regimes that each principal must regularly negotiate in their schools and work spaces, which I explore in the next section.

Tracing the operation of disciplinary practices for Ruth and Judy

> Discipline makes individuals; it is the specific technique of a power that regards individuals both as objects and as instruments of its exercise.
>
> (Foucault, 1977b, p. 170)

Foucault argues that discipline is an important aspect of governmentality, particularly in the management of a population in its depths and details (Foucault, 1991b). In this section I examine how the subject (principal) is placed in a range of discursive and particularly disciplinary practices that constitute daily life for the two school principals. Foucault's notion of disciplinary power allows for the promotion of the productive and enabling side of power as well as the coercive and oppressive aspects as emphasised by more 'statist' or sovereign perspectives (Foucault, 1981a). Similarly much of the leadership literature discussed in Chapter 3 also relies on a more sovereign view of power, so it is hoped that the analysis in this section can help to elaborate more fully the range of pressures and mechanisms brought to bear on and through principals in their day-to-day work. While the specific purpose of this section is disciplinary power and panopticism, it is important to acknowledge that discipline does not 'represent all power relations and all possibilities of power relations' (Foucault, 1986, p. 380).

Foucault describes discipline as a political anatomy of detail in its creation of docile bodies. By this he is referring to the 'mechanics of power' that produces subjected and practised bodies by defining 'how one has a hold over others' bodies to do not only what one wishes but also to operate as one wishes, with the techniques, the speed and the efficiency that one determines' (1977b, p. 138). The docile body, according to Foucault, is one that may be subjected, used, transformed and improved, and its docility lies at the intersection of the analysable body and the manipulable body (1977b, p. 136). It was during the classical age, Foucault argues, that the body came to be discovered as both object and target of power, not as a sudden discovery but rather through a gradual multiplicity of processes across many different fields and locations (1977b, p. 138). The idea that the principal can be perceived as a docile body, just as any child, is one that has not been sufficiently explored. Principals are uniquely placed in that they are docile bodies themselves but are also a part of disciplinary mechanisms that construct their staff members and the students as docile bodies. We are all docile bodies in one way or another, but it is the particular forms and expectations of docility that are important to examine.

Discourses and contexts of schooling have played an influential role in the docility of both principals as they have already been made docile through the schooling system, Judy as a teacher, and Ruth as a teacher then as a teaching principal. This teaching-principal role is one that is often undertaken by new principals in the government system so they may gain experience before moving on to a larger site. This was confirmed in an interview with the Executive Director of Schools for the district, as she states:

> The principals who start there will generally have worked at a small school before then, they always have, really. They will usually have had a small school where they may have been by themselves and had a teacher aide or a teacher aide/admin assistant. Then they generally go to another school that has a couple of teachers, then, they get to their Band 7[2] schools with 15 teachers.

These placements in small rural schools can be very challenging for novice principals, as they must combine a substantial teaching commitment with the necessary administrative duties (Clarke and Wildy, 2004; Ewington et al., 2008). The location in rural settings in most cases can also provide added complexities for the new principal, particularly in terms of isolation and adjusting to new contexts. Clarke, Stevens and Wildy (2006), in their study of novice teaching principals in rural settings, argue for a more formal handover structure between outgoing and incoming principals where the new principals are given appropriate information on the school's context and the interaction with the community. Without these forms of intervention, a new principal is then on a steep learning curve with the complexities of the position and is also expected to imbibe the roles and responsibilities advocated by Education Queensland in their *Teaching Principal's Guide* (1999c) so that they may then become suitable for transfer to a larger school down the track. Ruth had been a teaching principal for a number of years and comments on the high turnover of people in teaching principal positions:

> A lot of people don't stay in the teaching principal role for very long. I think Education Queensland trades on that a bit, they're a bit like cannon fodder. People burn out in those, they either burn out and go back to the classroom or go for promotion so their voice is lost to that argument as new young guns come through with new enthusiasm. But there are more people who are staying in Band 5 schools, that's their

career in those small schools so they're driving some of those arguments saying 'look I've been doing it for twenty years and I'm still overloaded, it's not me being ineffective, it's the role'. Particularly with school based management in small schools, because they're still doing the same compliance documents as Band 11 schools and they're having to do them in the same detail and you might have, you know, 10 kids. There needs to be some thought about that. They're also often first time principals so they don't have the basic knowledge that I've got now and you're trying to learn finance, trying to learn the facilities, trying to learn the teaching, everything, all the bits. You're often in remote places so they're really challenging. Like, I saw nobody when I was at Birdsville for nearly 6 months, from district office, etc. They were on the phone a bit. You're pretty much on your own when you arrive there and there's this school to run and you've never been a principal before and it's like 'good luck'.

The already-embodied docility of principals through exposure to the schooling system may be one of the most powerful factors in the disciplining of principals, first as a teacher and then for many as a teaching principal. Gronn (1999) uses the terms *formation* and *accession* to describe these preparatory stages in the development of educational leaders and while these terms are useful it may be problematic in some cases to view the progression of leaders into their roles in such a linear fashion. This type of linear career model of leadership, I feel, is inappropriate to describe the experiences of both the principals in the case studies. Judy, for example, experienced a very unusual entry into the position of principal (see Chapter 1), although she had previously been a head of department.

Ruth experienced a more traditional (in the state system) entry into the position from having been a teaching principal for a number of years and then moving up into a larger school. While this appears to follow Gronn's progression, it would be difficult to argue that issues surrounding leadership formation and accession ceased then to play an important part of Ruth's leadership in the new context. I would also argue that using Gronn's linear model, entry into a teaching principalship simultaneously involves both processes of formation and accession as well as the later stages of incumbency and divestiture due to the high turnover of some principals in those positions. Such models of leadership can prove to be problematic and viewing the principal as a docile body within different contexts may help to break up such a linear pathway and expose power relations for the principal that otherwise may go unnoticed. The result of moves by authorities as Education Queensland to promote their leaders through the ranks in this manner can be a normalisation of principals through being made docile bodies to the system. In recent years, according to the Executive Director of Schools, Education Queensland has also started to move from viewing principals as managers to now advocating principals as 'curriculum leaders':

They very much need to be curriculum leaders now, they balance human resources and finance management but in a school they must not lose sight of the fact that they are curriculum leaders, first and foremost. Their jobs are not managers anymore, they are leaders of learning and that's probably been a shift in the last few years, we've been very focused on selecting, fostering and developing managers and many would absolve their responsibility to others and leadership would be done by someone else.

I am not sure whether Ruth would wholly agree with this statement as, even though she has acknowledged the importance of curriculum to me on a number of occasions, there is still a large part of the job that consists of managerial types of tasks that can be, at times, distracting and all-encompassing.

The subjection of the principal as a docile body and the producer of docile bodies is important for the school under disciplinary regimes. As such, both Judy and Ruth are in the position of being subject to a number of disciplinary techniques through surveillance from students, parents, the community and governing bodies, as well as being a mechanism of surveillance over others. It is through such relations of power that the principal is constructed and maintained under scrutiny and scrutinises others. This is how governmentality can operate in both an upwards and downwards direction (Foucault, 1991b). From my observation and interview data with both principals, it is apparent that there are expectations for the principals of these schools to be readily available and approachable to students, parents and staff. In a very real sense the principal is not only a target for all these concerned parties but also the vehicle by which a number of governing mechanisms are carried out. This brings into play 'a whole set of techniques, methods and knowledge, descriptions and plans' (Foucault, 1977b, p. 141). Both principals of the case study schools identified the pressure on their time and body from these competing groups. This partly emanates from the principal being very much a symbolic representative of the school as well as having the responsibility for many of the day-to-day operations. For example, Ruth has often emphasised to me the importance of the many and varied relationships that need to be developed and maintained with staff, students and community groups as well as both the district and central offices of Education Queensland. Finding the time to devote to these relationships, however, is an issue that speaks loudly to Jane, a teacher at Pine Hills who had to fill in for the principal over the period of a few days, as she states:

The time constraints on the principals' roles is just horrific, they do PR, they're the community face of the school, they're the Education Queensland face to their staff, they're departmental dogs' bodies for paperwork, they're the finance manager, in charge of grants applications, everything falls to them to either ok or delegate some of that work. We have a fantastic administrative officer that goes through a steamroller load of work but the final buck stops with Ruth.

These everyday practices of the principal listed above can be conceptualised in terms of what Foucault (1977b) refers to as discipline being the political anatomy of detail. Here, he refers to the minute techniques and acts of everyday practices where the exercise of power is embedded in these practices of school life. For example, Ruth made a point of remaining visible in the school by doing a number of rounds of the school where both teachers and students could regularly see the principal outside of the administration offices throughout the day. Often this would involve checking up on problematic students, providing any needed assistance for casual or supply staff or to return errant students back to their classroom, as the school has long had a truancy problem. So this principal's personal supervision of these daily fragments of school life constitutes an emphasis of the small things which make up this surveillance, this attention to detail that is not necessarily a part of the official role of a principal, but for Ruth constitutes a political investment of the body. Similarly, Judy would often make a presence around the school in order to interact with students, staff and teachers. On a number of occasions I observed Judy taking students who had been out of class for a variety of reasons back to their classroom to personally make sure that they not only went back to class but to possibly discern if there were any problems.

It is through activities such as personally returning students to class that the principal 'embodies' the authority or 'discipline' of the school, and at the same time is visible in ways that also construct her subjectivity and docility. Some principals may rarely leave the confines of the administration block, which can also be, in itself, disciplinary. Ruth, however, considers this role of physical visibility as being very important even though it may result in time constraints and sometimes limiting the placement of resources in other areas. The significance for Ruth is that such actions can be productive for the running of the school and that makes this visibility significant for her. It is this rationality for the inspections and surveillance that brings into play a whole range of knowledges, particularly for the teachers and students who must feel the panoptic effects of these actions. Not only does the principal place him/herself under their gaze but withdrawing from that gaze can also be significant. Principals are certainly able to exercise power through both visibility and invisibility. This may be through locking themselves away in their office for periods of time or in fact finding other ways to avoid the constant interruptions. As Ruth comments:

In my last school I used to go to the District Office and say 'I'm just in here working on my three year plan', I might work in there with some of the people, human resource people or performance measurement people. That's not a bad model, to take yourself out of the loop and actually remove yourself from the site. But, yeah, I do a lot of work after school and I do take stuff home just about every night. I don't think I am working as effectively as I possibly can yet, I'm still trying to find the model that works. And as I said, the previous principal's model of maybe not coming in till 11:00 sometimes, knowing full well he's probably done four hours work but it's been uninterrupted and has probably been more valuable than ten hours here of interruptions and the world hasn't crashed when he hasn't been here.

This symbolic positioning of the principal's body can be interpreted by staff and students in a number of ways. As a part of this surveillance, some teachers may welcome the gaze of the principal during school while others may feel under pressure if they know the principal could visit at any time. It is this visible and invisible nature of disciplinary power through surveillance that can be more pervasive and significant than the view of the principal as the 'sovereign power' of the school. Interestingly, Jean Francois Lyotard argues that, in fact, 'administrative procedures should make individuals want what the system needs in order to perform well' (1984, p. 62). This idea is closely linked with Foucault's notion that power is productive, as Ruth's desire to personally see to the smooth running of small day-to-day operations and processes is achieved not through top-down policy but rather through everyday practices that make the principal's aspirations compatible with the state's overall educational design. Certainly the size and nature of the school play a significant part in the role and type of work-load for both principals in this study, but it is the analysis of these mundane day-to-day processes that reveal significant amounts of information and, importantly, may also provide a better understanding of the complex position faced by many principals whereby they are caught up in the regimes of power but also created as subjects by these same regimes (McKinlay & Starkey, 1998).

Any examination of gazes and surveillance needs to discuss the notion of panopticism, as it is a central feature of the functioning of disciplinary power. Foucault (1977b, p. 200) describes Bentham's panopticon, although never actually built, as the architectural figure of disciplinary power. As discussed in Chapter 2, the panopticon was a design incorporated into the prison during the eighteenth century, whereby at the centre of the structure is a tower and the building on the periphery is divided into cells that can be seen at all times from this tower. The purpose was to provide a state of permanent visibility so that there is an automatic functioning of power. For Foucault (1977b), the significance is that power should be both visible and unverifiable; visible in the sense that the inmate will constantly be able to see the central tower from which the prisoner is spied upon, and unverifiable because the inmates can never know whether they are being looked at and so believe it could be always the case. As a result:

It automatises and disindividualises power. Power has its principle not so much in a person as in a certain concerted distribution of bodies, surfaces, lights, gazes. Consequently, it does not matter who exercises power. Any individual, taken almost at random, can operate the machine: in the absence of the director, his [*sic*] family, his friends, his visitors, even his servants.

(Foucault, 1977b, p. 202)

Certainly the principal is a central feature of this permanent gaze as one can never be sure when the principal of either school may appear at the classroom or be looking out of the office window or wandering around the school grounds. It is not only the gaze of the principal that the teachers and students must look out for, but also the gaze of other teachers and students that make up this field of visibility. The principal is also subject to this gaze and surveillance from staff, students, parents and the Indigenous communities and this is possible though a range of mechanisms. For example, a significant factor in the operation of disciplinary power is the allocation of space and architecture, or what Foucault refers to as 'the art of distributions' (1977b, p. 141). To achieve this distribution of individuals, Foucault outlines the importance of several techniques: enclosure, partitioning, functional sites and rank (1977b, p. 141). The notion of enclosure involves maximising the efficiency of work by the construction of a workspace that is closed in upon itself and is responsible for its own specific tasks. The school itself, along with prisons and factories, is a classic example of this organisation of space.

For Foucault, partitioning refers to the allocation of smaller workspaces within the larger enclosure. More specifically, this corresponds with classrooms and, more relevant for this book, the administration block or building or section where all the administrative tasks take place. Certainly in large schools, more often than not these are whole buildings, but even in small schools such as the two studied for this book there is a designated area that is immediately identifiable as the administration offices. This is where administrative work can be more concentrated so as to maximise advantages and neutralise inconveniences (Foucault, 1977b). Partitioning is significant for the organising of space that allows for the analysis of individuals as:

Its aim was to establish presences and absences, to know where and how to locate individuals, to set up useful communications, to interrupt others, to be able at each moment to supervise the conduct of each individual, to assess it, to judge it, to calculate its qualities or merits. It was a procedure, therefore, aimed at knowing, mastering and using. Discipline organises an analytical space.

(Foucault, 1977b, p. 143)

The specific functioning of these spaces, for example school administration, allows these sites to correspond with particular tasks, to individualise the workforce for the purposes of efficiency and surveillance. This is what Foucault refers to as the notion of functional sites. The people within these sites are also 'ranked', such as school children organised into classes by age and further into streams by ability. School administration is also ranked by a chain of command that still exists in most schools today through the principal, deputy-principal, managers, teachers, heads of departments, finance officers, administration staff, secretaries and the like.

Both the case study schools have similar staff arrangements in their administration. Riverside has a deputy principal who relieves the principal from day-to-day duties one day a week while Pine Hills has a deputy who is part time in that role. Riverside has a full-time administrative officer as well as a receptionist/secretary, while Pine Hills has one person fulfil both those positions. Pine Hills has also recently appointed a full-time finance officer, through lobbying the district office, to help relieve the burden on the principal. However, that position is a one-year contract, not a permanent position. These arrangements are significant because they distribute individuals into networks of relations. Thus, what we have overall is the organisation of space that needs a specific architecture, hence the layout of most schools have a general similarity to their structure and design.

While Foucault highlights the importance of architectural design for the purposes of efficiency, there are some indications from both case study schools that indeed the functional site of the administration can also hinder many of the tasks that the principals consider to be important. The placement of the administrative staff together in close proximity, for the ease of locating individuals, organises the principal into an analytical space that produces both positive and negative effects. It is positive in that students, parents and staff know where to locate the principal, and by the same token, negative in that the expectation of constant availability can significantly affect the ability of the principal to focus on the task at hand as well as enabling constant interruptions and time demands. Certainly the size of the school is important too, as the administrative officer at Pine Hills remarked, 'The principal in, say, a high school has buffers around him [*sic*] whereas here in a small school Ruth has to be more on call, a more hands on approach.' Ruth also offers:

> Certainly here, it's the unpredictability of it too, like I can have a diary with the best made plans for spending some time writing a submission and then stuff happens, a parent comes up angry because something's happened and you just end up railroaded away from that thing and you have to prioritise.

Strategies to deal with such intrusions can be difficult to implement:

> Some days, and it's pretty rare, but I'll say to the deputy I just need two hours and I'm going to lock the door but even then like you've seen this morning you sort of tune in to what's happening out there.

In many cases it is in fact necessary to remove oneself completely from the school site in order to be able to complete certain tasks without interruption, as earlier interview transcripts from both principals indicate.

It can be seen from these excerpts that the architectural arrangement of space can work both for and against efficiency but it does serve effectively for the purposes of surveillance. Both administration offices and more specifically the principal's office in the case study schools were situated on the upper floors of school buildings where from one glance out the window or from the veranda one could survey large sections of the school. Frequently during my conversations with Ruth, she would look out the window at particularly noisy kids or to investigate incidents that sounded out of control. Judy could also see vast areas of the school from the veranda and would often signal to students and staff members without having to go down into the playground. Upon being quizzed about this, Ruth is aware of the 'invisibility' of the location of the principal's office within the school:

> Yeah, I don't know if that was a thought out thing at the time, it probably was, set up near a bank of classrooms, near a quadrangle, the kids forget I'm here. Being here I can even hear if there's an angry parent's voice coming up to the office and the admin person's the same.

Interestingly, Ruth also believes the structures and the condition of the buildings are very important to the overall ethos of the school, which is the 'Strong and Smart' message:

> It's important to keep the vision up in front of people and really break down the vision to what 'Strong and Smart' means, how will we know this is a strong and smart school? What does the admin look like? What do the buildings look like?

It is in this way that the architecture of the school permeates the school motto and overall vision for the school and has a direct influence on the bodies of everyone in the school. Foucault emphasises the importance of architecture as having a functioning role in the aims and techniques of the government of societies (Foucault, 2002e, p. 349). The role of the architecture of the school is a part of the discourses that construct the order and organisation of the school in its self-management.

The use of timetables in schools requires that divisions of time be allocated so that groups of people may be undertaking the same tasks at the same time. This is to ensure the effective use of time throughout the school day. Certainly this idea has more direct applications for school children and their teachers, as they are required to be in particular places undertaking particular tasks at a given time, than it does the principal. Most principals have a wide array of tasks and activities throughout the day, and it is very difficult to plan a regular timetable when there are issues constantly needing attention and the possibility of unexpected problems that may need a quick response or allocation of resources. Indeed, the nature of the principal's job may in fact be seen as a form of resistance to some disciplinary pressures that are exercised on other staff and the school children, such as the control of activity through timetables. That is not to say that time is not an issue for principals, as clearly the lack of time and the extraordinary workloads place significant disciplinary pressure on principals, as Thomson argues: 'Principals' work, as everyday practice, does not fall into neat little boxes. It is both messy and ecological-it is holistic, unpredictable, consuming and contradictory, pulling in all directions at once' (2001, p. 16).

Both principals work very long hours and also state that they work at home and on weekends. Both principals in this study remarked that although they work very long hours, they feel that the job is never done and the constant distractions at school mean that they have to try to allocate some time for certain tasks such as grant applications and budgets outside of school hours. For example, Ruth remarks:

> The nature of this job, and I've learnt because I've been a principal now for 10 years in a few different sites, is that it's never finished. You never feel like you can go home at the end of the day and the job's done. It's a constant ongoing job that you feel a bit like a plate spinner where you put a lot of effort into one project and then you put it onto something else but you still have to touch base so you end up with this ... or like juggling and you feel like if you take your eye off the ball, the whole lot will fall. So you've got to move your mindset really quickly, like if you wanted to chart my mindset really quickly this morning, I mean all before 11:30 a.m. across five or six different projects, and that's not unusual, that's a really common thing.

This sense of being responsive to constant demands and interruptions is a part of the disciplining of the principal as they are constantly juggling a whole range of tasks and being expected to respond to issues and crises as and when they happen.

The organisation of the body through training and techniques is also significant according to Foucault, as 'time penetrates the body and with it all the meticulous controls of power' (1977b, p. 152). Interestingly the school bell was located in the principal's office at Pine Hills and frequently it was either the principal herself or the administrative officer that pressed the bell to signal the start and end of classes, although there were some situations where one of the students was allowed to 'ring the bell'. In contrast, Riverside did not have a bell system except at the end of morning tea and lunch, and this was usually rung by one of the students. So even having the bell physically located in Ruth's office implies the penetration of time on the body of the principal as the principal gives approval for the bell to be rung. In contrast, at Riverside, time was disciplinary on bodies of the teachers, as they are the ones who have to keep track of time during their classes and signal the end of class.

Foucault emphasises that it is the correlation of the body and the gesture that maximises efficiency, that is, the correct use of the body. An example of this could be teaching children how to hold a pen correctly and teaching them how to sit at their desks to work efficiently throughout the whole day. The body of the principal is also disciplined to produce effective and efficient gestures in perhaps a less overt way but no less pervasive. The principal's body is regulated through everyday life and practices by the regulation of time and space but also through self-discipline and self-regulation, so as to make the principal and his/her routines, actions and gestures as efficient as possible.

It is this training of the principal's body that is crucial in the creation of effective practices in disciplinary societies. According to Foucault, discipline operates four techniques in doing so, and in turn operates through a number of techniques: it draws up tables, it prescribes movements, it imposes exercises and it arranges 'tactics' (1977b, p. 167). These tactics are especially significant, as Foucault argues: 'Tactics, the art of constructing, with located bodies, coded activities and trained aptitudes, mechanisms in which the product of the various forces is increased by their calculated combination are no doubt the highest form of disciplinary practice' (1977b, p. 167).

These tactics thus consist of such things as the architecture and layout of both the school and administration offices, and the way time penetrates the body of the principal, staff and students. Other mechanisms, more specifically techniques of normalisation, such as school performance tables, annual reviews, grant applications, submissions and the like, can be some of the most successful means of disciplinary power for precisely the reason that they appear harmless, but may also be the most pervasive and manipulative in their effectiveness. These seemingly simple mechanisms of hierarchical observation, normalising judgement and the examination are continuously disciplining principals while the principal also has to be monitoring the disciplining of others.

In this section, I have illustrated how both principals are positioned within disciplinary regimes via techniques of surveillance, architecture, time and the notion of docile bodies. Through these mechanisms, Ruth and Judy are both objects and instruments of this type of power. This is not to say that these processes operate necessarily through repressive or negative means but rather that they operate as a specific form of subjectification through the government of individualisation. In the next section, I examine the continual process of writing and managing submissions and grants as a form of governmentality that requires disciplinary procedures of examination, hierarchical observation and normalisation.

Discipline through documentation

An important part of governmentality is the behaviour and action of the principal, as it is through these practices of self-managing schools that the subject becomes manageable. Here the subject can be both the school and the principal. It is through the operation of power/knowledge that the education system constitutes a range of taken-for-granted practices that serve the rationalities of school-based management. Through such activities such as submissions, annual reports and accountability frameworks, schools and their principals become knowable, calculable and administrable objects. For example, both principals in this study spoke at length about the laborious and time-consuming task that was the constant writing of submissions for funding. It is for this reason that I have chosen this aspect of governmentality to demonstrate an example of how this technique of self-management functions in a disciplinary capacity and positions principals as subjects.

The process of grant and submission writing, along with the subsequent management of them along the way, is an example of a dividing practice that combines processes of examination, hierarchical observation and normalisation of principals as part of their self-management. One of the main aims of the disciplinary apparatus is the normalisation of individuals and these effects can be far-reaching. For example, for both Ruth and Judy, who state that they spend a large amount of time on writing and managing grants and submissions, there is a danger that these actions and requirements normalise them into a management-heavy paradigm of working which can take time away from other tasks such as addressing curriculum and pedagogy within their schools, which they both state they would like to be able to do more of.

Foucault defines the norm by the 'exacting and coercive role it can perform in the domains in which it is applied' (2003, p. 50). Therefore it is not defined by any natural property but by particular means in specific sites. Even within these sites there are different normalisations for different individuals, for example, the normalisations that exist for a child or a teacher in a school can vary greatly from those that exist for the principal. It is also important to remember that often, these normalisations are carried out by other individuals within the organisation, for example it may include surveillance from staff, students and the local community as mentioned earlier, and not necessarily be carried out by bureaucratic regimes. Foucault further argues that 'the norm is not simply and not even a principle of intelligibility; it is an element on the basis of which a certain exercise of power is founded and legitimised' (2003, p. 50). The power in this case is disciplinary power.

Foucault refers to disciplinary society as 'the age of social control' (2002a, p. 57), whereby the networks of power were designed no longer to punish individuals' infractions but to correct their potentialities. In order to achieve this, it is necessary for there to exist small penal mechanisms that could have corrective functions. For example, these include the submission-based funding that both principals stated they have to spend a considerable amount of time doing in order to gain funding for projects. These processes employ such mechanisms as normalisation and the examination to assess and evaluate not only the school but also the principal in the writing of these applications.

It is through the norm that disciplinary power wields its power, as Foucault argues, 'the perpetual penalty that traverses all points and super-vises every instant in the disciplinary institutions compares, differentiates, hierarchises, homogenises, excludes. In short, it *normalises*' (1977a, p. 183). It is not only the principal who is judged but also the school itself. In sub-missions for funding, the applications are judged and compared with those from other schools and other principals in competition for those funds. Cri-teria such as the quality of the proposal, the level of need, the history of the school in demonstrating its performance and management of previous grants are all examined and assessed through this process. Thus principals' work is also examined in their preparation of those submissions.

Such normalisations of the principal's work are not necessarily always functioning in a dominating or repressive manner through these disciplinary processes, but they also can shape the principal as a subject with particular desires and aspirations (Meadmore, 1993; Rose, 1990). As Ruth explains:

> A lot of our money that used to just come out is now submission based, you're writing submissions to try to get funds for extra things to your core business, like whether it be computer programs or anything that enhances your curriculum. It seems the way, particularly the last couple of years, it's gone that everything's competitive submission based. So trying to find the time to write the submissions, and then manage the funds when they come in as well. So we might have got a $70 000 grant come through recently that was submission based that's going to look at improving attendance and a whole lot of things. It's not just getting the grant, it's then managing that next $70 000 which will cost about five sub-programs, some involving employing people, some buying resources. In the schools with a lot of Indigenous kids you often get a lot of opportunity to apply for a lot of money, so the Indigenous Know-ledge Centre is a project, all our digital projects, our filming, then we've got to manage that program, and just various other ones that generally we're successful in if we apply. So a bit of a challenge is finding the time to do the application and then you do have to manage it if you get it.

This quotation illustrates how this changed form of the distribution of finances now requires activity from the principal that it did not before the move to self-management. This activity now forms the principal as self-managing rather than managed by the bureaucracy. The formation of the subject in this way is central to discourses of self-management and binds the principal into activities that form their own subject positions within the system, that is, principals who run self-managing schools. One consequence of this is that these 'new' activities do take the principal away from other tasks as well as requiring them to constitute themselves as 'autonomous' through this management activity which at the same time binds them into rules and regulations. The fact that it is Ruth who is primarily responsible for writing the submissions, and then managing the funds and reporting to governmental bodies and their respective communities about the achievements and progress of these programmes, has shifted her subject position as principal. The role of the principal has changed in this particular mix of centralisation and decentralisation. The centre now has to develop the 'tenders' and frameworks, receive submissions from principals, grant money, monitor and receive reports. The decentred unit now has to apply for tenders, make submissions, expend money and write reports. As a result, the relationships between Education Queensland and the school are reconfigured through this set of activities and regulations. This 'mentality' therefore shifts as subject positions become defined in different ways under self-management.

The fact that both schools serve Indigenous communities has further implications as this opens up a broader area for funding applications, but again these are done by both principals. Other staff members, however, are aware of this added complexity, as one teacher comments:

> That's another issue, because it's an Indigenous community school, you not only have the opportunity to spend all day everyday writing grant applications because there are so many things out there offering funding, you then have to have the checks and balances in place to meet the acquittals. A lot of the catch phrasing that goes with the funding is now that it's self funding within three years or that the outcomes have to be x, y and z.

It soon becomes apparent how the two principals are positioned differently in terms of government accountabilities. Ruth primarily has formal accountability pressures coming from central office in the preparation and managing of these submissions as a part of the self-management process. In contrast, as Riverside is not directly accountable to a central government body, Judy is able to 'play the field' to make choices for what she and the Board want the school to do. Judy expressed to me a range of thoughts on funding and the constant submission-writing as a part of the principal's role, as she states:

> Although we are an independent school, we don't have the finances that other independent schools do. The fact that because we are a school we can't tap into a lot of the funding that I believe we should be able to but can't because we're a school. For example, I used to do very well out of the gaming fund, that's how I did all the computers in the seminar

gallery room, for example, upgrading the computer room. Well schools are not allowed to access the gaming fund anymore. Sport and Recreation have money available for sports facilities but schools aren't allowed to access it. It's largely because they see it as EQ's [Education Queensland] responsibility to provide those facilities but unlike state schools we don't get that funding and in terms of AISQ [Association of Independent Schools Queensland] we are in competition with all of the elite private schools. So those are the conundrums that make things difficult.

Thus, Judy is in the position of constantly applying for funds from a variety of sources due to the particular nature of the school. She is also primarily responsible for the actual submission of grant applications as previously stated. This is particularly relevant, as this school is in the unusual position, for an independent school, of being completely reliant on funding from both the federal and state governments as well as searching for financial support from outside agencies. It has been the school's decision to implement a no-fee policy for parents in regard to programmes such as the nutrition and transport programmes. As a result the degrees of freedom for the school to be able to dedicate funds to such programmes must be robust enough to withstand the financial strains on the school. Each time Judy applies for funds for any given programme, she is taking upon herself certain financial liabilities and responsibilities on behalf of the school. In this system, Judy will always have to be in the process of raising money, applying for grants and making decisions about one sort of spending as opposed to another. In this way a private school principal is differently inserted in discourses of school management.

At the same time the principal is also under constant examination and scrutiny and it is through the examination that a powerful combination of both normalisation and hierarchical observation appears. The examination is one of the most important and pervasive disciplinary techniques in the field of education. It is highly ritualised and 'combines the ceremony of power, the form of the experiment, the deployment of force and the establishment of truth' (Foucault, 1977b, p. 185). It is through the examination that whole domains of power/knowledge are established. The examination may operate as the formal process of assessment that students undertake in schools or state-wide examinations such as the Year Three, Five and Seven tests, and the end of Year Twelve examinations. Examinations also take the form of yearly performance reviews and documents as grants and submissions. Through these examinations certain truths about the school and indeed the principal are established on a continual basis. The endless nature of examinations is also in itself disciplinary as it can be regarded as a constantly repeated ritual of power and exchanger of knowledge (Foucault, 1977b). Judy has found that examinations such as grant applications are a classic example of this ritual of power and exchanger of knowledge:

When we purchased this school I then made application again to Block Grant [part of the AISQ] for refurbishment of some of the buildings and on the first interview they had with me they said that our submission was far too great and that there were schools in far greater need than us and the thing that upset me the most really, was that they told me to do away with the nutrition program and the transport program because if I did away with those two key elements then we would be able to service a debt.

This new form of management means that 'debts have to be serviced', in other words, financial criteria have to cut across educational criteria. The school's commitment to a range of programmes to support their students and parents indicates not only a willingness to embrace both social and educational capital roles and opportunities for their students that they otherwise would not receive in the state educational system, but also the ability to negotiate and engage with a range of organisations and bodies for those applications.

The government of individualisation as a figure of power (Masschelein, 2004) is realised through the examination, as the examination is central to the production of individuality (Meadmore, 1993) through continuous evaluation as a part of the disciplinary apparatus. This normalisation of individuals is achieved through what Rose terms a 'grid of codeability of personal attributes' (1990, p. 133) and it is this objectification of the subject that ascribes norms. It is also through documentation that the examination exerts its disciplinary power, as Foucault argues:

> The examination that places individuals in a field of surveillance also situates them in a network of writing; it engages them in a whole mass of documents that capture and fix them. The procedures of examination were accompanied at the same time by a system of intense registration and of documentary accumulation. A 'power of writing' was constituted as an essential part in the mechanisms of discipline.
>
> (1977b, p. 189)

This proliferation of documentation, such as the constant grant applications for both case study schools, is closely linked to practices of government associated with self-government so that the individual can be more effectively disciplined (Meadmore, Limerick, Thomas & Lucas, 1995). This introduction of documentation also signals what Foucault terms the 'first stage in the formalisation of the individual within power relations' (1977b, p. 189). The whole apparatus that came with this formalisation of the individual within power relations opened up the possibilities for the individual to be under the gaze of a permanent corpus of knowledge and also the inventing of a system that could measure a whole range of characteristics not only between individuals and groups but also their distribution in a given population (Foucault, 1977b, p. 190). Thus the individual becomes a 'case' that may be described, measured and compared with others, and as a result it is the individual that needs to be corrected, classified, normalised or excluded (Foucault, 1977b, p. 191). By analysing the specifics of these mechanisms, it is possible to understand how it is that the individual becomes both subject and object to a realm of 'truth games' that are so pervasive throughout our society (Foucault, 1988, p. 15).

For Riverside Community School, Block Grants are administered by the AISQ, of which Riverside is a member. Judy has found that the membership of the AISQ has been problematic for the school, as there used to be a system where there were both Indigenous and Non-Indigenous Block Grants, whereas now all schools are applying for funding from the same pool. This is problematic because there is a huge variation in the schools that make up the AISQ, ranging from elite private schools to Riverside. When I asked Judy about the school being a member of the AISQ, she replied:

> Not by choice, but by the fact that you need to be affiliated with a professional body to make it easier to obtain certain funding but in terms of support I am sorry to say that the AISQ probably has let this school down quite badly and don't take an active role or active interest. I think that in the differences between them, their membership and this little school are too broad and then on their agenda are not the issues that affect us. I was quite amazed and interested ... I was invited to be a guest for a day on AISQ's Education Committee Meeting and there the things they were concerned about, and the things that were causing them the most angst ... I thought my god, if that's all I had to be concerned about, life would be completely different.

To obtain the Commonwealth funding the schools need to be a member, as Judy states:

> A lot of the newer schools are joining now because there is that requirement for registration now, that you do have an affiliation, so some of the newer schools coming online are becoming members of AISQ because if you're not then you can't apply then for block grant. But the fees aren't insubstantial either and I can show you some papers showing what this school gets for literacy and numeracy as opposed to other member schools. We're funded the least out of any school with AISQ. Years ago there were separate block grants. There were Indigenous block grants and non-Indigenous. In some ways we would have been better off if the two had remained separate and that we were competing for dollars amongst other Indigenous education providers as opposed to across the board. Because when we talk about need there is no comparison between this school and most of the schools that are members of AISQ.

Of significance for both principals is the power/knowledge at work in production of these submissions. Foucault argues that it is through the body that power/knowledge operates, to make it a productive and subjected body (1977b). It is through the body of the principal in the preparation and management of these grants that creates new subjects and new knowledges. It is easy to take such practices for granted under self-management systems, but it is important to recognise the new forms of principal subjectivity that occur through these discourses. It is through such mechanisms that governmentality works to govern or steer 'at a distance' (Ball, 1994; Miller & Rose, 1992). The initial submissions and the subsequent reporting on the use of those funds is how power/knowledge works to not only discipline principals but also normalise them into a way of working and managing that can take them away from other tasks. However, the power/knowledge nexus around funding regulation and submissions can also allow principals to use their knowledge to exert power in relation to the state. As such power/knowledge works both ways, as the extra programmes and services, such as the nutrition, transport and tutoring programmes, offered by Riverside demonstrate.

These 'everyday' practices of grant-writing form particular knowledges and create subjects through this formation of truth. In this case, grant submissions and documents such as the triennial review, which Pine Hills has recently submitted, form 'truths' about the schools and their teachers, students and principals. These truths are formed through a reconfiguration of the governance of finances to a more market-based approach whereby each school submits its grant application to be evaluated against other schools' applications. Pine Hills is competing for funds with other Education Queensland schools and also schools searching for funding specifically for Indigenous students. For Riverside, as Judy commented earlier, their school is in direct competition for funding with the elite private schools in the AISQ where membership of the AISQ has been problematic for Riverside, as previously stated.

With the new emphasis on outcomes and performance under regimes of self-management comes the pressure for schools and principals to be able to demonstrate significant gains in these areas, something that is often difficult to do in complex schools such as Riverside and Pine Hills which exercise significant social capital roles that are not as easily measured as educational outcomes. It is through attending to performance and outcomes that governmentality also operates:

> I would say the pressure of the responsibility to get outcomes has in the last two years, and not just at this school, in EQ in general if you look at education, the whole push by Brendan Nelson[3] has really put pressure on people for performance. You don't want to blame underperformance on context of schools but it has to be considered and in the consideration of it you have to then work out strategies that will minimise the damage of the context to those kids. But to do that, that could be somebody's

research for 10 years, but you are sort of expected to try and fast track all that and find the programs and professional development the people and then they leave and you are starting again. I think that pressure to get outcomes with no extra resources and no extra support. I've never been in a job where you just get thrown into it and you are just learning as you go as much as this one.

In this section I have demonstrated how principals are subjectified under the shifting regimes of self-management through using grant-writing and applications as an example. I have argued that while these practices normalise principals into a specific way of working, they also allow the principals to exert power in relation to the state. In the next section I examine the relationship with the community for these principals of self-managing schools and some of the complexities that these arrangements provide for the principals in the form of both constraints and productive aspects.

Community as a new site of governmentality

A significant feature of new school-management regimes involves the changing relationships between schools and their local communities. The history of schooling in Australia is one which has typically consisted of hierarchically structured systems and organisations (Gilbert & Dewar, 1995). As a result of recent moves to more public accountability within the school system under school-based management in Queensland, schools are expected to engage with their communities in more open discussion and collaboration (Education Queensland, 1999a, 1999b). Under these arrangements, communities are portrayed as figures of reason and sanity against old school structures. However, such inherently positive and unrealistic connotations of community involvement are problematic as they subscribe to idealised notions of community that have little to do with the complex arrangements of schools such as Pine Hills. Smyth (2009) argues that such a move towards community engagement activities is not the break with neo-liberal policy that it is often portrayed to be. He argues that the promotion of community engagement is a game of 'rhetorical flourish' that has little to do with addressing underlying social problems. The particularity of context in the case of Pine Hills is a significant factor in the school portrait as the local community acts as both an inside and outside dynamic upon the school. For the duration of the research undertaken for this book there was a political struggle within the community and the government education body concerning Pine Hills and its performance since the previous principal. Under the previous principal the school achieved a very high profile and the success of the principal and the school has been widely documented. With the arrival of Ruth, however, there has been constant criticism about the school and its performance from some sections of the community. This is the troubled environment in which Ruth has been operating and it can be seen from the interview material from her that this has been difficult for her to overcome and deal with on a day-to-day basis. I have tried as well as possible to avoid engaging with this issue and 'taking sides' but the contested political climate around Pine Hills is one that greatly infiltrates the portrait.

In this section I show how the community relationships with each of the case study schools are complex and far from the idealised view that is constructed through government discourses promoting community participation in school decision-making. The notion of community is contested and has been used to refer to a range of phenomena: for example, community as collective values (Plant, 1974) and the notion of the school as community (McLaughlin, 1991; Sergiovanni, 1994). Feminist authors have highlighted inequalities in communities (Fendler, 2001; Fraser, 1999) as well as the value of communities for collective action (Fraser & Lacey, 1993; Young, 2000). Bauman (2001) shows us that the notion of community is one that is inherently unstable and constantly eludes us, while Beck (1999) and Giddens (1998) maintain that communities are in flux with the changing needs of society. However, Lingard, Hayes, Mills and Christie (2003) argue that communities are good by nature but acknowledge that they are constructed by discourses with normalising effects. Rose's (2000) work is useful to define community as an affective and ethical field that, while not necessarily a geographical, social, sociological space, or space of services, may well link itself to any of these. According to such a notion, community is made up of relationships among groups of individuals and a commitment to a particular culture (Etzioni, 1997). Makuwira (2007) argues that within Indigenous communities in Australia, the conceptualisation of community is similarly problematic, but community is largely defined by geography, identity and issue.

Rose's (1999) notion of community as a field of *ethico-politics* is interesting to consider, and I use this in conjunction with Foucault's notion of *governmentality* to view community as a site of power relations whereby community is instituted as a new sector for the purposes of government. The use of community by the government is achieved through a range of programmes, policies and techniques that 'encourage and harness active practices of self-management, identity construction, personal ethics, and collective allegiances' (Rose, 1999, p. 176). Rose suggests that this new power game operates in a field of ethico-politics, which is concerned with the self-management techniques necessary for responsible government and the relations between one's obligation to oneself and one's obligation to others.

According to this power game, the community's gaze can function as both a normalising and disciplining mechanism of school-based management, albeit in different forms for both Pine Hills and Riverside. In this capacity, the local communities of these schools operate in both an enabling and constraining capacity for both principals. This is considered an important part of the self-managing school and can have direct implications for decisions made in these schools.

Identifying the communities of each of the schools is problematic but it is possible to discuss a range of factors and characteristics that contribute to the relationship between these groups and the two schools. Pine Hills has a community that is in close physical proximity to the school in its rural setting. Pine Hills State School is heavily embedded in this context. The town of Pine Hills is characterised by high levels of unemployment and welfare dependence. Domestic violence and alcoholism are issues of concern and there is also a significant issue of transience between this town and other Indigenous communities and settlements around Queensland. These sorts of factors create specific demands of Pine Hills and as a result the relationship between the school and its local community determines what needs to be done and also what can be done. In addition, the staffing demands of the school are dependent on the availability of teachers (there is generally a shortage in rural areas) who often travel long distances to work at Pine Hills. The high level of turnover of teachers makes it difficult to create levels of trust between the school and the local community.

One of the significant achievements under the previous principal at Pine Hills was the emphasis on and establishment of links between the school and the local community. This involved inviting Aboriginal Elders into the school as a symbolic as well as operational move, to employ local tradesmen and workers to undertake repairs on the school, to actively encourage and seek out local community members to be involved as teacher aides while skilling them under the Remote Area Teacher Education Program (RATEP), and also the employment of other cleaners and groundstaff under the Community Development Education Program (CDEP). This had the positive effect of valuing the contributions the local community can make to the school as well as valuing and celebrating their Aboriginality. In addition to this, Ruth explained to me how she and other staff members at Pine Hills regularly make home visits to keep in contact with members of the local community over issues that arise. At the same time, the infusion of community members into the day-to-day operations and running of the school has also been problematic for Ruth.

Such relations with Pine Hills' local community are very important for the school and the positioning of Ruth in these power games. Both principals of the case study schools are placed in a position that both constitutes and is constituted by their school communities (Lingard et al., 2003). As a result both Judy and Ruth occupy different speaking locations in these regimes, each with strengths and weaknesses.

For Riverside Community School, the 'community' actually consists of groups of people from all over Brisbane. When I asked a member of the School Board at Riverside about the community, he emphasised the notion of the school as a meeting place, as he states:

Well regardless of all those different locations, where the students are actually coming from, it's a place where we can all be one even though we are all different with different experiences, different backgrounds, circumstances, but there is something which is more of an acceptance, despite those differences there are things we have in common and it's the things we have in common that the school is about sharing. You know to be able to go and just talk to the principal.

In this case the word community designates their Aboriginality rather than a localised geographical space. This Indigenous community, like that of Pine Hills, is characterised by high levels of unemployment and welfare dependence. This has an impact on school policy and decisions made in that the school recognises these factors in their decision to do without a fee structure, having a transport system for the students and having a daily nutritional programme. It is also school policy to maintain at least 80 per cent of staff members of Indigenous origin. The school has also set up the Riverside Community Skill Centre, which is a centre located on the premises of Riverside that is an important part of the school's approach to Indigenous community development by offering a range of programmes, for example the development of digital literacies, in order to assist members of the Indigenous community into the workforce.

Both schools play a social capital role in their communities but the specific challenges around localised interactions and relationships appear more substantial for Pine Hills, as the Executive Director of Schools for the region explains:

> The school in the community like Pine Hills is playing a much greater role than just an educational role, it's playing a social capital development role. The complexities of principalship in that role means that you're liaising, leading and engaging with a pile of government and non government agencies and you often have accountabilities with that and you don't get that down the road and around the corner. So that's the biggest issue, so dealing with the communities, the challenges that are facing young kids in that community and working with the parents and dealing with the sheer breadth of the inter-agency dimension.

The locality of its community in relation to the school continues to have an impact on day-to-day life, as it has in the past. Pine Hills State School is still considered a state-run school with a particular legacy and history, as Ruth states:

> The community came through being a mission; they had a superintendent as it was very hierarchical and it was very controlled and I read a thing the other day when I was having one of my kids in 1984, the hospital down here, the dining room and that were still segregated. That's pretty recent in my history that this dining room and the kitchen and

that were segregated and I think that well a lot of my staff are women older than me who having their kids who have been through that system, in such recent memory.

The impact of the community on the school is something that the staff is particularly aware of, as this comment from a teacher demonstrates:

It's like well you might be at Pine Hills so well bite the bullet and get on with it. Do your job here or go somewhere else if they don't like it. Lots of community issues from what I can gather which causes a lot of upheaval.

The significance of this quotation illustrates a perception from some of those staff coming from outside the community that it is a troubled and difficult place to work, and as a result some staff may bring those expectations to the school with them every day. A number of other staff such as teacher aides and cleaners, however, do come from the local community and have little opportunity to 'go elsewhere'. They have a direct personal interest in seeing their community, their families and their children succeed despite large hurdles. I am certainly not advocating that the teachers from outside the community do not care or do not want their students to succeed, as this is far from the case, but it is not just the local community members and children that bring certain expectations and assumptions with them to school, the outside teaching and administrative staff do too. The difference for these students is that many will never leave the community and a large number will also not make it through to Year Twelve, and this is of great concern for the local community.

In contrast to this, Riverside offers schooling right up to Year Twelve for its students and only four years ago had its first two students graduate from Year Twelve. With increasing numbers of its students remaining at school throughout the high school years, it is expected that more numbers of its students will finish Year Twelve with the opportunity to go on to further study or employment. This is seen as an important aspect of the school, providing the necessary scaffolding and support to encourage its students through high school and even into university. As a primary school, Pine Hills' students tend to go to the nearest high school in a neighbouring town, but the drop-out numbers are very high.

It is impossible to separate the political climate around Pine Hills and its history from what happens on a daily basis in the school. Context is crucial. Such is the complexity of the community's involvement in Pine Hills that Ruth claims that some sections of the community are looking for any action to target and criticise the school for political gain whereas other members of the community are genuinely supportive of the current leadership. The perception from some of the community is that as a government school they are serving the interests of the white majority and given the historical context of

Pine Hills, this is understandable. The perception that Ruth is trying to 'whiten the school' is one that has been reiterated from certain sections of the community that have a political interest in the school, as Ruth explains: 'Some people see accountability and process as aligning with 'whiteness' and so the improvements in our audits we get hammered for because 'it's almost like a white school now'. But we have to make sure there's that balance.'

This political context is one that has plagued Ruth from the start of her position and has made it very difficult to be seen to be doing well and working towards productive outcomes for the school and students. This has certainly had a significant impact on her role and capacity to act as principal. She has repeatedly explained this situation to me on a number of occasions. For example:

> Still lots of challenges around being accepted here as far as, not by the majority of people but by a few people making mischief behind the scenes about me being here and the pattern seems to be when things start to settle down and run smoothly somebody will stir something up. It appears nearly purposely, it may not be, but a spanner's been thrown in the works to destabilise the place again. So that's continued and I guess people have got better dealing with it, more and more people are just appearing to get on with their job and not become involved in it. We've had a couple of people go off on stress leave because of the destabilisation affecting them so that's been sad because they're both good operators … Some of the Triennial School Review comments, most of the negative comments were very similar to each other as if they had been coached. One of the things that was said was that the principal should attend all community meetings but really if you went to all of them then you would be doing nothing else. So the balance of being visible in the community is against the availability here and you can't be out too much.

This testimony by Ruth was made at the end of 2006, a period of time that she often remarked to me as having been a long, difficult year. To make matters more difficult for the principal, she had also recently found out that her job had been readvertised, as she explains:

> They've readvertised my job. Out of the blue there was a decision to re-Band it to a Band Nine from a Band Seven and I was pretty taken aback by that as usually it takes eighteen months of consultation for that to happen. I still believe that it was done in a way to maybe get rid of me out of the school. Because usually you can only go up one banding with the school and this was two and if it is two then you have to reapply for the position. The mischief side of me says that it was a tricky way to try to get me not to apply or to lose in an application process. The corporate line was that they want the principal's role to become more complex and involve taking the good stories to the world and having interns and

hosting a lot of visitors so it is a more complex job. Maybe the truth is somewhere in between because they only got three applicants, they've decided not to fill it. So that's been really quite traumatic and stressful to deal with on top of running the school which is the normal thing. That's pretty much been the nature of it since I started so it's been a big couple of years of trying to improve things while dealing with this stuff that goes around the edges and the background. It's not necessarily conflict in your face but it's undermining, kicking your legs out from under people, putting down people when they are trying to do something so it's been quite damaging.

Since then, Ruth has faced an uncertain future at times, but has been kept on as principal since then. Such is the political environment of uncertainty that Ruth has been working under since her time at the school, as she explains in the following extract:

It's been the hardest principal's job I've ever had. Not because of the kids but because of the politics around it. There has been a lot of undermining in the community in some respects. Some people stood up when the re-banding was announced, a huge amount of letters went down and petitions from people here. There was quite a backlash which they weren't expecting. There are certainly people with different views depending on who they are aligned with.

From this quotation it can be seen that Ruth does acknowledge positive support from the community, so it appears as though it is very much a community divided. In response to some of these concerns, Ruth has made concerted efforts to improve community relations by getting a senior Indigenous staff member to take on a role similar to some of the practices of the previous principal:

The previous principal understood that fundamentally because he's Aboriginal and really reinforced that with the kids all the time. We use the Strong and Smart message a lot but the pride in Aboriginality, I get Joe often on parade to do that but I probably need to get more of that into my repertoire in valid ways so it's not just lip service to it. The way I have done it is to try and give the kids the things they are proud of like doing well at the Melbourne art thing.

Ruth does concede that she needs to be doing more to improve relations with sections of the community, however, to some extent she appears to be constrained in what she can and cannot say and do through the community's gaze and her 'whiteness'. This is particularly due to the fact that the community influence on Pine Hills stems from both those inside the school as well as outside the school. This is an example of what Rose terms 'government through community' (1999, p. 176). The community's gaze operates throughout the school day and upon Ruth's daily practices, whereas for Judy there are spaces at school where she can withdraw herself from this outside gaze.

The community influence and impact upon Riverside appears quite different from that of Pine Hills, and therefore positions Ruth differently according to these accountability regimes. Riverside does not have the same intensive relationship with its community as many of the students are bussed in from a large range of suburbs, so the physical closeness and impact is lessened somewhat. Again the ownership of the school by the Indigenous community and council seems to have had a huge impact on the community's expectations and relationship with the school, often perceived as a positive one. As Judy states:

> Support from the community generally and if you take, for example, at the end of last year, when the Aboriginal Tutorial Assistance Scheme (ATAS) funding was going to be cut and as you know having been here that this is the context that hasn't been changed. The Department was absolutely bombarded with letters and phone calls from a wide ranging cross-section of the community, not just the Indigenous community. There were even some Liberal politicians that got themselves involved so it was pretty amazing. Quakers. It was actually a Quaker who in the school's first year paid the teachers' wages. So the Quakers have long had an association with the school. 'Super Gran' she was called. So there has been a lot of interesting people involved.

As can be seen from the quotation above, there are a number of positives for Riverside that can be drawn from the community's direct involvement. The main one is being able to draw upon community members to be directly involved in the school, whether it be as teacher aides, groundstaff or cleaners. For many of the children, having family and community members at school can be of great benefit. Both schools draw upon staff who have connections with a student when an issue arises, as Judy states:

> We do say here in our staff meetings, well if you do have a child who is proving to be particularly difficult, think about what person on staff they may be related to, or have a family connection with, so engage them in terms of trying to make things better for this child. It is not unusual for a staff member if a child is doing something that is particularly wrong that they won't be sent up here to me, they'll be sent to Bob who might be an uncle, for example.

Perhaps some of these approaches contribute to an increasingly widespread view that organisations 'that have emerged from within the Aboriginal community and which reflect Aboriginal aspirations and priorities are functioning better than other structures that are imposed by the government' (House of Representatives, 1990, p. 45). By the same token, state schools, such as Pine Hills, are left to deal with the contradictions that government policies create (Ball, 1994), particularly in relation to discourses of community relationship and engagement with the school, which are different from Riverside. The principal's subjectivity in this process is one that precariously shifts through these competing discourses. The principal, as a speaking subject, is both the site for a range of possible subjectivities and also subjected to regimes of discourses which enable them to act in a particular way (Weedon, 1987). This terrain needs to be negotiated and is open to conflict, particularly where issues of power and culture are embedded in the tensions between Pine Hills and their local community.

Gaze and ethnicity

As both of these principals of Indigenous schools are white, I was interested to see to what extent this played a role in their positioning between school and their local community. Both principals have commented upon their 'whiteness' as having some significance in their subject positioning. For example, Ruth comments:

> My non-Indigenous status has been something that appears to have played more of a role here than it has in other schools, including both Indigenous and non-Indigenous schools. In other places it hasn't been such an issue. The division in black and white has been obvious here, not just in contentious things, it's often raised ... For example, I have just picked up teacher aides because we've had a lot of people away so I've just called on people we've used before. Now they happen to be non-Indigenous because we didn't have any Indigenous ones, so there was a bit of uneasiness because I was seen to be replacing an Indigenous person with a non-Indigenous person. The link was then made that I'm trying to 'whiten the place' whereas in reality it's none of that. The response to that is that I have to be conscious of that every time I make a decision, so rather than make a decision based on what's best for the kids with the most skilled person being in place, I have to constantly see it through that filter. My decisions are made through that filter, how other people will see that decision. It may be that I have to explain it more. That's probably been a challenging thing as it's frustrating when I get that thrown up at me when I don't believe it's true and I have the best interests of the kids at heart. You sort of wear it but it's frustrating sometimes. I try and keep stepping back and looking at the longer term view and think maybe these are blips and just hard days, teething problems but I am not necessarily convinced of that either.

Ruth's testimony indicates how she perceives her positioning as a speaking subject. If she makes a decision that is contentious with some members of the local community then her ethnicity becomes a factor. Nevertheless she cannot escape her 'whiteness' whether she likes it or not. In the example above, she perceives that educational factors take precedence over appeasing local concerns when she is looking for teacher aides. She explains that as a result, she views all of her decision-making within this mindset of 'how will members of the local community react'. The gaze of the local community is an important technique of government in this power game, in pursuing active practices of self-management on the part of the principal. The expectation from some vocal sections of the local community is that as the local community school, the teacher aides should come from that local community. This is a stance that was actively constructed by the previous principal. However, as a white principal, Ruth's subject positioning is different from that of the previous principal in this decision-making process.

The gaze of the community can be a powerful influence in this case as it informs what actions the principal takes in respect to the hiring of staff. It is not a matter any more of accepting staff placements from the central bureaucracy, the principal now has the key role in the hiring of staff, and the local community also perceives the principal to be directly responsible for these decisions. With funding being largely determined on enrolments under self-management, this then creates a situation of unease for the principal where concerns for funding and market forces can override issues of teaching and learning, as parents can withdraw their children from the school and send them to another school in the region. For Ruth, here it appears as if 'image and impression management are becoming as important as the educational process' (Ball, 1994, p. 51). To be seen to be working with the interests of the community is all important.

Judy has also commented upon the issue of being a white principal in an Indigenous setting and some of the constraints that places upon her job. However, she had difficulty thinking of a specific issue where this played out, as she states: 'I'm going to put my neck out on the line and say that as a non-Indigenous person what you can do in an Indigenous school is constrained by the fact that you are non-Indigenous.'

Judy's understanding of this issue was more based on speculation, whereas for Ruth, her example was directly related to issues of her professional practice. From the interview data it seems that the principals are aware of this positioning. Ruth is aware of the scepticism with which reforms from above are received within the school and local community and herself positioned as being compliant with the top-down reforms. On the other hand, Judy is aware when making decisions that her position as principal is one that has been not only elected by the school governance council but also continues to act on their behalf.

Judy speculates that as a white person there are some things you cannot do as a principal of an Indigenous school. While this is a perception that may or may not be the case, the importance of this statement is the principal's view on this issue determines directly the actions that she may or may not take in her daily practices. Depending on the issue and stance to be taken, the principal can be either constrained or enabled in their capacity to act through relations with their respective communities. This constant monitoring by the community and self-monitoring of their own practices by the principal is a key feature of the new way these school-management arrangements play out. Here, the principal is positioned in a web of complex and often contradictory discourses that reinforce the principal's subject position as the school's face to the community, albeit as a white face heading Indigenous schools. In Judy's case, her way of being and operating at Riverside indicates that there are different ways of being 'white' and it may be surprising to many outside the school to learn that she is not Indigenous.

As a member of the School Board at Riverside, Fred acknowledges that Judy's whiteness may be perceived as a problem for some Aboriginal people who believe that the principal of an Indigenous school should be an Aboriginal person, but he does not subscribe to that view, as he states:

> Some people, they would see that as being a problem. For me it doesn't, I mean with those sorts of arguments, I'd just say it's Murri people using European theories of race construction. It's got nothing to do with that, it's all about a mindset, when I hear Aboriginal people using that sort of argument, I think 'well you're saying it just like a white fella'. There are lots of white fellas who are very comfortable with Aboriginal communities simply because they can see the role that relationships have and they play out that role in relationships. This [points to skin] has got nothing to do with Aboriginality and if this is going to be a measure of it then it shows no understanding of what relationships are about. I'm sure it has impacted negatively for Judy but you've just got to have a look at all the old arguments of Indigenisation and what it does. Having people in a position simply because they are Aboriginal doesn't necessarily mean you are doing the job that you're required to do.

In contrast to Judy at Riverside, the contested political environment surrounding Pine Hills has somewhat positioned Ruth as the face of white government education that had been mediated through the much publicised transformation under the previous Indigenous principal. At Riverside, the principal is positioned as representing the Indigenous community as elected by an Indigenous Board of Elders. The knowledge that Riverside is an Indigenous-owned and -controlled school does have a direct impact on the community's view and perception towards the school. As Judy comments:

> The fact that it hasn't succumbed to the approaches from other agencies including the government, including the churches, we have maintained our independence. That it is seen in the community as being an Indigenous owned and controlled school and I think that has a significant bearing on how the kids see the school, and their sense of ownership of

the school. They do know that this is their school. The fact that that ownership then allows parents a sense of entitlement here which they wouldn't have in a state school, they don't expect to have a say in a state school whereas it's sort of an automatic given here. And parents are not backwards in coming forwards here and they're often here to complain but I don't mind the complaints because they feel as if they have got a voice here. They can come here and say 'I didn't like the way this happened or that happened', which I think is fabulous.

This indicates how, as a principal, Judy is constituted in a particular set of accountability relationships by the parents of an independent school. In contrast, Ruth and Pine Hills are accountable to the state education body as well as having a complex and intensive relationship with its community as constructed by the previous principal. In summary, I have argued in this section how the community, as a part of this new terrain of self-governance, can operate to discipline and create a new subjectivity for the principal, as white principals of Indigenous schools, through their whiteness, albeit to different extents for Ruth and Judy.

Conclusion

In this chapter I have demonstrated how each of the two school principals is inserted differently into the power regimes within school management. In doing this, I have given examples of daily work practices for both principals within self-governing schools. I then moved on to show how each principal is positioned within disciplinary power relations as a part of this governmentality using Foucault's notions of docile bodies, surveillance, time and architecture. Following this I proceeded to demonstrate how power operates on and through the principals through submission-based funding mechanisms. This is an example of how governmentality can function through the conduct of conduct of these school principals. In the final section, I argued how the notion of community, examined as the notion of a new power regime of community participation under self-governance, indicates that community relations are significantly more complex than idealised notions within government policy and in this way could be better viewed as a new sector for the purposes of government. Within this section I further illustrated how each principal's 'whiteness' creates new subjectivities and can function as a disciplining mechanism as a part of this regime.

In the next chapter I use Foucault's notions of ethics and technologies of the self to understand how it is possible to contest and respond to the proliferation of practices that serve under this governmentality framework to decontextualise and normalise the work of principals. I examine how issues of gender are relevant in these technologies of the self and how these inform their leadership practices. I do this with the view to disrupt the traditional notions of leadership as put forward by much of the leadership literature examined in Chapter 3, and illustrate how the leadership and work displayed by the principals of the case study schools is complex and constantly shifting and is able to move beyond the constraining views of principals' work represented through traditional leadership and managerialist discourses.

5   Leading and managing as ethical work

> One could not form oneself as an ethical subject in the use of pleasures without forming oneself at the same time as a subject of knowledge.
>
> (Foucault, 1992, p. 86)

The previous chapter explored the different ways that the two school principals were inserted and positioned within discourses of school management and used the examples of the writing of submissions and grants, and school–community relations, as forms of governmentality. However, governmentality is concerned with not only practices of governing others but also practices of the self (Dean, 1999). In this chapter I examine these practices of the self and how the two school principals exercise such practices to become ethical subjects. Specifically I use Foucault's notions of ethics and technologies of the self to understand how it is possible for the two school principals to contest and respond to the proliferation of practices that can serve to discipline and normalise them under notions of governmentality. In addition, I examine how issues of gender are relevant in technologies of the self and how these inform their leadership practices. This is done with the view to disrupting the traditional notions of leadership put forward by much of the leadership literature examined in Chapter 3, and to illustrate how the leadership and management work displayed by the principals of the case study schools is complex and constantly shifting in ways that are not captured by the constraining views of principals' work represented through traditional leadership and managerialist discourses.

A principal's work is highly ethical and an understanding of how principals act with regard to their own actions as well as in relation to those of others, such as teachers, parents, children, colleagues and community groups, is important. It is necessary to remember that Foucault's genealogy of ethics was undertaken using discourses of Greek antiquity, and while I would not go so far as to say that these discourses directly translate to today's society, they do provide ways of critically analysing thoughts and actions in relation to the self and others that can open up possibilities for change (Hoy, 1986).

The first section of this chapter examines Foucault's four aspects of ethical work on the self that were introduced in Chapter 2, that is: concepts of ethical substance, mode of subjection, forms of elaboration and telos. The second part of this chapter takes the notion of telos of the ideal principal and the ethical work it entails for each of the two principals. This telos is shaped partly by discourses of the principalship in literature, community expectations and systemic documents such as those produced by Education Queensland, and also in a more personal way by the kind of principal that both Judy and Ruth want to be, and what has to be worked upon to achieve that. The third and fourth sections specifically examine how each principal constitutes herself as a moral subject using Foucault's notions of ethical substance, the modes of subjection, and then the forms of elaboration.

Foucault's construct of ethics

Foucault's notion of ethics is concerned with the relationship one has with oneself and processes of self-formation in response to a range of prescribed codes of action (Foucault, 2000a). It is this relationship that needs to be seen as important rather than the codes of behaviour themselves. For Foucault, ethics is:

> A process in which the individual delimits that part of himself [*sic*] that will form the object of his moral practice, defines his position relative to the precept he will follow, and decides on a certain mode of being that will serve as his moral goal. And this requires him to act upon himself, to monitor, test, improve and transform himself.
>
> (1992, p. 28)

Thus, Foucault's notion of ethics stands against any understanding of ethics that defines itself as an abstract normative code or customary conduct (Bernauer & Mahon, 2005, p. 152). As principals, the two participants involved in this study are constantly making decisions in relation to codes of behaviour and action prescribed through agencies such as Education Queensland and the Board of Elders, as well as expectations from parents, staff, students and community groups. Being a principal involves a range of activities that need to be continually questioned and in doing so, principals and teachers are doing ethical work not only on themselves but also in relation to others for the good of the school and the students. Christie (2005, p. 40) employs a useful way of looking at the notion of ethics, for she argues that ethics is 'a disposition of continual questioning and adjusting of thought and action in relation to notions of human good and harm. It entails work on the self and consideration of how to be and act in relation to others.'

The importance of this notion of ethics is that it moves beyond an engagement with notions of ethics that are little more than sets of competences and capabilities, or a set of moral codes to which principals must subscribe (see, for example, Education Queensland, 1997, 2006; Independent Schools Queensland, 2006). Furthermore, Christie notes that ethics is concerned with notions of what constitutes human good and how to be and act in relation to others.

Foucault's genealogical work on ethics (1990, 1992, 2000a) proposes that ethics is about a relationship of self to self and how we constitute ourselves as moral subjects by our actions. Foucault demonstrates that there are four dimensions to this self-forming process. This is not to say that the content of this process is the same today as in Greek Antiquity, as we don't have the same notions of what we need to do to be ethical as the Ancient Greeks did. What is similar, however, is that we do undertake work on ourselves in the same four ways.

Using these four main aspects of Foucault's genealogy of ethics, I consider in this chapter the self's relationship to itself as a key notion of the way we examine principals' work. The first of these four aspects of ethical work Foucault puts forward is 'ethical substance', which refers to the part of oneself or of one's behaviour that is relevant for ethical judgement in order to achieve moral conduct. For example, feelings and emotions; or more specifically, the act linked with pleasure and desire. The second is the 'mode of subjection' or the way in which people are invited or incited to recognise their moral obligations. This may refer to divine law in a holy text such as the Bible or the Koran, social customs, natural laws or rationality. Other examples could include documents produced by Education Queensland for school principals and Indigenous community customs and expectations. Third is 'forms of elaboration', the self-forming activities by which we can transform ourselves into ethical subjects. Such activities can include a range of physical and mental techniques such as self-discipline, meditation, writing and training one's body. One example of this that I use later in this chapter is how Judy pushes certain tasks outside school hours so that she can be available for students and staff during the day. The fourth of Foucault's fourfold ethical framework is 'telos'. This refers to the achievement of a certain mode of being, a mode of being characteristic of the ethical subject. More specifically the accomplishment of a mastery over oneself, the sort of person one wishes to be (Foucault, 1992, 2000a; O'Farrell, 2005). For the two principals in this study it means the type of principal they wish to be.

Situating this notion of ethics within a framework of governmentality is important, for governmentality is concerned with not only practices of governing others but also practices of the self (Dean, 1999). In relation to Foucault's previous work, it should be emphasised that these practices and technologies of the self do not supersede disciplinary power but more function in a different way yet still operate as a form of governmentality, as Foucault states, 'what we call "discipline" is something really important in this kind of institution; but it is only one aspect of the art of governing people in our societies' (2000g, p. 177). Foucault (2000e) argues that it is the concept of governmentality that makes it possible to bring out the freedom of the subject and its relationship to others. This, he argues, is what constitutes ethical work. It is through these active practices of the self that the subject constitutes him/herself and these practices are not invented by the individual but by society, culture and social group (Foucault 2000e). Therefore, in this chapter, I use Foucault's notions of ethics and technologies of the self to understand how it is possible for each principal to contest and respond to the proliferation of practices that can serve to discipline and normalise these two participants within this governmentality framework.

The telos of the principalship

The essential aim of this chapter is to examine the two principals as moral subjects, and the work each does to form herself into a moral subject. This is defined by both the discursive norms of the leadership literature and employing authorities as telos, and also by their own personal telos or vision of what they would like to do and be in order to be considered moral in their own eyes. Using Foucault's fourfold ethical framework from the data I have gathered, it is clear that there are two sets of work that each principal does. The first is how the principal constitutes herself as moral subject, and second, the work she does to ensure the school as a moral institution through leading and managing. Therefore each section on the principal is divided into two according to these dimensions of ethical work that they do. First, however, I discuss notions of telos and the ideal principal.

Judy: telos of a 'good principal'

Judy's personal telos as a principal and the type of principal she wishes to be can be seen, in this section, through her interview responses, my observation field notes and an interview with other staff members. In the following interview transcript, Judy responds to a question about how she would describe her style of leadership, as she states:

> My style of leadership is often criticised from outside the school and I am seen as being too soft, not having a hard enough line but it has yet to be proven to me that by being a dictator you have any sort of better respect from your staff, so I try and lead by example. With obvious commitment to the core business here, and that's the children.

In this excerpt I interpret Judy's view of good personal leadership as involving the development of good relationships with staff and treating them with respect. She also refers to the core business as being the children, which, I believe, she means in relation to the school as a whole being devoted to the welfare of the children as well as herself, in terms of her personal relationships with the students. She also demonstrates her view that more authoritarian styles of leadership do not necessarily result in increased respect from staff even though that style of leadership is often expected from outside agencies and community groups. Judy attempts to demonstrate good leadership by modelling behaviour to staff and students, as she explains:

> I try to lead by example. The fact that I'm here every day, that I work hard, that I always treat the children with respect, that I always have time to listen to children and I'd like to think that people emulate that, emulate treating the children nicely and always taking the time not to make an immediate judgement but to listen and to let children think that they do have a say. Even if a staff member is in the wrong, I would never yell at anyone or demean them in front of others, if anything needed to be said I would always say it in private. I don't believe in belittling people, or making people feel worse than they already possibly do, and there is no harm in letting things ride for an hour or two so that you can deal with the matter in private. I also take an interest in the school after hours and by doing things like cleaning the toilets because I don't believe in any notion of hierarchy within the school and I would never ask somebody to do something that I myself wouldn't do or be seen to do. If the cleaners are sick or something has been forgotten, well that needs to be done so it doesn't matter who does it as long as it gets done. So staff see me cleaning the school, see me picking up rubbish so that makes it alright for everyone to do as well. It takes away from that attitude of 'I'm better than you', which can happen in schools. Even some teachers will sometimes say to me 'what are you doing, you shouldn't be cleaning the toilets', well why not, just because I hold a particular role doesn't make me any better than anybody else.

Judy emphasises notions of 'working hard', 'treating children with respect', listening to their concerns, forming positive relationships by 'not belittling people' and working against notions of hierarchy within the school. In addition, what is important for Judy is to be liked by the students: 'I suppose deep down, the fact that the kids like me [laughs]. It may not be unanimous throughout the school population, but I think it's fairly significant.'

One of the most powerful aspects of Judy's sense of self as a principal is to build positive relationships with the students, and her telos, or idea of a good principal, is one who takes the time to directly address students' concerns and takes the time to listen to them, and an indicator of this is the extent to which she perceives herself as being liked by the student population.

The other work that Judy does is in relation to the school functioning as an ethical institution. In terms of a telos of the school, Judy has expressed to me in interviews a commitment to more than just the educational achievements of the children. She argues for more social capital building capacities as a part of the school's core business. That is, to respond to the deep needs of many of the children attending the school. As she states in the following excerpt:

> I think the main philosophy is that all children need to be respected and that as an educational facility, an Indigenous educational facility, we are charged with the responsibility of looking after the whole child and not just their educational needs. That's why we do other things that most schools wouldn't do. I think the respect is the biggest thing. That's why we find it difficult, particularly with new staff, getting over that concept of consequences for certain behaviour because we believe that you have to take into account the background of the children, what particular things have happened to them.

In this case, Judy's expresses her intention and desire, as principal, to build a school that can take into account each child's situation when evaluating their behaviour at school and to respect each child accordingly. In the above transcript there is an element of satisfaction for Judy in the school being able to offer programmes such as the nutrition, transport and literacy programmes, and understandings of the needs of the children that other schools cannot. There is a moral sense of self in the principal's own contributions to these outcomes both in terms of providing the means for such programmes but also in her daily interactions and practices within the school, particularly in terms of relationships with the students. This moral self-regulation was evident during periods of observation of Judy at work, in interviews with her and also in interviews with other staff and board members of the school. For example, in an interview with a member of the school board at Riverside, I questioned him about Judy's leadership style and his response provides an insight into the telos of the school and how he perceives this principal's ethical work in relationship to that telos:

INTERVIEWER: How would you describe Judy's leadership in the school?
JOE: In my experience I think it's virtually accessible, accessible because of relationships being the foundation of the school itself. I think people find the roles, not so much in the positions they may hold within the school, but in the relationships dictated to in the nature of what the school is for. So I think Judy's leadership reflects the intent and purposes of the school. I suppose we say and hear it often in schools that it's all about the kids, and you know it's their school. The only way you do that, I think, is by providing that leadership which bases its relationships between staff and students.

The style of leadership through accessibility and relationships displayed by Judy is therefore seen to be based on the intent of creating an environment for the students and community that is reflective of the telos of the school, which is to address the needs of the children, not just in terms of educational outcomes but also social outcomes. Joe, in the following transcript, highlights the importance of these social outcomes for the students at Riverside:

> It certainly achieves in terms of outcomes here, obviously we want those sorts of educational achievements as well but there are other things which go along that such as self esteem, positive reflection of students themselves, confidence. It comes more from that accessibility, it's accessible for students to achieve those outcomes by being able to see a place and that relationship.

There are those at the school who argue that Riverside can provide a much better environment for Indigenous students than through the state system, as Joe states:

INTERVIEWER: Are there some things that Riverside can do that state schools cannot?

JOE: Oh, I think there are lots of things. Basically, a lot of the problems with state school education, I think, and this is in the way we look at deficiencies. If we just go literacy, numeracy, the main problem with the education system is the concern with educational achievements or a lack of educational achievements and what they tend to do is basically respond to the functions and functionality of literacy and numeracy. What Riverside Community School does differently is not only do we address those sorts of things but it's the ways in which you bring in a whole series of, and we come back to that word again, relationships which students bring with them into the classroom. And it's trying to address and have opportunities to address, respond and support those broader influences as well, and not just focus on the students' numeracy and literacy ability in the classroom. It's trying to combat a whole range of other influences. So the ways in which we do it, we have the tutoring programme with lots of one on one etc. a bit of commitment, it's hard work and it requires a lot of human resources and financial resources to do that. State school systems, I think will shy away from those sorts of commitments because it's other criteria to which they are being held accountable to. So those benchmarks are very different.

Here, Joe is largely referring to the school moving away from deficit models of students and Aboriginal people and trying to acknowledge a greater range of factors and influences upon their achievements at school.

The benchmarks for students' achievement, he argues, are very different for Riverside as opposed to state schools which must be accountable to literacy and numeracy benchmarks. In accordance with this philosophy, Riverside Community School chooses to implement a range of programmes to support this whole child development and the ethos of the school. These programmes are in response to the belief that the state system is incapable of doing similar ethical work due to systemic and accountability constraints. The sorts of decisions made by the principal and board at Riverside are ethical choices in response to the capacity of parents to contribute financially to these programmes. This is a substantial commitment by the school to sustain the financial burden this places on the school, and is not made lightly, but the school considers this financial risk to be acceptable in order to 'behave ethically'.

The telos of the school can also be found in the *Riverside School Handbook* (2005, p. 2). It states under the vision statement that the aim of the school is to: 'promote the development of Indigenous students as independent and skilled people who are culturally, morally and socially responsible; employable, capable of self-fulfilment and of contributing to society.'

In addition to this, the vision statement, which I detailed in Chapter 1, describes issues of 'empowerment, identity and success through education' (2005, p. 2). Crucial to achieving this is the importance the school places on valuing and respecting Indigenous heritage and culture. For example, the high school department describes its purpose as providing:

> A unique opportunity for Indigenous and non Indigenous high school students to be able to interact, develop and achieve in an environment that is conducive to their needs, firstly as custodians and reconcilers of Aboriginal and Torres Strait Islander traditions and protocol and secondly, as the future face of Indigenous culture, contributing positively to the development of Australian society in the new millennium.
>
> (*School Handbook*, 2005, p. 16)

From the above transcripts and documents, it can be seen that social capacity building, accessibility, relationships, financial policy, respect for Indigenous traditions and employability are all examples of the school's telos. These are some of the ethical dimensions that Judy works on as principal in terms of the telos of the school. The work that Judy must do on herself in terms of her personal telos certainly overlaps with this telos of the school but as a principal she is in a particular subject position and therefore must also work on herself to meet her personal telos to be an ethical being. In the next section I demonstrate more specifically the ethical work she engages in to become a moral subject and on the school to become a moral institution.

Judy: self-forming work

At the beginning of Chapter 4, I showed an example of the sorts of tasks Judy does on a day-to-day basis. From this it could be seen how direct inter-actions with students form a significant part of her day, and not just in a disciplinary, behaviour-management capacity. The following is another excerpt from my observational field notes from a different day. This excerpt consti-tutes only one morning, but I have chosen this day as an example of how Judy engages with and devotes time directly to students and their concerns, rather than delegate these responsibilities to other staff members. Through this example, I demonstrate how Judy becomes personally involved in a significant way in each of the issues that arise. These actions form an import-ant part of the self-forming work that she does. In this excerpt I have taken out the other tasks that Judy engaged in during the morning and have included just those activities directly involved with the students themselves:

Wednesday morning:

8:25 a.m.   Judy makes phone call to classroom teacher about an incident with a student yesterday

8:27   phone call to high school staff room

8:30   speaks to student about what happened yesterday. Making sure they're ok

8:35   having to deal with an incident (fight) between 2 students who are sisters, resulting in one walking home. Judy left her office to go to try to find her

8:45   found the girl and begins a discussion with them about what happened. During this time there were some interruptions involving consoling a student who accidentally hit their head (gave them a big hug, made sure they were ok, then sent them on their way); getting some wayward students into class

8:55   a visit from a teacher to discuss the fight between the two sisters

8:55   Judy makes a phone call to the canteen to ask the lady in charge what she may have seen and if she knows anything

9:00   a couple of students still not in class, Judy personally takes them to their classroom

9:05   visit to family worker to find out if she knows anything in rela-tion to the sisters fighting

9:25   staff member comes in to inquire about the use of the pool. Judy outlines the requirements in terms of insurance and supervision

9:30   Judy rings classroom teacher to send up two students involved in an incident on Monday which resulted in another student refus-ing to come to school yesterday

9:42   Judy questions the two students about Monday's incident

9:55   phone call to teacher to see if the student is ok, teacher is going to ring back

10:00	phone call from teacher. Apparently student was kicked and then had his shoes taken but didn't tell anyone at school on Monday. He then didn't come to school yesterday
10:30	talks with two girls who were fighting
10:50	Judy has a long chat with a student who is seen as being 'at risk' (this student has a carer outside of school hours). He is only coming to school for the middle session at the moment but Judy says that she wants him to try hard and be able to come back for the whole day. He says he will try.
11:00	another talk with a student who seems very upset, Judy takes her back to class.

The significance of this excerpt is that Judy devotes a significant amount of time on these students' concerns and not just delegating them to another staff member. What is not readily apparent from the excerpt is the extent to which Judy personally consoles and comforts each of the students in a time of crisis and displays genuine concern for their welfare. With the incident between the two sisters, for instance, Judy made sure to find out as well as possible what really happened by phoning a range of other staff members and also took the time to sit down and discuss what happened and why with the girls themselves.

As stated in the previous chapter, and as can be seen in the above excerpt, Judy devotes a lot of her time to dealing directly with the students and their concerns and the students know that they are able to just 'turn up' at the office and usually see her directly during morning tea and lunch breaks. The way that Judy regulates these activities; these processes of subjectification in terms of what Foucault refers to as 'need', 'timeliness' and 'status' (1992, pp. 53–62) determine the manner in which Judy manages herself through these modes of subjection. In terms of need, the moderation of Judy's activities is not based on any code or prescriptive set of behaviours but through the self-regulation of activities based on their need as the situation arises. Judy's accessibility to the students, staff and parents is subject to moral and self-regulation. There is no prescription outlining that Judy should designate a certain length or period of time each day to such issues but rather she has to get the balance right of mixing these activities with the other daily tasks that need to be accomplished. It is here that it is up to Judy to determine when it is necessary to act and which course of action under the circumstances in order for her to be the kind of principal she aspires to be. For Foucault, 'in the use of pleasures, morality was also an art of the right time' (1992, p. 58). He then goes on to argue that this form of moderation belongs particularly to those with rank, status and responsibility. As principal, it is up to Judy to determine the appropriate level of action and response to certain issues that come up. To spend too much time dealing directly with students can take away from other tasks and issues whereas not spending enough time with students' concerns and relationships can also lead to criticism. Such is the complex inter-relation of pleasure and quantity as a mode of subjection. Pleasure can then also become part of the disciplining processes that Judy is subject to.

The emphasis on relationships within the school also operates in the way the school addresses behaviour management issues, as Judy states:

> In terms of behaviour management, I don't like that term, I would rather talk about teaching and learning engagement and the things we need to do to teach the children and have the children actively engaged in learning. So we do say here in our staff meetings, well if you do have a child who is proving to be particularly difficult, think about what person on staff they may be related to, or have a family connection with, so engage them in terms of trying to make things better for this child. It is not unusual for a staff member if a child is doing something that is particularly wrong that they won't be sent up here to me, they'll be sent to Bob who might be an uncle, for example. I also often call on the tutors if things aren't working in class for a child, as they have a relationship with their tutor. I'll often ring down to the co-ordinator and say 'Oh, is Greg free?' to spend time with someone, and that can have a calming effect on the kids. It can often change what can be a volatile situation into something that is being calmed right down.

The school will often call upon the tutors in the literacy programme to help with any issues the student may be having at school as each child in the primary school will have at some point been involved in the literacy programme. One of the main aims of the literacy programme is the development of a one-on-one relationship between tutor and student and this relationship is very important in the achievement of students within this programme.

In the previous chapter, Judy reported how she often shifted more managerial tasks to outside school hours. Using Foucault's framework, this could be seen as an example of Judy's ethical work, the work she performs on herself in order to transform herself into the ethical subject of her behaviour. Foucault uses the term *enkrateia* (1992, p. 63) to signify the dynamics of domination of oneself by oneself to make proper use of the ethical subject. In Judy's case, she enters into a relationship with herself to push other types of work and tasks to a time that is less likely to affect the accessibility she so desires in her relationships with the students, staff and parents. This is the ethical work, a self-forming activity that Judy does in order to transform herself into an ethical subject. Closely following Foucault's fourfold framework one could say that Judy's telos is one of accessibility for staff and students throughout the school day, so she works on her time management (ethical substance) by pushing more managerial tasks outside school hours (forms of elaboration) and she is often reminded from the school's community, parents and board that as the principal of this school, she needs to be available for them to come and personally see her (mode of subjection).

In her telos as principal of the school, Judy also stated that she sees responsible financial stewardship of the school as important. From the following interview excerpts, it can be seen that Judy chooses to implement these sorts of decisions with this telos in mind:

> Financially, with keeping the buses on the road, the increase in petrol costs has affected us. So the rising cost and funding not keeping abreast with that is problematic. See the funding bodies don't take that into consideration with us because most schools don't provide those services at no charge. Other schools that provide a bus service, there is a charge to parents and as the petrol goes up so does what they charge the parents. But the majority of our parents don't have the capacity to pay, so there are some of the issues ... We could have a bursar here but I would rather have low class numbers and employ a teacher and I don't think I'd change that. But I suppose that in terms of a succession plan it makes it a little bit more difficult because I am familiar with all the accounting and software packages, because I do the payroll too. Not that that takes you a long time nor is it any wonderful skill, but it is a skill that the person would need to have.

Judy's ethical work here involves taking on the responsibility of doing all the finances rather than employing someone specifically to do that job. She states that she would take on more work and responsibility in order to have lower class numbers which will have a positive impact on their learning. Thus, her forms of elaboration here consist of her work in taking on this responsibility, for example personally doing budgets, accounts, audits, payrolls, etc., instead of hiring someone specifically for that job. In doing so she reminds herself of the low socio-economic background of many of the parents and then tries to work a solution to managing the limited financial resources available to her.

One of the most significant aspects to Judy's ethical substance is actually the notion of leadership itself. So far in this chapter I have outlined extensively how Judy perceives her leadership and what it means to be a good principal through her telos. By using phrases such as leading by example, developing relationships, being accessible and being too soft, Judy is recognising that leadership is an ethical substance that needs to be worked on to be a good principal. Her modes of subjection in terms of leadership are her relationships with the students and staff and also, importantly, discourses of leadership. She clearly demonstrates an understanding of these leadership discourses in an earlier interview excerpt where she states that she is often criticised from outside the school for being too soft. This demonstrates the power of more authoritarian discourses emanating from literature, other principals and community expectations of how a principal should be, that have made her aware of her own leadership and how she perceives such an authoritarian style of leading to be no more effective, in her opinion. In order to obtain specific examples of some of Judy's work as a leader in the school, I asked her if there was any particular example where she felt she displayed good leadership – she responded:

> I think there's no one particular example, it's just how you interact with people generally, and I suppose the power that you give individual people within the school. So I may well ask a groundsperson to perform what would be seen as outside their realm, for example, when I went to the meetings about upgrading the tennis court facility, well I didn't ask the two deputies to go with me, I asked the two groundsmen to go with me because they're the ones who interact with the children on that level. They're the ones that know what other community members would use the facility so it's kind of doing things so that everybody has an equal role within the school and that may not happen in their day to day tasks but they can have that in day to day decisions, and giving all staff members that kind of responsibility in terms of the bigger picture of the school.

Thus the ethical work that Judy does here in terms of forms of elaboration is giving responsibility to all members of staff in the school and this is also working towards her telos of breaking down hierarchy within the school.

The terrain of ethics that Judy must engage with on a regular basis is constantly shifting and she recognises the continual need for self-reflection and adjustment to these shifting and sometimes competing concerns. This issue of self-reflection is another part of Judy's ethical substance and is concerned with the work she needs to do on herself to be able to provide the kind of close relationship she wants with every student as circumstances change. This is also about what's required of the school as an institution, that it stay small enough to know every child if this telos of care is to be maintained. As the following excerpts from an interview with Judy demonstrate:

> I wish sometimes that I had a counselling background because increasingly children are presenting with some issues that I am fearful of dealing with, in case I make it worse, particularly when you enter areas of sexual abuse, long term violence ... That's one thing that bothers me a little is that there are some children now that I don't know intimately and, you know, five years ago I could say to you that I know every single kid in this school and I knew who their family

was, I knew what had happened to them but there are kids I don't know that of anymore. And that's why I am fearful of this school ever getting too big because I think if it ever gets to big we'd lose what we are able to do.

I sometimes worry about myself becoming out of touch with what is happening in the real world because I very rarely leave this school, in fact, I don't leave this school. That's sort of been borne out of ... I always hated when I was a teacher the fact that the principal never was there, was always away at meetings, off on conferences and to be perfectly frank I've been to many of those conferences and I think to myself, 'I would have been better off at school'. And I don't say that with any snobbery attached but very few of those conferences can offer ... perhaps if I was teaching in white mainstream school it would, it would have offered me something but very little of it is applicable to our situation. Some of it you can take and mutate and change but I think, and I'm not being funny, that this school is so far ahead in terms of Indigenous education that when I go to things on Indigenous education I think 'Oh my god! That's practice from twenty years ago!' I am amazed and shocked when I hear 'don't look Aboriginal children in the eye' and 'they're all visual learners', what a crock! That's like saying that all white Australians learn in a particular way, we moved away from those antiquated notions a long time ago.

The above quotations demonstrate a number of practices of self-problematising and disciplining that are introduced in order for the individual to enable them to engage with their conduct as ethical subjects (Hunter, 1994; Masschelein, 2004). These practices are closely associated with what Foucault refers to as pastoral power. This idea of governing people is similar to the notion of the shepherd tending a flock of sheep. It must also be mentioned that the work Judy has to do to be 'the shepherd' and the work she has to do on the school as an 'institutional shepherd' are both different and overlapping at the same time, as implied from her personal and the school's telos. In this notion of pastoral power, the shepherd keeps watch over the flock both as a whole and also each individual member. This idea originated in Egyptian, Assyrian, Messopotamian and Hebrew cultures, but was transformed by European Christianity whereby every aspect of people's lives was taken care of from birth to death (O'Farrell, 2005). Foucault also argues that these practices of pastoral government still characterise the exercise of power in the West (Foucault, 2000e). Hunter goes further to state that the school has in fact been 'assembled from the moral and material grab-bag of Western culture; providing a means of dealing with specific exigencies; and capable of nothing more than contingent solutions to limited problems' (1996, p. 148). The modern school, according to Hunter, has been characterised by the adoption of Christian pastoral guidance in order to actualise self-realisation as a central disciplinary objective (1996, p. 149). Thus, as a part of this historically shaped development of the school, the principal holds a discursive position as a site of power relations but then also works on herself to produce a form of subjectivity.

This notion of an ethics of care for each individual student while caring for the school body as a whole is one that Judy sees as important as she expresses concern at not being as familiar with all of the students in the school due to the increase in numbers. It is interesting that Judy says she is concerned with the school getting too big as she has also stated that as part of her vision she wants to offer a broader curriculum in the high school, but to do that there needs to be a level of growth in student numbers to support that element of choice. Judy also self-problematises herself as not having enough of a counselling background to be able to address a number of concerns that are increasingly presenting themselves at school. In the following excerpt, Judy outlines a number of issues of concern that, she argues, seem to be increasing in recent years:

INTERVIEWER: What do you consider some of the changes facing the school and you, as a principal?

JUDY: To be perfectly frank, some of them are not very pleasant. Over the last two years we've had a very significant increase of the number of children being taken into care. We are starting to see problems and issues that I never had to deal with when I first came to the school. In the high school, for example, drugs are becoming an issue. Sniffing is becoming an issue, not across the population but there are children engaging in those kinds of behaviours which is concerning. Young pregnancies are becoming an issue. We are losing young girls, at fourteen, because of pregnancy. That is also an issue.

These issues that are arising have a direct impact on Judy's telos of caring for each student, as with larger numbers of students come a wider variety and increasing number of such issues, particularly among high school students. Judy has expressed to me in other interviews how she is aware that she herself and the school shouldn't ever become complacent, even though the school is achieving very sound academic results. She is always looking to get better, to improve one's practice. Such issues of self-reflection need to be viewed as a particular form of governing others, resulting from this work on the self. In terms of self-reflection, I asked Judy how she knows if she is doing a good job and her response was:

I suppose I don't [laughs]. The things that I measure myself on are keeping the school afloat, so the fact that I manage to do that gives me some feeling of satisfaction. The fact that we have those new buildings there, which gives me some sense that I have achieved something, there are other little things like, I don't play any real role in the literacy intervention programme but I do keep the funds coming so that it can operate. I did start the programme. The fact that we now have ex-students who we are supporting through university; the fact that a lot of staff have improved their educational standings since they have been here; the fact that I encourage staff who I think have a particular talent to go to university to get qualifications and return to the school in other capacities.

This self-reflection on the part of Judy is in fact one way in which power operates productively through self-government, not through repressive structures. Power is operating through this self-reflexivity. Lyotard (1997) also emphasises the importance of the modern critical subject as a part of a productive system. In this way, governmentality, particularly pastoral power, operates through self-critique and reflection by the principal resulting in a specific form of subjectification.

In summary, I have demonstrated in this section how Judy constitutes herself as a moral subject following Foucault's four dimensions of ethical work. I have argued that Judy's telos of a good principal revolves around the ideas of being accessible, leading by example, showing respect, being liked by the students and having an ethics of care. In terms of the telos of the school that Judy must work on, issues such as the school having a social capital role, valuing relationships, knowing each child and financial steward-ship are considered the most important. Following this I argued that self-reflection, self-regulation and leadership are examples of Judy's ethical substance, while modes of subjection consisted of the Indigenous community's expectations, including students, parents and the school board, as well as documents such as the *School Handbook*, and leadership discourses. Finally, examples of Judy's forms of elaboration were pushing administrative work to outside school hours, personally being in charge of the financial matters, making time to be available and accessible for staff, students and parents. In the next section, I use this same framework to examine the way that Ruth constitutes herself as an ethical subject.

Ruth: telos of a 'good principal'

Like Judy, Ruth's ethical work on herself in terms of self-regulation of beha-viour and leadership is aimed at being the kind of principal she wants to be. It is this process that determines the end product or telos (Hofmeyr, 2006). The telos to which Ruth aspires can be demonstrated in the following inter-view transcript:

INTERVIEWER: So what's your definition of a good principal?
RUTH: Someone who is a really good people person because relationships are a really big part of the job. Relationships with the children, with the

staff, with the community, and further afield with District Office, Central Office, other people in joint ventures, being able to build those relationships and maintain them is probably a really important thing. I think it's important that you're fairly unflappable and steady because when all hell's breaking loose people rely on you to steady the ship. If you're someone who gets carried away with the highs and lows of the situation then you're probably not of a lot of benefit. I mean it's good to be passionate about stuff but it's important that you can be calm in a storm and you have to be confident in your own ability and your own judgements.

Ruth clearly states that she believes a good principal builds good relationships with staff, students, colleagues and state education authorities. A good principal, in her view, is also someone who can be calm in difficult situations by controlling their emotions. This excerpt comes from my first interview with Ruth when she began at the school, and it can be seen in the next transcript how Ruth's view of an ideal principal has slightly changed as her time and experience in this school has evolved over the last few years. She appears to have shifted her emphasis from relationships with people to issues of delegating and operating procedures as characteristics of her ideal self as principal, as she states:

A principal that knows when to delegate and when to take things on myself. Somebody that manages to care for people's welfare in the school, to be able to be alert for everybody and how they are travelling. Knowing how to run a really professional school where there are some protocols around how we operate as a staff. We've tried a few things, like tried having Alice make appointments and it just doesn't seem to work very well at this place. I'm too accessible here, if I was in another building, but people can hear you and see you and they will stand outside until they can get you. I'd really like to make sure I have people operating in a professional way with each other when we're having a discussion about curriculum, for example, no put downs.

Relationships are still important for Ruth, but the emphasis here is on being able to delegate, having an ethics of care and acting in a professional manner. Ruth acknowledges the difficulties for her in moving up from a small school to being a principal of a larger school in terms of relationships with a larger number of staff. It is interesting to note how Ruth considers herself too accessible, whereas for Judy, being accessible was a part of her telos.

Coming into a school which had been run by the previous principal who, she perceived, had a very authoritarian style of leadership has also been challenging, as she has emphasised to me on a number of occasions how she believes the relationships between staff, students and parents to be very important, and how she has been used to operating in a very open, consultative style of leadership. As a result she has had to alter her ways of working (forms of elaboration) to some extent to reflect staff and community expectations (modes of subjection). That is, she isn't able to be the type of ethical subject she would like to be. As a result, Ruth is then adjusting and accommodating the work she does on herself without necessarily changing her telos. It is in this way that leadership operates as a part of Ruth's ethical substance that I discuss in the next section.

The arrival of a new principal into any school requires a delicate balance of respect for the previous principal combined with a new enthusiasm and vision for the school. In this sense, the work and style of the previous principal can function as a mode of subjection. In Hall's study of female headteachers in Britain (1996), she found that when examining each woman headteacher's experiences of moving into a new headship, gender was a complicating factor on top of the other issues and expectations. Hall found that the gender and style of the previous head and senior colleagues did impose some constraints for these principals. For Ruth, the gender, ethnicity and style of leadership of the previous principal has created some constraints for her entry into the school. Ruth has acknowledged that there were some systems that were not in place when she became principal, such as special education provision, assessment and facilities, which has made some aspects of her job difficult. Not only this but the fact that the legacy of the previous principal has been widely documented in the media and educational circles has created an unenviable position for the incoming principal. A number of staff members at Pine Hills have remarked on the change-over and different operational styles of the two principals. For example:

> He was charismatic. He had the vision and he could share the vision. Ruth's the next step on from that where she has the vision but she's going to put the infrastructure there for everybody. I think the team achieves without her having to do a big song and dance about it. She's just got everything motoring along without it looking like she's had to pull a lot of ropes but she's made it so that people have got non-contact time to get the work done that they need to do. She's happy to step into a class to teach or model something for somebody who's finding it a little bit difficult. So that's a bit different where the previous principal was more the PR, he had the contacts, the ability to attract funding to the school.

And the following:

> She's had to break down the barriers being a white female here. Following the previous principal has been a really big step for her. Ruth is a

head of department, a principal, parent liaison officer, she's got many different roles. As of this year though, she has put more structure in giving people more responsibilities. Even enrolment has gone up this year as opposed to last year and just by restructuring, the troublesome kids we had last year are in class now and even coming up showing their great work.

From these transcripts it can be seen that these two staff members see Ruth's leadership in a very different light to that of the previous principal's leadership which was very much being out there doing the PR, whereas Ruth has 'everything motoring along without any fuss'. These teachers see Ruth as being a very much hands-on type of principal, and I think this appropriately describes her work practices and behaviours that I observed. For example, whenever I arrived at the school, the last place I would find Ruth would be in the principal's office or even in the administration building. She was always out in the playgrounds talking to students and staff, and she seemed most comfortable and relaxed while doing so.

The following interview excerpts from two other staff members reveal a deep respect for Ruth and the way she has handled the transition into this school:

> She's a very good people person. I find that she's very open to suggestions and ideas. She's willing to give people a go. I think she brings out the best in people. She finds a strength in people and she works on it. I'm more an authoritarian person. I don't think I'd ever be a wonderful leader because I want it done this way, I want it done yesterday, I want it done now. Now, Ruth, because she can take in all of the factors, take in the reality of what we'd like to do to what we have time to do in very small steps and she has that kind of patience and it's the subtle changes that people probably don't appreciate that if you've been here in the long term you can actually see. She has a lot of strengths and a leadership style that I admire.

And also from another staff member:

> Good because she doesn't lay the law down but she's got a friendly approach. She's open to offers and open to criticism or help. She has an open door for everyone. She's a laid back type of person. She offers her ideas and puts it out to everyone for discussion. I really take my hat off to Ruth, I have a lot of respect for her, while she's here I'm here. Having worked in the education system since 1989, I rate Ruth very highly.

These interview excerpts from staff members at Pine Hills indicate how Ruth has been able to garner support from the staff through actions and practices such as consultation and negotiation rather than orders from above. This has also led Ruth to receive criticism from some sections of the community who believe the principal needs to be 'strong' and 'give the orders'. This notion is certainly a legacy from the previous principal who was able to operate in that capacity, however, Ruth has a very different way of working from him and this has been recognised by many staff at the school. These perceptions of the principal from community members act as modes of subjection in relation to Ruth's practices and ethical work as principal.

Additionally, these transcripts from staff members indicate that they consider Ruth's style of leadership to be effective and desirable. Ruth, however, indicates that she thinks she needs to be 'more pointy' in her approach in some matters, as she states in the following excerpt:

> Good leaders know when they need to be pointy and make a decision 'right this is what we're doing' and they know when they need to be flat and I guess I'm feeling very clumsy, it's like beginning teachers, they have a limited repertoire of ideas. It's like this grab bag of ideas and you sort of draw on them when you need to. The big drama of my class distribution thing was an example I was being pointy and making a decision and I needed to be flatter, but at the time I was trying to operate in this pointy mode which is very clumsy to me because I am not good at it and the flatter one is where I normally operate but because at the time there was a lot of pressure to take the lead and make decisions about things and so I clumsily made a decision about that and I won't do it again probably. But as your grab bag of leadership skills develops more you know when to use which ones. When I first started staff meetings, when the previous principal first left, I was sort of like 'well what do you all think about that?' whereas now I say 'we have to do this and this…' and I used to be really panicky about staff meetings at one stage. Now I will just get there five minutes before and I just rattle through the list on the board and I know which ones I need to ask for everyone's ideas and other ones I will just say well here's what we're going to do.

Part of this transcript relates to an incident at the end of 2005 where Ruth decided to distribute certain classes to teachers for the next year without consultation. Normally she would have consulted and negotiated with everyone and worked the classes out for next year. On this occasion, however, she was trying to implement a 'pointier' model of leadership and tell each teacher which classes they will be taking. The ensuing uproar over this issue is something that both Ruth and the Executive Director of Schools spoke about to me and were able to laugh at in hindsight, however, indicating that certain approaches were favourable for certain circumstances.

This transcript also indicates that Ruth is aware that many leadership discourses promote a top-down, transformational leadership style and that she is uncomfortable with this style of operating. However, she feels that it is necessary for her to adopt this type of approach because she suggests that it is expected in the community and that powerful leadership discourses dictate that that kind of model should be used. The leadership documents circulated to principals by Education Queensland such as the *Standards Framework for Leaders* (1997) and *Leadership Matters* (2006) are also heavily influenced by these types of traditional models of leadership. These documents and discourses are then operating as a mode of subjection.

It is important to recognise that gender plays an important part in leadership as ethical substance and also the modes of subjection. For instance, the community can have certain expectations on their idea of how the principal should look and behave, as Ruth states:

> Sometimes you have got to have this front of Ruth the principal in the community, to have this persona you have to hold and that is a bit of a mismatch sometimes. At my last school they said to me 'Oh miss you don't wear principal's clothes!' cause they had only had blokes, and I said 'what are they?' and they said 'those long socks miss and those leather shoes'. So they had a picture of what a principal is, the same as the people do here. I think there is still this charismatic leader type of person that they think a principal should take here whereas my model of principalship is very parallel with more leadership density in it where you are working more alongside people and I've had to try to play this role of 'yes, I'm the leader' and I'll walk in and make a decision. You're really working in a model that's not your preferred model. The Executive Director of Schools says it's good to have that awareness of it all. So I sometimes have to put this different hat on. Probably the people I have the best relationships with are the cleaners who come in the morning because no one else is here, there are no expectations, no parents and it's just very relaxed. In other schools I have been in, that's often the case but then you have to play these other roles. This is probably the most different I've had to be in any of the principal's jobs.

Ruth is also aware of how gendered leadership discourses can affect her way of being and working as a principal:

> So I guess the male model is more to give orders and expect them to be obeyed and I wonder to a degree whether the people want and expect that even though they're more than capable to do it themselves. I guess I've sort of thought that some of the people have been working here for 15 years and I feel out of place telling them what to do but in a way I think there's a bit of an overlay where people expect you to. So

trying to work out where that all fits and I've probably been the one to alter my leadership style more than they've altered their operational style because I've been the one who can alter that more quickly. And I've had to make that alteration but my goal and vision is for it to be as flat as it was at my last school. And in some ways I think I am getting there when I see people take some initiative in things and I think well that's good. So my goal would be to work people towards understanding and wanting to participate, density of leadership where different people are leading different projects in the school where it's not just me leading everything. And I'm not sure because I worked a few months with the previous principal but my feeling is very much that he was the person up there, the leader, and people needed or felt comfortable with that.

Here, Ruth is using the gendered discourse of male leadership as a mode of subjection to reflect on and be aware of how she conducts her leadership in the school. As a result she alters her forms of elaboration through adopting different styles of leading because she believes it is easier for her to change rather than change school culture. This is, then, reflective of her telos which is trying to achieve leadership density where everybody is participating rather than her being at the top giving direction. Like Judy, she is trying to work against the hierarchical structure of schooling.

So far I have mentioned Ruth's telos as being one of care, acting in a professional manner, knowing when to delegate and alter her leadership style and building strong relationships. In addition to these, Ruth also considers her relationships with the students to be particularly important. As with Judy, it is important to Ruth that she be liked by the children, as she states: 'It's important for me to be well liked by the kids, have a good relationship with them and not lose that contact with the kids.'

From the above interview excerpts, it can be seen that Ruth's personal telos of a good principal is primarily concerned with being liked by the kids, being accessible, displaying a calm and professional demeanour and displaying an ethics of care for the children in the school, having a range of leadership skills to draw upon and delegating tasks and responsibilities.

In addition to this personal telos of a good principal, Ruth must also play an important role, in the form of leading and managing the school, as part of the fourfold work that the school needs to do to be an ethical institution. The telos of the school can be summarised by the following quotation from Ruth:

It's about getting our kids, teachers and teacher aides, all our staff and our school community are, I guess, stronger and smarter. It's about doing everything we can and working out how best to teach our kids so they get the best outcomes and the best life chances. All that we do should really be aimed about making a better life chance for these kids and education is so important in that.

Ruth has often explained to me how she still emphasises the 'Strong and Smart' motto that has been carried over from the previous principal. Through this motto, Ruth sees very much the importance of being able to empower Indigenous people and having an ethics of care through this social capital role of the school.

Ruth's self-forming work

Two important parts of Ruth's ethical substance are her emotions and self-reflection. Managing her emotions is an aspect of self-reflection that Ruth has commented on extensively in her conversations with me. She has explicitly stated as part of her telos to be a good principal that it is important to control one's emotions. School leadership is undoubtedly an emotion-filled activity and how school principals deal with and manage their emotions is an area that is often neglected in much of the literature on educational leadership (Blackmore & Sachs, 1998), though notable exceptions include Beatty (2000a, 2000b, 2000c), Blackmore (1995, 1996, 2004), Boler (1997, 1998, 1999), Gronn (2003), Hargreaves (1995, 1997, 2004), Mills (2009) and Zorn and Boler (2007). The emotional demands placed on school principals by staff, students, parents, members of the community, peers and governmental and school bodies are enormous. The multiple and often competing demands means that school principals are expected to be able to cope with such demands in more efficient and effective ways. Both principals in this study have stated how they do significant work activities outside school hours and frequently at home. As a result, the split between the personal and professional lives of these principals has become blurred (Blackmore & Sachs, 1998). This resulting emotional burden placed on school principals can play a significant role in their work practices and how they self-regulate and monitor their behaviour in the work environment.

This emotional work of principals is important for both male and female principals. However, research by Blackmore and Sachs (1998) shows that the ways in which school principals respond to such demands and the expectations of principals is highly gendered. This process of managing one's emotions can be seen as a disciplinary process as a means of self-regulation that operates differently for men and women. This is because there are fewer risks for men in the embodiment of masculinist forms of leadership such as transformational leadership (Lambert, 2007) as they already do embody masculinity as the norm (Blackmore, 1999). To display emotions in the workplace for women is often seen as weak and non-rational, and portrays women leaders as vulnerable (Blackmore & Sachs, 1998).

Ruth, in particular, noted how she regulates her behaviour and emotions to be seen to be 'in control', particularly in times of stress and conflict. For example, the perception that the principal is 'in control' is one that Ruth has worked hard to maintain, in the face of criticism from some parts of the community (a mode of subjection):

> I've come in here and I've purposefully kept up the façade because I was really winging it for the skill levels in some areas, in some things I felt quite confident like curriculum, kids and behaviour but for some of the people management I've left the façade up, I'm learning all the time, kind of like the duck looking serene but paddling like hell underneath. Even some of the parent stuff, where you've got cranky parents, I haven't had cranky parents like this for years so you're learning on the run with some of those things but people needed me to look calm and in charge. I've purposely had that armour around me to a degree but it was a conscious decision to keep that façade there to serve a purpose.

Noteworthy points here include how Ruth uses phrases like 'keeping up the façade', 'looking calm and in charge' and 'the duck looking serene but paddling like hell underneath'. These types of statements indicate that Ruth believes that to let one's emotions be visible is linked to losing one's professionalism and being seen to display weakness. This is an example of the ethical work she does on herself in order to become what she considers a 'good principal' to be. This type of belief of controlling one's emotions is consistent with other research into the emotions of female administrators (Blackmore & Sachs, 1998). For example, Marian Court (1995) argues how displays of anger are culturally acceptable for men but not for women. As a result, Court argues, such silences shore up male privilege. This self-moderating of one's emotions are even specifically spelled out as desirable capabilities necessary for school principals to have in Education Queensland's recent document *Leadership Matters* (2006). This document functions as a mode of subjection for Ruth, as it is circulated to all government school principals. This document clearly states the importance of personal capabilities of school principals, for example, that they 'are emotionally mature' and they 'remain composed in challenging and complex situations'. At first glance these capabilities appear to be self-evident in the day-to-day challenges that unfold for school principals. However, when read as part of the whole document, one senses that there is a strong undercurrent of masculinist, transformative types of characteristics being put forward as the ideal model of a school principal. Other words and phrases throughout the document include 'confident', 'inner strengths and qualities', 'courage', 'inspire', 'to persuade and influence others', 'clever thinking, sound judgement and wise decision making'. All of these types of capabilities one could expect to find in a 'Transformational and Charismatic Leadership 101' course.

As stated in Chapter 3, such documents as *Leadership Matters* serve to decontextualise the work of principals into different capabilities that are to be implemented at every school site. Lambert (2007) even goes as far as to say that transformational leadership can be seen as a means of regulation and containment rather than a source of enablement and democratisation. In particular, it is the masculinised emotions of transformational leadership that are disciplinary for women principals. In addition, as I have stated earlier, it is the self-regulation of emotions that are an important mechanism of this type of regulation. For example, Ruth states:

> You need to be steady when all hell's breaking loose, you've got kids going mad, staff arguing with each other, you need to be steady so, underneath you might have a bit of turmoil happening, plus you are dealing with your confidence in your own ability to deal with this. A lot of the time you don't have the opportunity or time to be able to ring people for advice, if you've got parents coming up, you've got a teacher here, kids upset, and they're all here together, you don't get the time to say 'well how will I deal with this?' Other things you do get time to say that and get some strategies but I'm still pretty clumsy with them, like grievances and complaints I've never had to deal with before I came here. There's a whole process around it that you need to learn so the emotions are the highs and lows here and probably it's good to get back into the rooms. You need to be aware of your emotions and really alert to 'yes I feel like crap because I just got hammered over this' and try and step back and see the bigger picture and keep the vision.

Clearly, though, Ruth's engagement with modes of subjection such as the documents for principals from Education Queensland has been an important aspect in her ethical work or forms of elaboration. Reading through the above transcript it becomes apparent that Ruth perceives good leadership to be about keeping one's emotions invisible. This contributes to the silencing of the emotional aspect of educational leadership. These discourses work as subtle technologies of control on the behaviours of both male and female principals. In order to be a good leader and taken seriously, one has not only to control one's emotions but to be seen to be in control in difficult situations. While this discourse operates in a normalising capacity for Ruth, it is also an important aspect of self-management in order to be able to manage others and the school. As Foucault argues, in order to govern others you must be able to govern yourself. I would add that it is also important to be seen to be able to govern yourself.

Another important aspect to Ruth's self-reflection is how she is made aware of her performance as principal. I asked Ruth the same question that I asked Judy, in terms of self-reflection towards her job:

INTERVIEWER: How do you know that you're doing a good job?

RUTH: I don't, that's something I struggle with all the time. I guess when I was a teacher I was a pretty good teacher and a principal in a small school, I probably struggled with it when I first started thinking, 'Oh god, I'm hopeless at this', but then you get good at it and I've been a principal in three small schools. But then this is the next step up. I think I'm probably doing a good job with the kids and I think I'm doing a good job with the facilities and some of that stuff. I don't think I'm doing a good job with the adults but that's probably the area where the biggest change is when you come into a bigger school. It's also compounded here by the fact that a lot of the systems that would help you do that well are not in place here.

From this quotation it is possible to discern a mode of subjection as well as her telos. That is, through answering this question, she sets out the criteria by which she judges her action and achievements, in particular what invites and incites and what type of being she wants to be as principal. For example, she judges her performance as principal on her relationships with the children as well as keeping the facilities in sound condition. She also confesses her need to do more work on her relationships with the adults at the school. Again, it is evident here that she judges her performance on the quality of her relationships with the students, staff and parents associated with the school. This relationship with the parents and adults is a powerful mode of subjection for Ruth. As a result, Ruth must do specific work in terms of this accountability, as she states:

I've spent a fair bit of time going out and visiting parents and trying not just to go when there's a negative thing, maybe catching up with some parents for positive stuff and in some schools I've been in you get a lot of the parents coming in through the school so you meet them there ... Sometimes you feel a bit guilty trekking off to Cairns or Mt Isa or something in case people think that you're just gallivanting around. So you have to make sure that it really will add value to what you do and people see it as valuable. And the community so if they know that I'm not here, they know that I'm there for a reason, so I'd be going and sharing that with council.

Ruth regulates her behaviour and work practices according to criteria and expectations set by the local community. These technologies of the self in which Ruth acts upon herself in relation to the languages, criteria and techniques available to her are crucial to her subjectivity formation. It is this symbiotic relationship between technologies of subjectivity and techniques of the self that is important in terms of management of the self (Rose, 1999, p. 11). In order to meet her own telos of care, Ruth engages in activities within the local community such as home visits and attending local community meetings and also making herself available for students, staff and parents throughout the school day. Like Judy, she also pushes work such as administrative tasks and answering email to outside school hours; however, on occasion she does 'lock herself away' to complete particularly pressing tasks. These relations with the local community can also be seen as Ruth's work in order to maintain the telos of the school, that is, there is significant overlap across these types of forms of elaboration.

As well as doing work such as visiting parents, Ruth often travels to the school early because a number of the children at Pine Hills arrive at school very early in the morning for a variety of reasons. As part of her telos of care for the children she considers this as an important part of forming good relationships with a number of these children. As she states: 'Some of our kids are here at 6:30, kids coming from 6:30 onwards and they come up and want to have a yarn because obviously they left home at 6:00 and maybe there's been nobody there.' This is very much some of the specific work (forms of elaboration) that Ruth does as part of her ethics of care. This carries on throughout the day, not just before school, as Ruth comments: 'I certainly like to be in the rooms and seeing what the kids are doing because it gives you a really good understanding of how your classes and your teachers are doing.'

Through visits to classrooms, personally attending to students' needs throughout the day, arriving early before school, making home visits and such practices are all ways in which Ruth attempts to know and be able to care for each of the students in the school. She must regulate and reflect on her actions and behaviour as a means of behaving ethically with the end result of improving the outcomes for the students and teachers at Pine Hills.

In support of this telos of care and empowering Indigenous people, Ruth must constantly make decisions to do with the Aboriginality of both students and teachers, and the community more generally. For example, Ruth has discussed with me how she makes a concerted effort to suspend fewer children from school; she concedes that, in fact, she could actually suspend many more than she does. This is part of what she states is her belief to empower Indigenous people through a mindset of trying to keep these children in the system because, if they leave school, there will be very few options open for them. Another dilemma for Ruth is the issue of employing people from the local community, as she states:

> The issues around colour when you advertise something and you should go with merit selection but you may veer towards the Indigenous person because we are in an Indigenous school. Sometimes you will see that as important but other times you need the absolute best quality person with the skills, again there's that balance of 'Well I'll give three people jobs but I will give this person the job because we really need the skills

for the job' and you might get a couple of local people to work with them to learn the processes.

These sorts of issues are heavily impacted upon by the contested political terrain of a school like Pine Hills that I have discussed in more detail in earlier chapters. Ruth is also concerned with each of the teachers and being able to support them on a day-to-day basis, and sometimes this may be in conflict with her relationships with the students. Such a complex ethical terrain needs to be negotiated on a daily basis:

> So it's my job I guess to support people so they don't feel so down that they just have days off and not function as well. Support them through that tricky time either by just moral support or for example, skilling if it's in behaviour management, skilling in the curriculum about the best ways to teach our kids here and also make sure our computers are working, make sure the grounds look nice and inviting. So it's a bit of the maestro pulling all the bits together to keep the vision moving. And I guess lobby with central office and district office for the best deal we can get with staffing, if we can get an extra teacher that could really enhance our 'strong and smart' stuff because it can make smaller classes. Or if we negotiate some special needs time to test kids so that now our kids are identified and getting programs that match.

It is interesting to note that while Ruth emphasises relationships as important, she acknowledges that this is an area that she has found to be particularly difficult in Pine Hills and needs improvement, as she states:

> Managing people's probably my area I'm least experienced in, so it's also the area that's the most challenging here. Maybe it is because I'm less experienced at it or maybe it is a challenging place to do that. I'm not sure which one it is, but it's certainly an area I'd ask for support or advice from my boss or from other people. I've got some Indigenous staff that I consult with in regards to dealing with a specific issue, so it's being open to get the information from those people, which is pretty important.

Foucault's work on the notion of 'care of the self' (see Foucault, 1990, 2005) is important here, as this attending to the self can be seen as a social practice in that the rationality of governing the self is the same rationality as governing others. It is necessary to be able to govern oneself properly in order to govern others and this is a formation of knowledge about the self. Foucault (1990) also points out that this care of the self has a medical aspect to it, among other aspects, whereby there is a particular attention to the body and its ills. This idea of taking care of the self in order to take care of others is typified by the following interview transcript by Ruth:

> I've seen a lot of people crash and burn out from this job, you need to pace yourself. Because it's never finished I consciously go and have a weekend off from it, I'll just leave it here and say no I'm not taking it home. Some people come in with a big bang and do wonderful things and then they burn out. You have to be able to stick the pace day after day and year after year because you're no good to anyone if you burn out. You also have to be able to jolly people along a bit, it is week 5 of term 4 but you can't act it. There's got to be a strength there that you need and just ride out some of the tough times so you don't end up a big stress bag.

In this quotation, Ruth is acknowledging how, as a principal, she needs to look after herself as she states, 'you're no good to anyone if you burn out'. Ruth is aware that she needs to be able to care for herself in order to care for the rest of the school. She also regards this as a constant attitude that one must take towards oneself (Foucault, 1990, p. 63) in order to survive over long periods of time. It is in this manner that Ruth exercises an ethics of control over herself to 'ride out some of the tough times'.

A key factor for Ruth's work on this care of the self is the context of Pine Hills and how it impacts on her work practices. The nature of Ruth's job, among other things, is heavily defined by the size and structure of the school. As a Band 7 school, Pine Hills has particular complexities and difficulties for the principal, as she has explained that there are no real administrative layers and structures to devolve and distribute some of the administrative load of being a principal, as I have discussed in earlier chapters. When questioned about the difficulties of being a principal of a school such as Pine Hills in terms of leadership, the Executive Director of Schools responded:

> Yes it is because there are no layers of leadership, you're it. Having done it myself, it is very difficult, you don't have a registrar, you don't have a deputy, you don't have a head of curriculum. You don't have any of that and you're everything, it is physically extremely demanding.

At a time when discourses of leadership are proliferating around issues of distributing and devolving work and responsibilities, the structure and hierarchy of schools like Pine Hills seems to be working against that. The staffing of Band 7 schools means that it is the principal who must personally be involved in every facet of school life. This type of responsibility resting with the principal has a profound effect on their leadership and work practices in order to be a 'good principal'. This would be a dramatically different scenario than, say, a principal of a large high school where layers of administration exist to formally devolve tasks and responsibilities.

In response to such constraints as having no layers of leadership, Ruth has set up a 'leadership team' within the school consisting of herself, the part-time deputy, the head of special education and behaviour management and the finance officer on contract from Education Queensland. In doing this Ruth is attempting to be able to delegate a range of tasks and responsibilities so that she can devote more time to what she terms the core business of the school, which is about curriculum and teaching and learning. Setting up this team is an example of Ruth's ethical work to become, in her view, a good principal who is able to delegate and devolve work to others. There is also significant overlap here with the work Ruth must do in terms of leading and managing others to work on the ethics of the institution of the school.

By these actions, Ruth is acknowledging that one person cannot hope to do all the tasks expected of the principal. This form of leadership dispersal (Lingard, Hayes, Mills & Christie, 2003) or distributed leadership (Crowther, Hann, McMaster & Ferguson, 2000; Gronn, 2003; Leithwood & Jantzi, 2000b; Louis & Riley, 2000) can help to create a sense of value and purpose to the work of those involved in this leadership team. However, it remains to be seen how this will be perceived by the rest of the school and community, who are 'outside of' the team (Gronn, 2003b) particularly when the majority of this team is white. As discussed in the previous chapter, this issue can be a sensitive one for some members of the local community.

One of the reasons why Ruth has set up this additional leadership structure is to attempt to reconcile the complex and sometimes competing tensions between leadership and management tasks by separating them into different categories. Ruth has expressed concerns about the extraordinarily large and difficult job of managing a school like Pine Hills, but remains optimistic that she will be able to focus more on the leadership side of things once some of the management pressure has been relieved, as she states:

> I think when you get the nuts and bolts of a school worked out, like the management parts of it, then you can toy a bit more with the leadership styles. When I'm not thinking about whether the pay slips have gone in for tomorrow, then I think I'd like to revisit some of the leadership stuff I have done before ... Challenges around leadership/management is to get as much of the management out of my desk as possible and on to other people if it's ok to do that, so that I'm not bogged down in the management things, getting our audit stuff up to speed; so getting best practice basically across all management systems from facilities to finance to human resources and that's a huge job. When that's in place it'll allow us to lead rather than manage, so that's a real challenge for us, Education Queensland have been really supportive in helping to resource that so it's a hard slog still at the moment but we can see light at the end of the tunnel.

From this excerpt it can be seen that Ruth is aware of the dangers of managerialism that can take time and resources away from the core business of schooling, and is using the 'leadership team' to do much of this administrative legwork so that she can lead and promote the vision. However, in a school of this size and staff structure there are always going to be ongoing managerial concerns and issues. These tensions between management and leadership need to be recognised and worked with (Christie, 2004) rather than viewed as something to be 'gotten out of the way'. Krantz and Gilmore (1990) also argue that splitting management and leadership by valorising one over the other, as Ruth does, can in fact prevent the integration of the vision and the means for realising that vision. Ruth has expressed (in an earlier excerpt) the need for a range of structures (such as the leadership team) to be implemented in order to be able to concentrate on improving the teaching and learning, but these will need ongoing management.

In this section, I have identified the work that Ruth does to become a moral subject as well as contributing to the school becoming a moral institution according to their respective telos. Ruth's personal telos was concerned with being liked by the children, building positive, professional relationships with staff, having an ethics of care for the children and keeping control of her emotions. In terms of her role in the school's telos, she sees herself as supporting staff through relationships and delegating tasks, empowering Indigenous people and the school having a social capital building capacity. Important elements of her ethical substance include her emotions, self-reflection and self-regulation of work practices. I also argued how Ruth's modes of subjection consist of the community's expectations, relevant documents by Education Queensland and the students themselves. I then demonstrated examples of the specific work that Ruth does in order to be that moral subject. These included having a constant physical presence around the school, being accessible for students, staff and parents, making home visits, arriving at school early, delegating tasks through setting up a leadership team, and often pushing more administrative tasks to outside school hours.

Conclusion

The main focus of this chapter has been to explore the way that both principals work on themselves in relation to Foucault's notion of ethics. I have done this by initially outlining Foucault's work on ethics and then demonstrating each principal's telos in relation to their own self and in terms of the school as a moral institution. I then proceeded to outline how they go about working towards this idea of what they perceive a 'good principal' to be. Even though Ruth and Judy had similar concepts of what a good principal does – for example, building positive relationships, working against hierarchical structures, being accessible, and being liked by the children – often the work they do to achieve this is different. This is perhaps largely due to the different political spaces produced through different accountabilities and power/knowledge processes inherent in the context of Pine Hills that produces Ruth as a subject and principal of an Indigenous government-run school and Judy as being inserted in self-governance discourses differently as principal of an Indigenous independent school. Hence, in addition to doing the will of the community, Ruth is faced with the often competing tension of doing the will of the system (Wildy, 1999). This demonstrates how important the situational dimension of leadership is to the work that each principal does. Even though both principals have a telos of working to respect Aboriginality, for example, they are required to do different things because of the different histories and particularities of each school and their local communities.

It is interesting that for Ruth, managing emotions seems to be an important part of her telos, whereas Judy makes no mention of emotions in her views on what makes a good principal. Perhaps this is due to the different modes of subjection for each principal, as Ruth has expressed to me how she uses Education Queensland's *Leadership Matters* document which emphasises being in control of one's emotions, whereas Judy, being a principal of an independent school, does not follow this mode of subjection. It is also important not to forget the different individual beliefs of each principal that profoundly influence the work they do to be a 'good principal'.

6   'Doing' leadership differently

> I take care not to dictate how things should be. I try instead to pose prob-
> lems, to make them active, to display them in such a complexity that they
> can silence the prophets and lawgivers, all those who speak for others or to
> others.
>
> (Foucault, 2002b, p. 288)

Many books have been written about leadership generally and also leadership
in education. In fact there is a whole industry of leadership studies through
various policy institutes, postgraduate courses in educational leadership and
administration as well as academic and some not so academic scholarship. It
does not take too much effort to find a plethora of books on 'exceptional
leaders' on bookstore shelves. Whether it is an autobiographical account of
politicians or biographies of famous sportspeople there is a huge market for
these stories. In my conversations with a number of school principals, it is
apparent that many of them do look to a range of 'best-practice' and 'self-
help' texts to try to negotiate their way through what is a very multi-faceted
and difficult job. While these books may make for an interesting read, for
the purposes of illuminating the work of everyday people in leadership positions in schools, these stories may as well be works of fiction. The business
world is similarly replete with accounts of CEOs telling how they became
successful leaders. Like others in leadership positions in the corporate world,
many school principals are also looking to these types of books for inspiration and answers in their workplace. This has become particularly the case
with the corporatisation of education in a number of Western countries,
especially the UK. However, the apparently seamless transfer of leadership
and management ideas from the business world into education must be seen
as heavily problematic and do not reflect the particularities of educational
matters or understand the complex, messy world of day-to-day life in
schools.

It has been pointed out by a number of scholars that the lack of supply of
principals and aspirant school leaders is a problem now and seems to be possibly getting worse, particularly in areas of high student diversity and low

socio-economic status. Therefore instead of simply transplanting 'leaders' from other fields as some have suggested, what is required is further detailed empirical study of the issues that make the job complex and demanding to the extent that many do not want to take up these positions. The analysis presented throughout this book provides one way of exploring and theorising the complexity and messy reality of the job. The portraits of the two school principals presented throughout this book are not intended to be an illustration of exceptional leaders or examples of 'best practice', although there is much to be admired in the way they go about their work in what are very challenging contexts.

What these portraits show is that principals' work is complex and challenging, and their subjectivities are a constantly shifting and flexible phenomenon rather than fixed as is constructed through numerous leadership policy documents. To reduce these principals' leadership within such models of leadership ultimately normalises their work to simplistic, generic competences or capabilities that continue to perpetuate inappropriate and problematic understandings of educational leadership. Rather than subscribe to presenting and interpreting these principals' work practices as transformational, instructional, moral or any of the other current models on the market today, through these portraits and the work of Foucault, I have demonstrated the different ways that these principals' subjectivities are created through a range of particular discourses, power relations and work practices.

As indicated in the Introduction, the use of portraits of both schools and their principals allows for a rich and in-depth analysis of their work practices. There are certainly 'stories' to be told about these and other school principals, and while recognition is given to imperfections or how things might be done better, the emphasis through the portrait is on highlighting successes and good work. It is through the portraiture method that I believe these stories become of interest to school principals themselves. It is certainly clear that few school principals trawl through formal research reports and academic articles, as they feel much of this work does not relate to their circumstances. It is my hope that many school principals can find similarities in the experiences of Judy and Ruth and this can help and enhance their understanding of their competing subjectivities, thus enabling them to reflect and work on their practice for the betterment of their students, schools and themselves as principals. This I believe is a more authentic way for principals to engage professionally with their roles and jobs rather than problematic attempts to implement a decontextualised list of things to do and ways to be a better school principal. Rather, the emphasis here has been on providing rich examples of others in the workplace that can facilitate an understanding of constraints, subject positioning and the work on the self towards a particular telos as principal.

Both principals' thoughts and practices throughout this book were influenced by discourses of leadership and management, as well as community expectations around leadership and Indigenous governance. These factors created a complex and unstable subject positioning for these principals that made for very challenging work, particularly so for Ruth. Leadership, according to Christie and Lingard (2001), is a dynamic process where forces that are conscious and unconscious, rational and irrational play out in complex social situations. This perspective is a useful one to describe the complex nature of school leadership for both Judy and Ruth.

In using the work of Foucault my aim in this book has been to disrupt traditional understandings of educational leadership, and to bring to light new ways of examining the principalship. In the field of leadership, 'theory' has usually consisted of the models I discussed in Chapter 3. Instead, I believe there is significant value to be found outside the field in order to broaden existing knowledge about educational leadership. Specifically, by theorising how principals are created subjects reveals how power and authority are critical to educational leadership. I move away from simplistic notions of power to show how Foucault's notion of webs of power provides a more nuanced understanding of power that moves beyond hierarchy and position. Power is thus exercised to provide agency to principals that work against the normalising discourses of education and leadership that focus on particular modes of performance and examination. The situatedness of the daily work practices of the principals is also illustrated through the disparity between the ways each of the principals' actions were viewed by their local communities. It seems that current modes of governmentality tended to be more constraining than empowering as they are concerned with the managed self and thus tap into the desires of educational leaders to do well for their communities. In addition, ethics is central to the production of these principals' subjectivities, and that their subjectivities are shaped by their telos, that is, a sense of what type of principal they wanted to be and the practices this requires. Furthermore, the idealisation of culture and community in the schools produced discourses that 'disciplined' these principals, but differently in each school due to differing legacies and institutional narratives. This is an important fact of school leadership that continues to be ignored in the mainstream literature.

It also needs to be acknowledged that while it is problematic to present a 'Foucauldian approach' to any particular field, I have endeavoured to present one way of using a number of his concepts as a toolkit. There is an abundance of material upon which one could draw to analyse and explain other phenomena and my challenge is certainly there for others to use Foucault's work rather than continue to rehash existing leadership models. With the continuation of Foucault's lectures at the Collège de France now being translated and printed it is a very exciting time for anyone undertaking analyses using Foucault's work, as these lectures provide significant additional material to help explain and provide background and context to his previously printed material.

Through the posing of 'problems' associated with leadership, it is my aim that others working in the field of educational leadership will be able to see similarities between the complexities and difficulties faced by Judy and Ruth and their own circumstances. It is therefore through this type of analysis that others may attempt to reconcile their own difficulties just as Judy and Ruth attempt to in their schools. Contrary to most of the leadership books available today, I do not attempt to prescribe solutions to problems that cannot be 'solved' through the next model or 'theory' that claims the truth about leadership. I also realise that such a stance may not be a popular one among scholars and practitioners looking for the latest book on best practice to assist them with their day-to-day work. However, if we are to gather more nuanced, theoretically rigorous understandings of the complexities faced by school leaders, then a wider net must be cast in terms of approaching, researching, theorising and analysing educational leadership. Helen Gunter has recently expressed concerns about the decline and possible death of educational leadership in the UK (Gunter, 2010). She argues that while theory does not immediately solve the dilemmas of what decisions can be made and implemented at 9.00 a.m. on Monday morning, it does allow possibilities for teachers and principals to generate new and interesting perspectives on this phenomenon we call leadership. Equally important, she argues, are the benefits from undertaking critical social thinking, creating possibility for action (2010, p. 520). It is my hope that this book can achieve the goals of not only addressing a gap in the educational leadership literature but also showing the importance of the relationship between theory and practice which is sorely lacking in leadership studies. As Foucault (1977c, p. 208) says, 'theory does not express, translate or serve to apply practice: it is practise.'

Notes

1 Introduction

1 Recent work by Spillane and Zuberi (2009) has shown some interesting methodological issues about conducting research focusing on the activities and practices of principals.
2 This body of work is vast but some good examples include: Ball (1990a), Hunter (1994), Masschelein (2004), McNicol Jardine (2005), Peters and Besley (2007), Popkewitz and Brennan (1997, 1998) and Usher and Edwards (1994).

2 A Foucauldian toolbox for educational leadership

1 Other writers who have effectively used this notion of governmentality include Burchell, Gordon and Miller (1991), Dean (1999), Holmes and Gastaldo (2002), Hunter (1994, 1996), Meadmore (1993), Meadmore et al. (1995), Miller and Rose (1992, 1993), O'Malley (1996), Rose (1990, 1999) and Simons and Masschelein (2006).

3 Discourses of educational leadership

1 For example, see Allix (2000), Bass (1985, 1990b), Bass and Avolio (1993, 1994), Bennis (1984), Burns (1978), Gronn (1995, 1996), Hallinger (1992), Ladomski (1995), Lambert (2007), Leithwood (1992), Leithwood et al. (1999), Murphy and Hallinger (1992), Silins (1994), Tichy and Devanna (1990).
2 For example, see Barnett, McCormick and Conners (2001), Bass (1985, 1990b), Bass and Avolio (1994), Bennis (1984), Hallinger (1992), Leithwood (1992), Leithwood and Jantzi (2000), Leithwood et al. (1999), Murphy and Hallinger (1992), Silins (1994), Silins and Murray-Harvey (1999).

4 Disciplinary regimes under self-governance

1 The term 'Murri' is often used to refer to Indigenous people in the state of Queensland in much the same way that 'Koori' is used in New South Wales.
2 The term 'Band' refers to the size of the school based on student enrolments. The smaller the band number, the smaller the school.
3 Brendan Nelson was the then Federal Minister for Education, Science and Training.

Bibliography

Acker, J. (1998). The future of gender and organisations. *Gender, Work and Organisation*, 5(4), 195–206.

Allan, E. J., Gordon, S. P. & Iverson, S. V. (2006). Re/thinking practices of power: The discursive framing of leadership in *The Chronicle of Higher Education*. *The Review of Higher Education*, 30(1), 41–68.

Allix, N. M. (2000). Transformational leadership: Democratic or despotic? *Educational Management and Administration*, 28(1), 7–20.

Alvesson, M. & Billing, Y. D. (1997). *Understanding gender and organizations*. London: Sage.

Anderson, G. L. (2009). *Advocacy leadership: Toward a post-reform agenda in education*. London & New York: Routledge.

Anderson, G. L. & Grinberg, J. (1998). Educational administration as a disciplinary practice: Appropriating Foucault's view of power, discourse, and method. *Educational Administration Quarterly*, 34(3), 329–353.

Angus, L. (1993). Democratic participation or efficient site management: The social and political location of the self managing school. In J. Smyth (Ed.), *A socially critical view of the self managing school*. London: Falmer Press.

Angus, L. (1994). Sociological analysis and educational management: The social context of the self managing school. *British Journal of Sociology of Education*, 15(1), 79–92.

Angus, L. (1996). Cultural dynamics and organisational analysis: Leadership, administration and the management of meaning in schools. In K. Leithwood, J. Chapman, D. Corson, P. Hallinger & A. Hart (Eds.), *International handbook of educational leadership and administration*. Boston: Kluwer Academic Publishers.

Ball, S. J. (Ed.). (1990a). *Foucault and education: Disciplines and knowledge*. London & New York: Routledge.

Ball, S. J. (1990b). Management as moral technology: A luddite analysis. In S. J. Ball (Ed.), *Foucault and education: Disciplines and knowledge*. London & New York: Routledge.

Ball, S. J. (1994). *Education reform: A critical and poststructural approach*. Buckingham: Open University Press.

Barnett, K., McCormick, J. & Conners, R. (2001). Transformational leadership in schools: Panacea, placebo or problem? *Journal of Educational Administration*, 39, 24–46.

Barry, A., Osborne, T. & Rose, N. (Eds.). (1996). *Foucault and political reason: Liberalism, neo-liberalism and rationalities of government*. London: UCL Press.

Barty, K., Thomson, P., Blackmore, J. & Sachs, J. (2005, December). Unpacking the issues: Researching the shortage of school principals in two states in Australia. *The Australian Educational Researcher, 32*(3).

Bass, B. M. (1985). *Leadership and performance beyond expectations*. New York: Free Press.

Bass, B. M. (1990a). *Handbook of leadership: A survey of theory, research and managerial applications*. Revised and Expanded. New York: Free Press; London: Collier Macmillan.

Bass, B. M. (1990b). From transactional to transformational leadership: Learning to share the vision. *Organisational Dynamics, 18*(3), 19–31.

Bass, B. M. & Avolio, B. J. (1993). Transformational leadership: A response to critics. In M. M. Chemers & R. Ayman (Eds.), *Leadership theory and research: Perspectives and directions*. San Diego, CA: Academic Press.

Bass, B. M. & Avolio, B. J. (Eds.). (1994). *Improving organisational effectiveness through transformational leadership*. Thousand Oaks, CA: Sage.

Bassey, M. (1999). *Case study research in educational settings*. Buckingham: Open University Press.

Bauman, Z. (2001). *Community: Seeking safety in an insecure world*. Cambridge: Polity Press.

Beatty, B. (2000a). The emotions of educational leadership: Breaking the silence. *International Journal of Leadership in Education, 3*(4), 331–357.

Beatty, B. (2000b). *The paradox of emotion and educational leadership*. Keynote address presented at the British Educational Administration and Management Annual Conference, Bristol, 22–24 September.

Beatty, B. (2000c). *Emotions matters in educational leadership*. Paper presented at the Australian Association for Research in Education Annual Conference, Sydney, 3 December.

Beatty, B. (2002a). *Emotional epistemologies and educational leadership: A conceptual framework*. Paper presented at the annual meeting of the American Educational Research Association, New Orleans, 1–5 April.

Beatty, B. (2002b). *Emotion matters in educational leadership: Examining the unexamined*. PhD thesis, Ontario Institute for Studies in Education, University of Toronto.

Beck, U. (1999). *The reinvention of politics: Rethinking modernity in the global social order*. Cambridge: Polity Press.

Bennis, W. (1984). Transformative power and leadership. In T. Sergiovanni & J. Corbally (Eds.), *Leadership and organisational culture*. Urbana & Chicago: University of Illinois Press.

Beresford, Q. & Partington, G. (Eds.). (2003). *Reform and resistance in Aboriginal education*. Crawley, WA: University of Western Australia Press.

Berkowitz, L. (Ed.). (1978). *Advances in experimental social psychology*. New York: Academic Press.

Bernauer, J. W. & Mahon, M. (2005). Michel Foucault's ethical imagination. In G. Gutting (Ed.), *The Cambridge companion to Foucault*. New York: Cambridge University Press.

Best, S. & Kellner, D. (1991). *Postmodern theory: Critical interrogations*. New York: Guilford Press.

Billing, A. D. & Alvesson, M. (1994). *Gender, managers and organizations*. Berlin & New York: Walter de Gruyter.

Billing, A. D. & Alvesson, M. (2000). Questioning the notion of feminine leadership: A critical perspective on the gender labelling of leadership. *Gender, Work and Organization,* 7(3), 144–157.

Bishop, P. & Mulford, B. (1999). When will they ever learn? Another failure of centrally-imposed change. *School Leadership and Management, 19*(2), 179–187.

Blackmore, J. (1989). Educational leadership: A feminist critique and reconstruction. In J. Smyth (Ed.), *Critical perspectives on educational leadership.* Sussex: Falmer Press.

Blackmore, J. (1995). Breaking out of a masculinist politics in education. In B. Limerick & B. Lingard (Eds.), *Gender and changing educational management.* Rydalmere: Hodder Education.

Blackmore, J. (1996). Doing emotional labour in the education market place: Stories from the field of women in management. *Discourse,* 17, 337–350.

Blackmore, J. (1997). *Leadership in 'crisis': Feminist insights into change in an era of educational restructuring.* Working paper, Deakin University.

Blackmore, J. (1999). *Troubling women: Feminism, leadership and educational change.* Buckingham: Open University Press.

Blackmore, J. (2004). Leading as emotional management work in high risk times: The counterintuitive impulses of performativity and passion. *School Leadership and Management, 24*(4), 439–459.

Blackmore, J. (2005). 'The Emperor has no clothes': Professionalism, performativity and educational leadership in high-risk postmodern times. In J. Collard & C. Reynolds (Eds.), *Leadership, gender and culture in education.* Maidenhead: Open University Press.

Blackmore, J. & Kenway, J. (Eds.). (1993). *Gender matters in educational administration and policy.* London: Falmer Press.

Blackmore, J. & Sachs, J. (1998). You never show you can't cope: Women in school leadership roles managing their emotions. *Gender and Education, 10*(3), 265–279.

Bleiker, R. (2003). Discourse and human agency. *Contemporary Political Theory, 2,* 25–47.

Boler, M. (1997). Disciplined emotions: Philosophies of educated feelings. *Educational Theory, 47*(2), 203–227.

Boler, M. (1998). Towards a politics of emotions: Bridging the chasm between theory and practice. *APA Newsletter, 98*(1).

Boler, M. (1999). *Feeling power: Emotions and education.* New York: Routledge.

Bouchard, D. F. (Ed.). (1977). *Language, counter-memory, practice: Selected essays and interviews by Michel Foucault.* New York: Cornell University Press.

Boyatzis, R. E. (1982). *The competent manager.* New York: John Wiley.

Britzman, D. P. (1995). The question of belief: Writing poststructural ethnography. *Qualitative Studies in Education, 8*(3), 229–238.

Brundrett, M., Burton, N. & Smith, R. (Eds.). (2003). *Leadership in education.* London: Sage.

Burchell, G., Gordon, C. & Miller, P. (1991). *The Foucault effect: Studies in governmentality.* Chicago: University of Chicago Press.

Burns, J. M. (1978). *Leadership.* New York: Harper & Row.

Calder, B. J. (1977). An attribution theory of leadership. In B. M. Staw & G. R. Salancik (Eds.), *New directions in organizational behavior.* Chicago: St. Clair.

Caldwell, B. J. (1993). *Decentralising the management of Australian schools.* Canberra: National Industry Education Forum.

Caldwell, B. J. (2005). *School-based management.* Brussels/Paris, The International Academy of Education/UNESCO, The International Institute for Educational Planning, Education Policy Series, 3.

Caldwell, B. J. (2006). *Re-imagining educational leadership.* Camberwell, Vict.: ACER Press.

Caldwell, B. J. & Spinks, J. M. (1988). *The self-managing school.* London: Falmer Press.

Caldwell, B. J. & Spinks, J. M. (1992). *Leading the self-managing school.* London: Falmer Press.

Caldwell, B. J. & Spinks, J. M. (1998). *Beyond the self-managing school.* London: Falmer Press.

Carmody, H. (1992, 12 November). No job for a woman. *ABC Four Corners.*

Chapman, J. (Ed.). (1990). *School-based decision-making and management.* London: Falmer Press.

Chemers, M. M. & Ayman, R. (Eds.). (1993). *Leadership theory and research: Perspectives and directions.* San Diego, CA: Academic Press.

Cheng, Y. C. (2006). *School effectiveness and school based management: A mechanism for development.* London: Falmer Press.

Christie, P. (2004). *Complexity in school leadership: What does this mean for Catholic schools?* Bishop Hans Brenninkmeijer Memorial Lecture.

Christie, P. (2005). Education for an ethical imagination. *Social Alternatives, 24*(4), 39–44.

Christie, P. & Lingard, R. (2001). *Capturing complexity in educational leadership.* Paper presented at the American Educational Research Association Conference, Seattle, 10–14 April.

Clarke, S. & Wildy, H. (2004). Context counts: Viewing small school leadership from the inside out. *Journal of Educational Administration, 42*(5), 555–572.

Clarke, S., Stevens, E. & Wildy, H. (2006). Rural rides in Queensland: Travels with novice teaching principals. *International Journal of Leadership in Education, 9*(1), 75–88.

Clegg, S. (1990). *Modern organisations: Organisation studies in the postmodern world.* London: Sage.

Clements, C. & Washbush, J. B. (1999). The two faces of leadership: Considering the dark side. *Journal of Workplace Learning: Employee Counselling Today, 11*(5), 170–175.

Collard, J. & Reynolds, C. (Eds.). (2005). *Leadership, gender and culture in education.* Maidenhead: Open University Press.

Connell, R., Ashenden, D., Kessler, S. & Dowsett, G. (1982). *Making the difference: Schools, families and social division.* Sydney: Allen & Unwin.

Court, M. (1995). Good girls and naughty girls: Rewriting the scripts for women's anger. In B. Limerick & B. Lingard (Eds.), *Gender and changing educational management.* Rydalmere: Hodder Education.

Crowther, F., Hann, L., McMaster, J. & Ferguson, M. (2000). *Leadership for successful school revitalisation: Lessons from recent Australian research.* Paper presented at the American Educational Research Association conference, New Orleans, April.

Crowther, F., Kaagan, S. S., Ferguson, M. & Hann, L. (2002). *Developing teacher leaders: How teacher leadership enhances school success.* Thousand Oaks, CA: Sage.

Daniher, G., Schirato, T. & Webb, J. (2000). *Understanding Foucault.* Sydney: Allen & Unwin.

Davidson, A. I. (2005). Ethics as ascetics. In G. Gutting, *The Cambridge companion to Foucault* (2nd ed.). New York: Cambridge University Press.

Davies, B. (Ed.). (2005). *The essentials of school leadership.* London: Paul Chapman.

Day, C., Harris, A., Hadfield, M., Tolley, H. & Beresford, J. (2000). *Leading schools in times of change.* Maidenhead: Open University Press.

Dean, M. (1999). *Governmentality: Power and rule in modern society.* London: Sage.

Department for Education and Skills. (2004). *National standards for headteachers.* London: DfES.

Diamond, I. & Quinby, L. (Eds.). (1988). *Feminism and Foucault: Reflections on resistance.* Boston: Northeastern University Press.

Dimmock, C. (2003). Leadership in learning centred schools: Cultural context, functions and qualities. In M. Brundrett, N. Burton & R. Smith (Eds.), *Leadership in education.* London: Sage.

Dimmock, C. & Walker, A. (2005). *Educational leadership: Culture and diversity.* London: Sage.

Downey, P. & Hart, V. (2000). Aboriginal owned schools: Still exotic mirages on the Australian education landscape. *New Horizons in Education, 102,* 15–29.

Dreyfus, H. L. & Rabinow, P. (1983). *Michel Foucault: Beyond structuralism and hermeneutics.* Chicago: University of Chicago Press.

Duignan, P. (2003). *Formation of capable, influential and authentic leaders for times of uncertainty.* Paper presented at the Australian Primary Principals' Association national conference, Adelaide.

Duignan, P. (2004). Forming capable leaders: From competence to capabilities. *New Zealand Journal of Educational Leadership, 19*(2), 5–13.

Earley, P. & Weindling, D. (2004). *Understanding school leadership.* London: Paul Chapman Publishing.

Education Queensland (1990). *Focus on schools.* Brisbane: The State of Queensland (Department of Education).

Education Queensland (1997). *Standards framework for leaders.* Brisbane: The State of Queensland (Department of Education).

Education Queensland (1998). *Future directions for school based management in Queensland state schools.* Brisbane: The State of Queensland (Department of Education).

Education Queensland (1999a). *Implementation of school based management in Queensland state schools.* Brisbane: The State of Queensland (Department of Education).

Education Queensland (1999b). *School based management in Queensland state schools.* Brisbane: The State of Queensland (Department of Education).

Education Queensland (1999c). *Teaching principal's guide.* Brisbane: Education Queensland.

Education Queensland (2000). *Queensland state education: 2010.* Brisbane: The State of Queensland (Department of Education).

Education Queensland (2001). *Three frames workbook.* Brisbane: The State of Queensland (Department of Education).

Education Queensland (2005). *Leadership matters: Leadership capabilities for Education Queensland principals technical paper.* Queensland Government: Department of Education and the Arts.

Education Queensland (2006). *Leadership matters: Leadership capabilities for Education Queensland principals.* Queensland Government: Department of Education and the Arts.

Ehrich, L. C. & Knight, J. (Eds.). (1998). *Leadership in crisis? Restructuring principal practice*. Flaxton, Qld: Post Pressed.

Elders, F. (Ed.). (1974). *Reflexive water: The basic concerns of mankind*. London: Souvenir Press.

English, F. (2000). A critical appraisal of Sara Lawrence-Lightfoot's portraiture as a method of educational research. *Educational Researcher, 29*(7), 21–26.

Etzioni, A. (1997). *The new golden rule: Community and morality in a democratic society*. London: Profile.

Evans, M. G. (1970). The effects of supervisory behaviour on the path-goal relationship. *Organisational Behaviour and Human Performance*, 5, 277–298.

Evans, M. G. (1974). Extensions of a path-goal theory of motivation. *Journal of Applied Psychology, 59*, 172–178.

Ewington, J., Mulford, B., Kendall, D., Edmunds, B., Kendall, L. & Silins, H. (2008). Successful school principalship in small schools. *Journal of Educational Administration, 46*(5), 545–561.

Faubion, J. D. (Ed.). (2000). *Essential works of Foucault 1954–1984, Volume 3: Power*. Harmondsworth: Penguin.

Feeney, A. (1998). A case study of educational leadership under school-based management. In L. C. Ehrich & J. Knight (Eds.), *Leadership in crisis? Restructuring principal practice* (pp. 89–95). Flaxton, Qld: Post Pressed.

Feidler, F. E. (1964). A contingency model of leadership effectiveness. In L. Berkowitz (Ed.), *Advances in experimental social psychology* (pp. 149–190). New York: Academic Press.

Feidler, F. E. (1967). *A theory of leadership effectiveness*. New York: McGraw-Hill.

Feidler, F. E. (1978). The contingency model and the dynamics of the leadership process. In L. Berkowitz (Ed.), *Advances in experimental social psychology* (pp. 59–112). New York: Academic Press.

Fendler, L. (2001). *Others and the problem of community*. Paper presented at the conference on Philosophy and History of the Discipline of Education: Evaluation and Evolution of the Criteria for Educational Research, Leuven, Belgium.

Fleishman, E. A. & Harris, E. F. (1962). Patterns of leadership behaviour related to employee grievances and turnover. *Personnel Psychology, 15*, 43–56.

Ford, J. (2006). Discourses of leadership: Gender, identity and contradiction in a UK public sector organisation. *Leadership, 2*(1), 77–99.

Foucault, M. (1967). *Madness and civilisation: A history of insanity in the age of reason*. London: Tavistock.

Foucault, M. (1970). *The order of things*. London: Tavistock.

Foucault, M. (1972). *Archaeology of knowledge* (A. M. Sheridan, Trans.). London: Routledge.

Foucault, M. (1974). Human nature: justice versus power. In F. Elders (Ed.), *Reflexive water: The basic concerns of mankind*. London: Souvenir Press.

Foucault, M. (1975). *The birth of the clinic: An archaeology of medical perception*. New York: Vintage.

Foucault, M. (1977a). Nietzsche, genealogy, history. In D. F. Bouchard (Ed.), *Language, counter-memory, practice: Selected essays and interviews by Michel Foucault*. New York: Cornell University Press.

Foucault, M. (1977b). *Discipline and punish*. London: Penguin.

Foucault, M. (1977c). Intellectuals and power. In D. F. Bouchard (Ed.), *Language, counter-memory, practice: Selected essays and interviews by Michel Foucault.* New York: Cornell University Press.

Foucault, M. (1980a). Two lectures. In C. Gordon (Ed.), *Power/knowledge: Selected interviews and other writings, 1972–1977.* Sussex: Harvester Press Ltd.

Foucault, M. (1980b). Truth and power. In C. Gordon (Ed.), *Power/knowledge: Selected interviews and other writings, 1972–1977.* Sussex: Harvester Press Ltd.

Foucault, M. (1981a). *The history of sexuality vol. 1: An introduction* (Robert Hurley, Trans.). London: Penguin.

Foucault, M. (1981b). The order of discourse. In R. Young (Ed.), *Untying the text: A post-structuralist reader.* London: Routledge.

Foucault, M. (1983). The subject and power. In H. L. Dreyfus & P. Rabinow (Ed.), *Michel Foucault: Beyond structuralism and hermeneutics.* Chicago: University of Chicago Press.

Foucault, M. (1986). Politics and ethics: An interview. In P. Rabinow (Ed.), *The Foucault reader.* Harmondsworth: Peregrine.

Foucault, M. (1988). Truth, power, self: An interview. In L. Martin, H. Gutman & P. Hutton, *Technologies of the self: A seminar with Michel Foucault.* Amherst: University of Massachusetts Press.

Foucault, M. (1990). *The history of sexuality Volume 3: The care of the self.* London: Penguin.

Foucault, M. (1991a). Questions of method. In G. Burchell, C. Gordon & P. Miller (Eds.), *The Foucault effect: Studies in governmentality.* Chicago: University of Chicago Press.

Foucault, M. (1991b). Governmentality. In G. Burchell, C. Gordon & P. Miller (Eds.), *The Foucault effect: Studies in governmentality.* Chicago: University of Chicago Press.

Foucault, M. (1991c). Politics and the study of discourse. In G. Burchell, C. Gordon & P. Miller (Eds.), *The Foucault effect: Studies in governmentality.* Chicago: University of Chicago Press.

Foucault, M. (1992). *The use of pleasure: The history of sexuality Vol. 2.* London: Penguin.

Foucault, M. (1993). About the beginnings of the hermeneutics of the self: Two lectures at Dartmouth. *Political Theory, 21*(2).

Foucault, M. (1994). Prisons et asiles dans le mécanisme du pouvoir. In *Dits et écrits* (vol. 11, pp. 523–524). Paris: Gallimard. [This passage trans. Clare O'Farrell]. Retrieved 18 March 2010, from www.michel-foucault.com/quote/2004q.html.

Foucault, M. (1996). The birth of a world. In S. Lotringer (Ed.), *Foucault live: Collected interviews, 1961–1984.* New York: Semiotext(e).

Foucault, M. (2000a). On the genealogy of ethics. In P. Rabinow (Ed.), *Ethics: Subjectivity and truth: The essential works of Foucault 1954–1984, Volume 1.* Harmondsworth: Penguin.

Foucault, M. (2000b). Candidacy presentation: Collège de France, 1969. In P. Rabinow (Ed.), *Ethics: Subjectivity and truth: The essential works of Foucault 1954–1984, Volume 1.* Harmondsworth: Penguin.

Foucault, M. (2000c). Self writing. In P. Rabinow (Ed.), *Ethics: Subjectivity and truth: The essential works of Foucault 1954–1984, Volume 1.* Harmondsworth: Penguin.

Foucault, M. (2000d). Technologies of the self. In P. Rabinow (Ed.), *Ethics: Subjectivity and truth: The essential works of Foucault 1954–1984, Volume 1.* Harmondsworth: Penguin.

Foucault, M. (2000e). The ethics of the concern for self as a practice of freedom. In P. Rabinow (Ed.), *Ethics: Subjectivity and truth: The essential works of Foucault 1954–1984, Volume 1*. Harmondsworth: Penguin.

Foucault, M. (2000f). Polemics, politics and problematisations. In P. Rabinow (Ed.), *Ethics: Subjectivity and truth: The essential works of Foucault 1954–1984, Volume 1*. Harmondsworth: Penguin.

Foucault, M. (2000g). Sexuality and solitude. In P. Rabinow (Ed.), *Ethics: Subjectivity and truth: The essential works of Foucault 1954–1984, Volume 1*. Harmondsworth: Penguin.

Foucault, M. (2002a). Truth and juridical forms. In J. D. Faubion (Ed.), *Essential works of Foucault 1954–1984, Volume 3: Power*. Harmondsworth: Penguin.

Foucault, M. (2002b). Interview with Michel Foucault. In J. D. Faubion (Ed.), *Essential works of Foucault 1954–1984, Volume 3: Power*. Harmondsworth: Penguin.

Foucault, M. (2002c). Truth and power. In J. D. Faubion (Ed.), *Essential works of Foucault 1954–1984, Volume 3: Power*. Harmondsworth: Penguin.

Foucault, M. (2002d). Omnes et singulatim. In J. D. Faubion (Ed.), *Essential works of Foucault 1954–1984, Volume 3: Power*. Harmondsworth: Penguin.

Foucault, M. (2002e). Space, knowledge and power. In J. D. Faubion (Ed.), *Essential works of Foucault 1954–1984, Volume 3: Power*. Harmondsworth: Penguin.

Foucault, M. (2003). *Abnormal: Lectures at the Collège de France, 1974–1975*. New York: Picador.

Foucault, M. (2005). *The hermeneutics of the subject: Lectures at the Collège de France, 1981–1982*. New York: Picador.

Fraser, E. (1999). *The problems of communitarian politics: Unity and conflict*. Oxford: Oxford University Press.

Fraser, E. & Lacey, N. (1993). *The politics of community: A feminist critique of the liberal-communitarian debate*. Toronto: University of Toronto Press.

Freebody, P. (2003). *Qualitative research in education: Interaction and practice*. Thousand Oaks, CA: Sage.

Fullan, M. (1993). *Change forces: Probing the depths of educational reform*. London: Falmer Press.

Fullan, M. (1999). *Change forces: The sequel*. London: Falmer Press.

Fullan, M. (2001). *Leading in a culture of change*. San Francisco: Jossey-Bass.

Fullan, M. (2003). *The moral imperative of school leadership*. Thousand Oaks, CA: Corwin Press.

Gale, T. (2001). Critical policy sociology: Historiography, archaeology and genealogy as methods of policy analysis. *Journal of Education Policy, 16*(5), 379–393.

Gane, M. & Johnson, T. (Eds.). (1993). *Foucault's new domains*. London: Routledge.

Gay, L. R. & Airasian, P. (2003). *Educational research: Competencies for analysis and applications* (7th ed.). Upper Saddle River, NJ: Merrill Prentice Hall.

George, J. M. (2000). Emotions and leadership: The role of emotional intelligence. *Human Relations, 53*(8), 1027–1055.

Gerwitz, S., Ball, S. J. & Bowe, R. (1995). *Markets, choice and equity in education*. Buckingham: Open University Press.

Giddens, A. (1998). *The third way: The renewal of social democracy*. Cambridge: Polity Press.

Gilbert, R. & Dewar, J. (1995). Community and the politics of participation. In B. Limerick & H. Nielson (Eds.), *School and community relations*. Marrickville: Harcourt Brace & Company.

Goleman, D. (1995). *Emotional intelligence: Why it can matter more than IQ*. New York: Bantam Books.

Gordon, C. (Ed.). (1980). *Power/knowledge: Selected interviews and other writings 1972–1977 by Michel Foucault*. Sussex: Harvester Press Ltd.

Gordon, C. (1991). Introduction. In G. Burchell, C. Gordon & P. Miller (Eds.), *The Foucault effect: Studies in governmentality*. Chicago: University of Chicago Press.

Grace, G. (1995). *School leadership: Beyond education management – An essay in policy scholarship*. Washington, DC: Falmer Press.

Grace, G. (2000). Research and the challenges of contemporary school leadership: The contribution of critical scholarship. *British Journal of Educational Studies, 48*(3), 231–247.

Gronn, P. (1995). Greatness re-visited: The current obsession with transformational leadership. *Leading and Managing, 1*(1), 14–27.

Gronn, P. (1996). From transactions to transformations: A new world order in the study of leadership? *Educational Management and Administration, 24*(1), 7–30.

Gronn, P. (1999). *The making of educational leaders*. London: Cassell.

Gronn, P. (2002). Distributed leadership as a unit of analysis. *Leadership Quarterly, 13*(4), 423–451.

Gronn, P. (2003a). Leadership: Who needs it? *School Leadership and Management, 23*(3), 267–290.

Gronn, P. (2003b). *The new work of educational leaders*. London: Sage.

Gronn, P. (2006, 30 October). The significance of distributed leadership. *BC Educational leadership Research, 7*. Retrieved 18 March, 2010, from www.slc.educ.ubc.ca/eJournal/Issue7/index7.html.

Gunter, H. (2010). A sociological approach to educational leadership. *British Journal of Sociology of Education, 31*(4), 519–527.

Gunter, H. & Ribbins, P. (2002). Leadership studies in education: Towards a map of the field. *Educational Management and Administration, 30*(4), 387–416.

Guskey, T. & Huberman, H. (Eds.). (1995). *Professional development in education*. New York: Teachers College Press.

Gutting, G. (Ed.). (2005). *The Cambridge companion to Foucault* (2nd ed.). New York: Cambridge University Press.

Haber, H. F. (1994). *Beyond postmodern politics*. New York: Routledge.

Hackmann, D. G. (2002). Using portraiture in educational leadership research. *International Journal of Leadership in Education, 5*(1), 51–60.

Halford, S. & Leonard, P. (2001). *Gender, power and organisations*. New York: Palgrave.

Hall, V. (1996). *Dancing on the ceiling: A study of women managers in education*. London: Paul Chapman Publishing.

Hall, V. (1997). Dusting off the phoenix: Gender and educational leadership revisited. *Educational Management, Administration and Leadership, 25*(3), 309–324.

Hallinger, P. (1992). The evolving role of American principals: From managerial to instructional to transformational leaders. *Journal of Educational Administration, 30*(3), 35–48.

Hallinger, P. (2003). Leading educational change: Reflections on the practice of instructional and transformative leadership. *Cambridge Journal of Education, 33*(3), 329–351.

Hallinger, P. & Heck, R. (1996). Reassessing the principal's role in school effectiveness: A review of empirical research, 1980–1995. *Educational Administration Quarterly, 32*, 5–44.

Hammersley, M. (2006, March). Ethnography: Problems and prospects. *Ethnography and Education, 1*(1), 3–14.

Harding, J. & Pribham, E. D. (2002). The power of feeling: Locating emotions in culture. *European Journal of Cultural Studies, 5*(4), 407–426.

Harding, J. & Pribham, E. D. (2004). Losing our cool? Following Williams and Grossberg on emotions. *Cultural Studies, 18*(6), 863–883.

Hargreaves, A. (1995). Development and desire: A postmodern perspective. In T. Guskey & H. Huberman (Eds.), *Professional development in education*. New York: Teachers College Press.

Hargreaves, A. (1997). Rethinking educational change. In A. Hargreaves (Ed.), *Positive change for school success, the 1997 ASCD yearbook*. Alexandria, VA: Association for Supervision and Curriculum Development.

Hargreaves, A. (2000). Mixed emotions: Teachers' perceptions of their interactions with students. *Teaching and Teacher Education, 16*, 811–826.

Hargreaves, A. (2001). Emotional geographies of teaching. *Teachers College Record, 103*(6), 1056–1080.

Hargreaves, A. (2004). Inclusive and exclusive educational change: Emotional responses of teachers and implications for leadership. *School Leadership and Management, 24*(2), 287–309.

Harris, A. (2005a). Leading from the chalk-face: An overview of school leadership. *Leadership, 1*(1), 73–87.

Harris, A. (2005b). Distributed leadership. In B. Davies (Ed.), *The essentials of school leadership*. London: Paul Chapman.

Hartley, D. (2007). The emergence of distributed leadership in education: Why now? *British journal of Educational Studies, 55*(2), 202–214.

Hartsock, N. (1990). Foucault on power: A theory for women? In L. J. Nicholson (Ed.), *Feminism/Postmodernism*. New York: Routledge.

Hatcher, R. (2005). The distribution of leadership and power in schools. *British Journal of Sociology of Education, 26*(2), 253–267.

Hayes, D. (2005). *Telling stories: Sustaining whole school change in schools located in communities with deep needs.* Paper presented at the Australian Association for Research in Education annual conference, Parramatta.

Heck, R. H. & Hallinger, P. (2005). The study of educational leadership and management: Where does the field stand today? *Educational Management Administration and Leadership, 33*(2), 229–244.

Hersey, P. & Blanchard, K. H. (1974). Measuring how you behave in a situational leadership framework. *Training and Development*, February, 22–37.

Hersey, P. & Blanchard, K. H. (1993). *The management of organisational behaviour* (4th ed.). Englewood Cliffs, NJ: Prentice Hall.

Hindess, B. (1996). *Discourses of power: From Hobbes to Foucault*. Oxford: Blackwell.

Hofmeyr, A. B. (2006). The meta-physics of Foucault's ethics: Succeeding where Levinas fails. *South African Journal of Philosophy, 25*(2), 113–125.

Holmes, D. & Gastaldo, D. (2002). Nursing as a means of governmentality. *Journal of Advanced Nursing, 38*(6), 557–565.

House, R. J. (1971). A path-goal theory of leader effectiveness. *Administrative Science Quarterly, 16*, 321–339.

House, R. J. (1996). Path-goal theory of leadership: Lessons, legacy, and a reformulated theory. *Leadership Quarterly, 7*, 323–352.

House, R. J. & Dressler, G. (1974). The path-goal theory of leadership: Some post hoc and a priori tests. In J. Hunt & L. Larson (Eds.), *Contingency approaches to leadership*. Carbondale: Southern Illinois University Press.

House, R. J. & Mitchell, T. R. (1974). Path-goal theory of leadership. *Contemporary Business, 3*, 81–98.

House of Representatives Standing Committee on Aboriginal Affairs (1990). *Our future our selves*. Canberra: AGPS.

Howard, A. & Bray, D. W. (1988). *Managerial lives in transition: Advancing age and changing times*. New York: Guilford Press.

Hoy, D. C. (Ed.). (1986). *Foucault: A critical reader*. Oxford: Blackwell.

Hughes, C. (2007). The pleasure of learning at work: Foucault and phenomenology compared. *British Journal of Sociology of Education, 28*(3), 363–376.

Hunt, J. & Larson, L. (Eds.). (1974). *Contingency approaches to leadership*. Carbondale: Southern Illinois University Press.

Hunter, I. (1994). *Rethinking the school: Subjectivity, bureaucracy, criticism*. Sydney: Allen & Unwin.

Hunter, I. (1996). Assembling the school. In A. Barry, T. Osborne & N. Rose (Eds.), *Foucault and political reason: Liberalism, neo-liberalism and rationalities of government*. London: UCL Press.

Independent Schools Queensland. (2006, June). Code of conduct. Reproduced in *Board Shorts, 1*(2).

Kanter, R. M. (1977). *Men and women of the corporation*. New York: Basic Books.

Katz, D., Maccoby, N., Gurin, G. & Floor, L. (1951). *Productivity, supervision and morale among railroad workers*. Ann Arbor: Survey Research Center, University of Michigan.

Katz, D., Maccoby, N. & Morse, N. (1950). *Productivity, supervision and morale in an office situation*. Ann Arbor: Survey Research Center, University of Michigan.

Keeves, J. P. (Ed.). (1988). *Educational research, methodology and measurement: An international handbook*. New York: Pergamon.

Kendall, G. & Wickham, G. (1999). *Using Foucault's methods*. London: Sage.

Kerr, S. & Jermier, J. (1977). Substitutes for leadership: Their meaning and measurement. *Organization and Human Performance, 22*, 374–403.

Kotter, J. (1990, May–June). What leaders really do. *Harvard Business Review*, 103–111.

Krantz, J. & Gilmore, T. N. (1990). The splitting of leadership and management as a social defense. *Human Relations, 43*(2), 183–204.

Ladomski, G. (1995). Leadership and learning: From transformational leadership to organisational learning. *Leading and Managing, 1*(3), 211–225.

Lambert, L. (1998). *Building leadership capacity in schools*. Alexandria, VA: Association for Supervision and Curriculum Development.

Lambert, C. (2007). New labour, new leaders? Gendering transformational leadership. *British Journal of Sociology of Education, 28*(2), 149–163.

Land, R. (1998). An ethical analysis of leadership competence for a competitive educational market. In L. C. Ehrich & J. Knight (Eds.), *Leadership in crisis? Restructuring principal practice* (pp. 43–51). Flaxton, Qld: Post Pressed.

Lawrence-Lightfoot, S. (1983). *The good high school: Portraits of character and culture*. New York: Basic Books.

Lawrence-Lightfoot, S. & Davis, J. H. (1997). *The art and science of portraiture*. San Francisco: Jossey-Bass.

Leithwood, K. (1992). The move toward transformational leadership. *Educational Leadership, 49*(5), 8–12.

Leithwood, K., Chapman, J., Corson, D., Hallinger, P. & Hart, A. (Eds.). (1996). *International handbook of educational leadership and administration*. Boston: Kluwer Academic Publishers.

Leithwood, K. & Jantzi, D. (2000a). The effects of transformational leadership on organisational conditions and student engagement with school. *Journal of Educational Administration, 38*, 112–129.

Leithwood, K. & Jantzi, D. (2000b). The effects of different sources of leadership on student engagement in school. In K. S. Louis & K. A. Riley (Eds.), *Leadership for learning: International perspectives on leadership for change and school reform*. London: Routledge.

Leithwood, K., Jantzi, D. & Steinbach, R. (1999). Transformational leadership as a place to begin. In *Changing leadership for changing times*, Buckingham: Open University Press.

Limerick, B. (1991). *Career opportunities for teachers in the Queensland Department of Education with special reference to the under-representation of women in senior management positions*, Queensland Department of Education, Brisbane.

Limerick, B. (1995). Accommodated careers: Gendered career paths in education. In B. Limerick & R. Lingard (Eds.), *Gender and changing educational management*. Rydalmere: Hodder Education.

Limerick, B. & Cranston, N. (1998). En/gendering leadership: Reconceptualising our understandings. In L. C. Ehrich & J. Knight (Eds.), *Leadership in crisis? Restructuring principal practice* (pp. 36–42). Flaxton, Qld: Post Pressed.

Limerick, B. & Lingard, R. (Eds.). (1995). *Gender and changing educational management*. Rydalmere: Hodder Education.

Limerick, B. & Nielson, H. (Eds.). (1995). *School and community relations*. Marrickville: Harcourt Brace & Company.

Lincoln, Y. S. & Guba, E. G. (1985). *Naturalistic inquiry*. Thousand Oaks, CA: Sage.

Lingard, R., Hayes, D. & Mills, M. (2002). Developments in school-based management: The specific case of Queensland. *Australian Journal of Educational Administration, 40*(1), 6–30.

Lingard, R., Hayes, D., Mills, M. & Christie, P. (2003). *Leading learning*. Maidenhead: Open University Press.

Lingard, R., Ladwig, J., Mills, M., Bahr, M., Chant, D., Warry, M., et al. (2001). *The Queensland school reform longitudinal study*. Brisbane: The State of Queensland (Department of Education).

Lotringer, S. (Ed.). (1996). *Foucault live: Collected interviews, 1961–1984*. New York: Semiotext(e).

Louis, K. S. & Riley, K. A. (2000). Relational leadership for change. In K. S. Louis & K. A. Riley (Eds.), *Leadership for learning: International perspectives on leadership for change and school reform*. London: Routledge.

Lyotard, J. F. (1984). *The postmodern condition*. Minneapolis: University of Minnesota Press.

Lyotard, J. F. (1997). *Postmodern fables*. Minneapolis: University of Minnesota Press.

Mac an Ghaill, M. (1994). *The making of men: Masculinities, sexualities and schooling*. Buckingham: Open University Press.

Macbeath, J. (2005). Leadership as distributed: A matter of practice. *School Leadership and Management, 25*(4), 349–366.

Makuwira, J. (2007). The politics of community capacity-building: Contestations, contradictions, tensions and ambivalences in the discourse in Indigenous communities in Australia. *Australian Journal of Indigenous Education, 36,* 129–136.

Marks, H. & Printy, S. (2003). Principal leadership and school performance: An integration of transformational and instructional leadership. *Educational Administration Quarterly, 39*(3), 370–397.

Marshall, J. (1984). *Women managers: Travellers in a male world.* New York: John Wiley.

Marshall, J. (1995). *Women managers moving on: Exploring career and life choices.* London & New York: Routledge.

Marshall, J. (Ed.). (2004). *Poststructuralism and education.* Dordrecht: Kluwer.

Martin, L., Gutman, H. & Hutton, P. (Eds.). (1988). *Technologies of the self: A seminar with Michel Foucault.* Amherst: University of Massachusetts Press.

Martin, R., McCollow, J., McFarlane, L., McMurdo, G., Graham, J. & Hull, R. (1994). *Devolution, decentralisation and recentralisation, the structure of Australian schooling.* Melbourne: The Australian Education Union.

Masschelein, J. (2004). How to conceive of critical educational theory today? *Journal of Philosophy of Education, 38*(3), 351–367.

Maxcy, S. J. (1991). *Educational leadership: A critical pragmatic perspective.* New York: Bergin & Garvey.

Maxcy, S. J. (Ed.). (1994). *Postmodern school leadership: Meeting the crisis in educational administration.* Westport, CT: Praeger.

Maxwell, J. A. (2005). *Qualitative research design: An interactive approach* (2nd ed.). Thousand Oaks, CA: Sage.

May, T. (2005). Foucault now? *Foucault Studies, 3,* 65–76.

Mayrowetz, D. (2008). Making sense of distributed leadership: Exploring the multiple usages of the concept in the field. *Educational Administration Quarterly, 44*(3), 424–435.

McConaghy, C. (2000). *Rethinking Indigenous education.* Flaxton, Qld: Post Pressed.

McGregor, D. (1960). *The human side of enterprise.* New York: McGraw-Hill.

McHoul, A. & Grace, W. (1993). *A Foucault primer: Discourse, power and the subject.* Melbourne: Melbourne University Press.

McInerney, P. (2001). *Moving into dangerous territory? Educational leadership in devolving education systems.* Paper presented at the Australian Association for Research in Education annual conference, Perth.

McKinlay, A. & Starkey, K. (1998). Managing Foucault: Foucault, management and organisation theory. In A. McKinlay & K. Starkey (Eds.), *Foucault, management and organisation theory.* London: Sage.

McLaughlin, M. W. (1987). Learning from experience: Lessons from policy implementation. *Educational Evaluation and Policy Analysis, 9*(2), 171–178.

McLaughlin, M. W. (1991). *Strategic sites for teachers' professional development.* Paper presented at the annual meeting at the American Educational Research Association, Chicago, April.

McNay, L. (1994). *Foucault: A critical introduction.* Cambridge: Polity Press.

McNicol Jardine, G. (2005). *Foucault and education.* New York: Peter Lang.

Meadmore, D. (1993). The production of individuality through examination. *British Journal of Sociology of Education, 14*(1), 59–73.

Meadmore, D., Limerick, B., Thomas, P. & Lucas, H. (1995). Devolving practices: managing the managers. *Journal of Education Policy, 10*(4), 399–411.

Merriam, S. B. (1988). *Qualitative research and case study applications in education.* San Francisco: Jossey-Bass.

Miller, G. (1997). Building bridges: The possibility of analytic dialogues between ethnography, conversation analysis and Foucault. In D. Silverman (Ed.), *Qualitative research: Theory, method and practice.* London: Sage.

Miller, P. & Rose, N. (1992). Political power beyond the state: Problematics of government. *British Journal of Sociology, 43*(2), 173–205.

Miller, P. & Rose, N. (1993). Governing economic life. In M. Gane & T. Johnson (Eds.), *Foucault's new domains.* London: Routledge.

Mills, M. (2009). *Gender and school reform: The emotional labour of principals.* Paper presented at the Australian Association for Research in Education annual conference, Canberra.

Mills, M., Martino, W. & Lingard, B. (2004). Attracting, recruiting and retaining male teachers: Policy issues in the male teacher debate. *British Journal of Sociology of Education, 25*(3), 355–369.

Mills, S. (1992). Negotiating discourses of femininity. *Journal of Gender Studies, 1*(3), 271–285.

Mills, S. (1997). *Discourse.* New York: Routledge.

Mills, S. (2003). *Michel Foucault.* London: Routledge.

Murphy, J. & Hallinger, P. (1992). The principalship in an era of transformation. *Journal of Educational Administration, 30*(3), 77–88.

Niesche, R. (2003). Power and homosexuality in the teaching workplace. *Social Alternatives, 22*(2), 43–47.

Niesche, R. (2005). Disengaging leadership: Educational administration and management as a field of scientific knowledge. In J. Yamanashi & I. Milojevic (Eds.), *Researching identity, diversity and education: Surpassing the norm.* Teneriffe: Post Pressed.

Niesche, R. & Jorgensen, R. (2010). Curriculum reform in remote areas: The need for productive leadership. *Journal of Educational Administration, 48*(1), 102–117.

Nussbaum, M. C. (2000). *Women and human development.* Cambridge: Cambridge University Press.

O'Farrell, C. (1989). *Foucault: Historian or philosopher?* London: Macmillan.

O'Farrell, C. (2005). *Michel Foucault.* London: Sage.

O'Leary, T. (2002). *Foucault and the art of ethics.* London & New York: Continuum.

O'Malley, P. (1996). Indigenous governance. *Economy and Society, 25*(3), 310–326.

Ozga, J. (Ed.). (1992). *Women and educational management.* Milton Keynes: Open University Press.

Pang, I. W. (2008). School-based management in Hong Kong: Centralizing or decentralizing. *Educational Research for Policy and Practice, 7*(1), 17–33.

Patton, M. Q. (2002). *Qualitative research and evaluation methods* (3rd ed.). Thousand Oaks, CA: Sage.

Peters, M. A. & Besley, T. (Eds.). (2007). *Why Foucault? New directions in educational research.* New York: Peter Lang.

Pine Hills State School (2005). *Annual Report.*

Pine Hills State School (2006). *Annual Report.*

Plant, R. (1974). *Community and ideology: An essay in applied social philosophy.* London: Routledge & Kegan Paul.

Popkewitz, T. S. (1991). *A political sociology of educational reform.* New York: Teachers College Press.

Popkewitz, T. S. & Brennan, M. (1997). Restructuring of social and political theory in education: Foucault and a social epistemology of school practices. *Educational Theory, 47*(3), 287–313.

Popkewitz, T. S. & Brennan, M. (Eds.). (1998). *Foucault's challenge: Discourse, knowledge, and power in education*. New York: Teachers College Press.

Pradeep, P. & Standish, P. (Eds.). (2000). *Lyotard: Just education*. London: Routledge.

Quicke, J. (2000). A new professionalism for a collaborative culture of organisational learning in contemporary society. *Educational Management and Administration, 28*(3), 299–315.

Rabinow, P. (Ed.). (1986). *The Foucault reader*. Harmondsworth: Peregrine.

Rabinow, P. (Ed.). (1997). *Ethics: Subjectivity and truth: The essential works of Foucault 1954–1984, Volume 1*. New York: New Press.

Ransom, J. S. (1997). *Foucault's discipline: The politics of subjectivity*. Durham, NC & London: Duke University Press.

Riverside Community School (2005). *Riverside Community School handbook*.

Rizvi, F. (1993). Contrasting perceptions of devolution. *Queensland Teachers' Union Professional Magazine, 11*(1), May, 1–5.

Rose, N. (1990). *Governing the soul: The shaping of the private self*, London: Routledge.

Rose, N. (1999). *Powers of freedom: Reframing political thought*. Cambridge: Cambridge University Press.

Rose, N. (2000). Community, citizenship, and the third way. *American Behavioral Scientist, 43*(9), 1395–1411.

Ryan, M. K. & Haslam, S. A. (2005). The glass cliff: Evidence that women are over-represented in precarious leadership positions. *British Journal of Management, 16*, 81–90.

Said, E. (1986). Foucault and the imagination of power. In D. Hoy (Ed.), *Foucault: A critical reader*. New York: Pantheon.

Sawicki, J. (1991). *Disciplining Foucault: Feminism, power and the body*. New York: Routledge.

Sawicki, J. (1994). Foucault, feminism and questions of identity. In G. Gutting (Ed.), *The Cambridge companion to Michel Foucault*. New York: Cambridge University Press.

Sergiovanni, T. (1994). *Building community in schools*. San Francisco: Jossey-Bass.

Sergiovanni, T. & Corbally, J. (Eds.). (1984). *Leadership and organisational culture*. Urbana & Chicago: University of Illinois Press.

Shakeshaft, C. (1987). *Women in educational administration*. Newberry Park, CA: Sage.

Shakeshaft, C. (1989). The gender gap in research in educational administration. *Educational Administration Quarterly, 25*(4), 324–337.

Shakeshaft, C. (1995). Gendered leadership styles in educational organisations. In B. Limerick & B. Lingard (Eds.), *Gender and changing educational management*. Sydney: Hodder & Stoughton.

Sheridan, A. (1980). *Michel Foucault: The will to truth*. London: Tavistock.

Silins, H. (1994). The relationship between transformational and transactional leadership and school improvement outcomes. *School Effectiveness and School Improvement, 5*, 272–298.

Silins, H. & Murray-Harvey, R. (1999). What makes a good senior secondary school? *Educational Administration Quarterly, 37*, 329–344.

Silverman, D. (Ed.). (1997). *Qualitative research: Theory, method and practice*. London: Sage.

Simons, J. (1995). *Foucault and the political*. London: Routledge.

Simons, M. & Masschelein, J. (2006). The learning society and governmentality: An introduction. *Educational Philosophy and Theory, 38*(4), 417–430.

Sinclair, A. (1995). Sexuality in leadership. *International Review of Women and Leadership, 1*(2), 25–38.

Sinclair, A. (1998). *Doing leadership differently.* Melbourne: Melbourne University Press.

Sinclair, A. (2004). Journey around leadership. *Discourse: Studies in the Cultural Politics of Education, 25*(1), 7–19.

Sinclair, A. (2005). Body possibilities in leadership. *Leadership, 1*(4), 387–406.

Sinclair, A. (2007). *Leadership for the disillusioned.* Thousand Oaks, CA: Sage.

Sinclair, A. & Wilson, W. (2002). *New faces of leadership.* Melbourne: Melbourne University Press.

Skelton, C. (2002). The 'feminisation of schooling' or 're-masculinising' of primary education? *International Studies in Sociology of Education, 12*(1), 77–96.

Smart, B. (1985). *Michel Foucault.* London: Tavistock.

Smyth, J. (Ed.). (1993). *A socially critical view of the self-managing school.* London: Falmer Press.

Smyth, J. (2002). Unmasking teachers' subjectivities in local school management. *Journal of Education Policy, 17*(4), 463–482.

Smyth, J. (2009). Critically engaged community capacity building and the community organizing approach in disadvantaged contexts. *Critical Studies in Education, 50*(1), 9–22.

Southworth, G. (2003). Instructional leadership in schools: Reflections and empirical evidence. *School Leadership and Management, 22*(1), 73–92.

Spillane, J. P. (2006). *Distributed leadership.* San Francisco: Jossey-Bass.

Spillane, J. P., Camburn, E. M. & Pareja, A. S. (2007). Taking a distributed perspective to the school principal's workday. *Leadership and Policy in Schools, 6*(1), 103–125.

Spillane, J. P., Halverson, R. & Diamond, J. (2004). Towards a theory of school leadership practice: Implications of a distributed perspective. *Journal of Curriculum Studies, 36*(1), 3–34.

Spillane, J. P. & Orlina, E. C. (2005). Investigating leadership practice: Exploring the entailments of taking a distributed perspective. *Leadership and Policy in Schools, 4*(3), 157–176.

Spillane, J. P. & Zuberi, A. (2009). Designing and piloting a leadership daily practice log: Using logs to study the practice of leadership. *Educational Administration Quarterly, 45*(3), 375–423.

Stake, R. E. (1995). *The art of case study research.* Thousand Oaks, CA: Sage.

Staw, B. M. & Salancik, G. R. (Eds.). (1977). *New directions in organizational behaviour.* Chicago: St Clair.

Stenhouse, L. (1988). Case study methods. In J. P. Keeves (Ed.), *Educational research, methodology, and measurement: An international handbook* (1st ed.). New York: Pergamon.

Stephenson, J. (2000). *Corporate capability: Implications for the style and direction of work-based learning.* Working paper 99-14, Research Centre for Vocational Education and Training, Sydney University of Technology.

Still, L. (1995). Women in management. Glass ceilings or slippery poles? In B. Limerick & B. Lingard (Eds.), *Gender and changing educational management.* Sydney: Hodder & Stoughton.

Stogdill, R. M. (1948). Personal factors associated with leadership: A survey of the literature. *Journal of Psychology, 25*, 35–71.

Stogdill, R. M. (1974). *Handbook of leadership: A survey of the literature.* New York: Free Press; London: Collier Macmillan.

Storey, A. (2004). The problem of distributed leadership in schools. *School Leadership and Management, 24*(3), 249–265.

Sturman, A. (1997). Case study methods. In J. P. Keeves (Ed.), *Educational research, methodology, and measurement: An international handbook* (2nd ed.). New York: Pergamon.

Tamboukou, M. & Ball, S. J. (Eds.). (2003). *Dangerous encounters: Genealogy and ethnography.* New York: Peter Lang.

Thomson, P. (2000) 'Like schools', educational 'disadvantage' and 'thisness'. *Australian Educational Researcher, 27*(3), 151–166.

Thomson, P. (2001). How principals lose 'face': A disciplinary tale of educational administration and modern managerialism. *Discourse: Studies in the Cultural Politics of Education, 22*(1), 5–22.

Thomson, P. (2002). *Schooling the Rustbelt kids: Making the difference in changing times.* Crows Nest, NSW: Allen & Unwin.

Thomson, P. (2009). *School leadership: Heads on the block?* London & New York: Routledge.

Thrupp, M. (2003). The school leadership literature in managerialist times: Exploring the problem of textual apologism. *School Leadership and Management, 23*(2), 149–172.

Tichy, N. M. & Devanna, M. A. (1990). *The transformational leader.* New York: John Wiley.

Tosi, H. L. & Kiker, S. (1997). Commentary on 'substitutes for leadership'. *Leadership Quarterly, 8*(2), 109–112.

Tzu, S. (2005). *The art of war* (S. B. Griffith, Trans.). London: Duncan Baird Publishers.

Usher, R. & Edwards, R. (1994). *Postmodernism and education.* London & New York: Routledge.

Visker, R. (1995). *Michel Foucault: Genealogy as critique.* London & New York: New Left Books.

Walzer, M. (1986). The politics of Michel Foucault. In D. C. Hoy (Ed.), *Foucault: A critical reader.* Oxford: Blackwell.

Watkins, P. (1989). Leadership, power and symbols in educational administration. In J. Smyth (Ed.), *Critical perspectives on educational leadership.* London: Falmer Press.

Weber, M. (1978). *Economy and society: An outline of interpretive sociology* (vol. 1). Berkeley: University of California Press.

Weedon, C. (1987). *Feminist practice and poststructuralist theory.* Oxford: Basil Blackwell.

Whitty, G., Power, S. & Halpin, D. (1998). *Devolution and choice in education.* Melbourne: Australian Council for Educational Research.

Wildy, H. (1999). Restructuring and principals' power: Neither the freedom from nor freedom to. *Leading and Managing, 5*(2), 114–124.

Wildy, H. & Louden, W. (2000). School restructuring and the dilemma of principals' work. *Educational Management and Administration, 28*(2), 173–184.

Wolcott, H. F. (1973). *The man in the principal's office: An ethnography.* New York: Holt, Rinehart & Winston.

Wolcott, H. F. (1999). *Ethnography: A way of seeing.* Walnut Creek, CA: AltaMira.

Wood, M. & Case, P. (2006). Editorial: Leadership refrains – again, again and again. *Leadership, 292*, 139–145.

Woods, P. A. (2004). Democratic leadership: Drawing distinctions with distributed leadership. *International Journal of Leadership in Education, 7*(1), 3–26.

Woods, P. A., Bennett, N., Harvey, J. A. & Wise, C. (2004). Variabilities and dualities in distributed leadership: Findings from a systematic literature review. *Educational Management Administration and Leadership, 32*(4), 439–457.

Yamanashi, J. & Milojevic, I. (Eds.). (2005). *researching identity, diversity and education: Surpassing the norm*. Teneriffe: Post Pressed.

Yeatman, A. (1994). *Postmodern revisionings of the political*. New York & London: Routledge.

Yin, R. K. (2003). *Case study research: Design and methods* (3rd ed.). Thousand Oaks, CA: Sage.

Young, I. M. (2000). *Inclusion and democracy*. Oxford: Oxford University Press.

Young, R. (Ed.). (1981). *Untying the text: A post-structuralist reader*. London: Routledge.

Yukl, G. A. (2002). *Leadership in organisations* (5th ed.). Upper Saddle River, NJ: Prentice Hall.

Zaleznik, A. (1977). Managers and leaders: Are they different? *Harvard Business Review, 55*(3), 67–78.

Zaleznik, A. (1983). The leadership gap. *Washington Quarterly, 6*(1), 32–39.

Zorn, D. & Boler, M. (2007). Rethinking emotions and educational leadership. *International Journal of Leadership in Education, 10*(2), 137–151.

Index

Aboriginal English 13
Aboriginal Tutorial Assistance Scheme (ATAS) 98
Aboriginality 93, 101, 135
accountability 28
Acker, J. 55
Allan, E.J. *et al* 49
Ancient Greek ethics 39
Anderson, G.L. and Grinberg, J. 5–6
Angus, L. 57
archaeology 18
architectural design 80–1
Association of Independent Schools Queensland (AISQ) 89
Australian Council of Educational Administration 21
Australian schooling 91

Ball, S.J. 6, 18, 44, 90, 100
Bass, B. 50
Bauman, Z. 92
Beatty, B. 55
Bentham's panopticon 26–7, 78
Best, S. and Kellner, D. 19
bio-power 33
Blackmore, J. 17, 42, 53; discourse description of 20; feminism 30, 54; and Sachs, J. 126
Blanchard, K.H. and Hersey, P. 47
Bleiker, R. 20, 22–3
body 73–4, 83; docile 73–4
Boler, M. and Zorn, D. 55
Burns, J.M. 47–9; concerns 49; leadership analysis 48; power 49; truth 49

Calder, B.J. 45

Caldwell, B.J. and Spinks, J.M. 59–61
Carmody, H. 54
Case, P. and Wood, M. 1
case studies 2–3, 7; *see also* Judy's narrative, Ruth's narrative
Christie, P. 105–6; and Lingard, R. 42–3, 48, 138
Clarke, S. *et al* 74
Clegg, S. 45
Clements, C. and Washbush, J.B. 50
Collaboartive School Management Cycle 60
community 64, 138; definition 92; engagement 91; gaze 100; governmentality 91–9
conduct 34
Court, M. 127
Crowther, F. *et al* 52

Dean, M. 34, 37
democracy 58–9
Diamond, I. and Quinby, L. 31
Dimmock, C. and Walker, A. 45
disciplinary power 26–30, 73, 84–5
disciplinary practices 30
disciplinary regimes of control 48
disciplinary society 26, 84–5
discipline 27, 36, 73, 83, 106–7; normalisation 83; tactics 83
discourse 19–20, 36, 41–63; leadership and management 21; pluralist approach 20
discursive field 22
distributed leadership 51–2; aggregated pattern 52; critics 52; emergence 51; holistic pattern 52

docile body 73–4
documentation 29, 84–91; grants and
    submissions 84–91

Education Queensland 1, 75, 124, 133;
    community engagement 91;
    Leadership Matters 61–3, 127–8;
    Standards Framework for Leaders 61
educational leadership 2, 17, 32, 48
educational research 3–4, 17–18
Edwards, R. and Usher, R. 19
emotions 126–8, 135; leadership 55,
    63
enclosure 79
ethics 16, 37–8, 104–5; elaboration 38,
    106; ethical substance 38, 106; mode
    of subjection 38, 106; moral 37; telos
    38, 105–6
examination 28–9, 29, 87, 88; formal
    29
Executive Director of Schools' narrative
    14–15, 74, 94, 132; curriculum
    leaders 75–6

Feeney, A. 58
female headteachers 121
feminism 30–1; leadership 53–5
Foucauldian concepts 7, 15–16, 40;
    toolbox for educational leadership
    17–40
Foucault's books as tool-box 4
functional sites 80
funding 85

gender 124
genealogy 4–7, 18, 24, 37
George, J.M. 55
Gilmore, T.N. and Krantz, J. 134
Gordon, C. 31, 34
government 34–6; schools 56
governmentality 19, 33–7, 60, 104,
    107, 138; community 91–9;
    outcomes 90–1; self 38–9
Grinberg, J. and Anderson, G.L. 5–6
Gronn, P. 1, 2; accession 75; charisma
    50; distributed leadership 52;
    formation 75; leadership 45; linear
    model 75
Gunter, H. 139; and Ribbins, P. 42

Haber, H.F. 45
Hackmann, D.G. 7
Halford, S. and Leonard, P. 54
Hall, V. 121
Hargreaves, A. 55
Hartley, D. 52
Hartstock, N. 31
Haslam, S.A. and Ryan, M.K. 54
headship 42
Hersey, P. and Blanchard, K.H. 47
history of the present 22
Hunter, I. 37, 56, 117–18; genealogical
    approach 37; modern school 117–18

Indigenous children 8, 85, 130
Indigenous community 86, 94, 101
Indigenous inhabitants 10–11
Indigenous Knowledge Centre 85
individual: distribution of 79;
    formalisation 88
inquiry 26
institutions 32

Jermier, J. and Kerr, S. 45
Judy's narrative: accessibility 113;
    administrative work 68; AISQ 89;
    ATAS 98; behaviour management
    114; breaking down hierarchy 116;
    children in care 118; cleaning school
    108; community ownership 101–2;
    disciplining 117; education
    co-ordinator 8–9; encounters 68;
    ethical work 114–15, 119; funding
    86–8; grants 90; independent school
    86–7; interacting with people 116;
    leadership style 107–9; modelling
    behaviour 108; personal involvement
    in student concerns 112–13;
    relationships 108; respect for
    children 109; responsibility 115;
    satisfaction 118–19; self-
    problematising 117; self-reflection
    118–19; sense of self 108; starting a
    school 9; student family connection
    98; student's problems 118; telos of
    good principal 107–8, 115, 119;
    time with students 65; whiteness
    100–1; work day 66–7, 112–13;
    worries 117–18

Kanter, R.M. 54
Kellner, D. and Best, S. 19
Kendall, G. and Wickham, G. 5
Kerr, S. and Jermier, J. 45
knowledge 23; power 23–5
Krantz, J. and Gilmore, T.N. 134

Lambert, C. 53, 128
Lambert, L. 52
leadership 1–2, 41–4, 136; capabilities
    62–3; charisma 50; definition 42;
    dispersed 52; distributed *see*
    distributed leadership; emotions 55,
    63; feminism 53–5; frameworks 2,
    48; glass ceiling 53–4; instructional
    52–3; management 44–5; models 41;
    ongoing life process 44; perspectives
    43; recruitment and selection 62;
    situational and contingency theories
    47; studies 1–2, 51, 136; survey
    questionnaires 50–1; theories 45–6;
    trait theories 46; transformational *see*
    transformational leadership
Leadership Matters (Education
    Queensland) 61–3, 127–8
Leonard, P. and Halford, S. 54
Lingard, R. and Christie, P. 42–3, 48,
    138; *et al* 17, 20, 41–3, 45, 92
Lyotard, J.F. 78, 119

McNay, L. 34
Makuwira, J. 92
management 44–5
Marks, H. and Printy, S. 53
Marshall, J. 55
Meadmore, D. *et al* 18, 24
Miller, G. 6
Miller, P. and Rose, N. 90
moral self-regulation 109
morality 37, 113

Nussbaum, M.C. 62

O'Farrell, C. 4

panopticon 26–7, 78
partitioning 79
pastoral power 37, 117
performance 30

Pine Hills community 10–13, 91, 93;
    insular 12–13; racial segregation 11,
    94–5
Pine Hills State School 10–15, 69–73,
    91–3; Aboriginal English 13;
    Aboriginality 93; administration 80;
    bell system 82; funding 90; home
    visits 13; location 10–11; motto
    'Strong and Smart' 12, 81, 125–6;
    political climate 95–6; principal *see*
    Ruth's narrative; staff 12–15, 93;
    staff narratives 121–3; teacher
    narratives 13–14, 95; typical daily
    events 70–1
pluralist approach 21
portraiture 7–8, 137
power 18–19, 23–5, 36, 40, 49, 57,
    78–9, 138; disciplinary 26–30;
    individuals 25–7; knowledge 23–5;
    mechanics of 73; pastoral 117;
    relations 4–5; visible 78
practices 5
Printy, S. and Marks, H. 53
punishment 24

Quakers 98
Quicke, J. 31
Quinby, L. and Diamond, I. 31

Ransom, J.S. 34–5
reason of state 37
resistance 33
Ribbins, P. and Gunter, H. 42
Riverside Community School 8–10,
    65–9, 110; administration 80; AISQ
    89; architecture 8; community 93–4;
    fee-free structure 9–10, 87; funding
    90; grants 89; high school 95, 111;
    literacy programme 114; nutrition
    programme 9–10, 109; observations
    65; policy 94; positive community
    factors 98; principal *see* Judy's
    narrative; programmes 88, 109–11;
    respect for Indigenous traditions 111;
    school board member's narrative 101,
    109–10; schooling experience 9; staff
    9, 69; staff meetings 69; students 65;
    telos 109, 111; time 82–3; typical
    daily events 66–7; vision 10

Riverside Community Skill Centre 94
Riverside School Handbook 111
Rose, N. 88, 92, 97–8; and Miller, P. 90
rural schools 74
Ruth's narrative 69–70; accessibility 120; accountability 129; breaking down hierarchy 132; burn out 132; calm in difficult situations 120, 127; challenges 96; classroom visits 130; community 11, 94–5, 129; consultation 123; decision-making 99–100; delegating tasks 133; early arrival to school 71–2, 130; emails 72; emotions 126–8; ethical work 119–20, 134; façade 127; first year 69; gender 124; goal 125; hiring staff 130–1; home visits 93, 129–30; intrusions 80; job readvertised 96–7; leadership style 123; long hours 71–2; looking after herself 132; male leadership 124–5; management pressure 133; managing people 131; motto 'Strong and Smart' 81, 125–6; nature of job 82; negative comments 96; office location 81; performance 129; politics 97; positive community support 97; previous principal 69–70, 78, 97; relationships 119–20, 125, 131; self-forming work 126–34; self-reflection 128–9; staff meetings 123; subjection 128, 134; submissions writing 85; systems 70; teaching principal role 74–5; technologies of the self 129; telos of good principal 119–20, 125, 134; uncertain future 97; visibility 69–70; whiteness 96–7, 99–100; work day 70; work practices 122; working effectively 77–8; workload 71–2, 82
Ryan, M.K. and Haslam, S.A. 54

Sachs, J. and Blackmore, J. 126
Sawicki, J. 4
school administration 79–80
school management cycle 60
school principals 2–3, 43, 136; accountability 86, 102; body 83, 90; centralisation 86; changing role 59; community 102; day-to-day work 15–16; decentralisation 86; disciplinary regimes 83; docile body 73–6; emotions 126; ethics 38, 104–5; expectations 76; gender issues 30–1; good principal concept 134–5; hiring staff 100; leadership 44, 61, 136–9; novice 74; office 43; permanent gaze 79; personal nature of job 72; power relations 58; reforms 58; regimes 64; relationships 76; resources 44; subjectivity 99–100; telos 107–11; time pressure 76; visibility 77; work practices 3, 6, 73, 76–7; *see also* Judy's narrative, Ruth's narrative
school reform 32
school-based management 33, 56–9; critics 56; facelessness 56; power regimes 64
self 38–9, 131; governmentality 38–9
The Self Managing School (Caldwell and Spinks) 59–60
self-governance 6, 34
self-management 42, 55–6, 85–6
Shakeshaft, C. 54
Sinclair, A. 43, 55; and Wilson, W. 43
Smyth, J. 57, 91
solutions 32
Spinks, J.M. and Caldwell, B.J. 59–61
Standards Framework for Leaders (Education Queensland) 61
Stick, M. 11–12
Still, L. 54
surveillance 76, 78

Thompson, P. 2, 7, 8; educational administration 21; educational publications 21; neoliberalism 58; principal's workload 82
Thrupp, M. 52
time 27–8, 82
timetables 81–2
transformational leadership 47–51, 59–60, 128
truth 25
Tzu, S. 1

Usher, R. and Edwards, R. 19

Veyne, P. 33
Visker, R. 5

Walker, A. and Dimmock, C. 45
Walzer, M. 32–3
Washbush, J.B. and Clements, C. 50
Watkins, P. 31
webs of power 138
Western educational climate 2
Western schools 17
Western society 39

Wickham, G. and Kendall, G. 5
Wilson, W. and Sinclair, A. 43
Wolcott, H.F. 46
Women in Educational Administration
  (Shakeshaft) 54
Wood, M. and Case, P. 1

Yeatman, A. 6
Yin, R.K. 6–7

Zorn, D. and Boler, M. 55